BLACK FUTURISTS
IN
THE INFORMATION
AGE

1-24-98

TO: POSTORIA

Now is the Time...
Our ancestors are calling
this!

Khephra &
am Moseti

Peace.

BLACK FUTURISTS
IN THE
INFORMATION
AGE

VISION OF A 21ST
CENTURY TECHNOLOGICAL
RENAISSANCE

TIMOTHY L. JENKINS
KHAFRA K OM-RA-SETI

KMT PUBLICATIONS
SAN FRANCISCO

UNLIMITED VISIONS, INC.
WASHINGTON DC

Cover Artwork by
Talibah Designs

First Edition

Library of Congress Catalog Card Number: 96-79952

ISBN 0-9635645-6-0

Published by KMT Publications, San Francisco
Unlimited Visions, Inc., Washington DC

Printed by Thomson-Shore, Inc.
7300 West Joy Road, Dexter, MI 48130-6216

Printed in the United States of America

CONTENTS

PART ONE
THE IMPACT OF THE INFORMATION
AGE REVOLUTION

PART TWO
PREPARATION FOR THE 21ST CENTURY
GLOBAL AGE

PART THREE
CHALLENGES OF THE NEW ERA

DEDICATION

In the memory of Ron Brown (1941-1996):
Secretary of the United States Department of
Commerce, African American internationalist, political activist, pioneer and global visionary. In the spirit
of our ancestors and of futurists building uplifting
bridges to the 21st Century, may Ron's vision and
life's mission help us to forge new unity and priorities
for the Information Age Revolution.

Hotep

ACKNOWLEDGEMENTS

In many ways the development of this project was a focused intellectual journey shared, to some extent, by many individuals along its pathways. Many thanks to Dr. Beverly J. Robinson and Dorothy Karvi of Black Filmmakers Hall of Fame, Leroy McCreary and Dr. Julian Earls of NASA, Black Filmmaker, A. Jacquie Taliaferro, Manu Ampim of Advancing The Research, Ronnie Prosser of Black Art Productions, political advisor and activist, Leon Thibeaux, Donald Jerrold, former president of the Black Data Processing Association, musician, Nate Justice, and Percy Earby for their collective support and research assistance on various phases of this project.

Special thanks and much appreciation to Saundra Anderson for providing her sharp editorial skills and consultation in polishing the final manuscript. And special thanks to my dear friend Geratha Ann McCreary, for her patient ability to provide thoughtful suggestions and recommendations on various issues. Many thanks to my father, Rev. James L. Davis (author and writer) for the mutual support we share in our writing and publishing endeavors.

Particular gratitude goes to Dr. Henry T. Sampson for his strong support in providing much clarity on the issue of black participation in the sciences. Likewise, special thanks to Dr. Ivan Van Sertima's tireless efforts in bringing forth critical research on black scientific achievements in the 20th Century.

I would also like to convey a sincere appreciation and great round of applause to the scientific traditions of our African ancestors and the great African Civilizations, and to the countless modern day black scientists, engineers, technocrats and others for their enormous contributions.

And finally, special thanks to the indwelling spirit of God for helping me to remain focused and patient in the production of this project.

Khafra K Om-Ra-Seti

FOREWORD

Andrew Young

The face of social injustice has many shapes and they change constantly. Today we are confronted by a very different image unlike any we have known in the past. It is a divided America without the necessity of active discrimination, but with painful results every bit as devastating.

Throughout the 20th Century, African Americans have continually struggled to overcome the forces that would stop their progress towards freedom, justice and equality in America. Over 35 years ago we marched on Washington, in a bold determination to bring about profound changes in our land. In the Civil Rights Movement of the 1960s, we changed the conditions of segregation in this country. We challenged this nation to abandon its practice of gross discrimination and racism, in the name of justice, fair play and civil decency. The signs came down, the South was transformed, and desegregation became the law of the land. Though we won many battles in our push for social and economic justice, we cannot say with conviction that our war of peaceful liberation has been won; "the badges and incidents" of discrimination cited in *Plessy vs. Ferguson* live on.

In the 1990s, we are confronted with a list of devastating statistics highlighting critical problems in black communities in America, which raise a number of perplexing questions for many in my generation. Indeed, if Martin Luther King Jr. were with us today, he would be outraged by the mindless killing in our communities among our young people, the debilitating drug scene, babies having babies, educational decline, job loss, homelessness and many other social pathologies. As I stated not so long ago, no nation as rich as ours should have so many people isolated on islands of poverty in such a sea of material wealth.[1] This is the dilemma that many black communities face as we approach the dawning of a new century. These disturbing trends must be reversed first by reversing the fundamental root causes.

Foreword

At the center of these causes are the increasingly marginal roles black people play in the economy of our nation.

Authors Timothy L. Jenkins and Khafra K Om-Ra-Seti are suggesting that many of our problems and our solutions can be found in the current Information Age Technological Revolution. As *Black Futurists*, they are seeking to raise our consciousness to the accelerating historic transformations that are taking place during the 1990s, in an effort to spotlight the significance of technological change as a fundamental cause for many expressions of social pathology. They not only point out the displacement of labor saving systems, robotic workers and devices are having on millions of African American workers, but they also warn that if educational decline continues at its current pace, those displaced (as well as millions of new African American workers) will be unable to function in the high-tech societies of the 21st Century. This dire prediction can only bring about dramatic increases in the problems I spoke of earlier. In chapter and verse, the authors explain how we are confronted with the forces of technological change on an astounding level and at a rapid pace, such that all previous expectations of an inclusive society may be at an end.

This book offers us an alternative *vision,* one that holds up a two-sided mirror to our face (one good, the other bad) and says, "choose the economic and technological mission of today, which is the way of the future." We are challenged to change our conditions by joining, on a grand scale, the technological revolution of our times. In the tradition of barrier breaking visionaries, the authors are issuing a *call* for a "Scientific and Technological Revolution" in the black world. They label that call *KyberGenesis,* a simultaneous revolution of the spirit and creative mind-set of African Americans to find and redefine themselves in the midst of the broad-sweeping informational changes reshaping our world for the 21st Century.

These authors argue that the spirit and mission of global deregulation (in many industries) is moving to create more market-driven economies for the global age of the 21st Century. Furthermore, with a vast majority of African Americans positioned as consumers and not producers, this represents a set of circumstances that is considered a formula for future economic disaster. African Americans have got to become, as a group, a more competitive and productive segment in the rapid emergence of the global age; the penalty for not responding to this challenge may present a state of economic suicide, particularly as governmental safety-net programs and affirmative action standbys are eliminated. The challenge, then, is to use our divinely inspired talents to create vibrant business, institutional and economic models utilizing information age technologies. They urge us to plant the seeds now during the remaining years of the 1990s, so that our harvest will be bountiful in the 21st Century. Thus, the leadership segment of the African American world is admonished to change its priorities and adapt to the profound implications of the Information Age Revolution. History has proven that African Americans have been resilient and resourceful since arriving to these shores over 400 years ago, now it remains for us to respond to this new *mission* and prepare ourselves for the 21st Century.

Changing times require adjustments in our behavior. We cannot expect to operate on the same agenda and platform in the future, if the world around us is shifting gears for higher levels of production and development. Jenkins and Om-Ra-Seti are correct in their assessment that major corporate restructuring and reengineering in the 1990s will leave millions of workers behind, as many companies struggle to become more competitive on a global basis. They seriously question whether the black community is prepared to survive this onslaught, and if not, what will be the strategy for future progress? Hence, *KyberGenesis* and the need for greater self-reliance and the creative use of many of these new technologies for educational systems, job training, entrepreneurial opportunities, and many other areas of practical use, which may very well offer the only realistic alternatives. With public education under heavy assault, and the imminent revision of our current welfare system that provides as much as a fifth to a third of black income, this call for economic and technological self-reliance is a timely alarm. Indeed, the "signs of the times" are again indicating a new direction, a spirit to promote something different beyond the limitations of the present era. I'm reminded of something I stated not too long ago, that the events that produce genuine change or meaningful success always involve a dimension that is beyond the obvious political, social, or personal forces. Something *ex*tra pulls all these energies and insights together creating something greater than the sum of its parts.

Perhaps this is what the authors are presenting to us, a vision whose time has come. They have articulated what we have been thinking about, and now is the time to put it all together. Our strategies and tactics will have to change in order to make a systematic adjustment to the historic "paradigm shift" that the authors are describing. From their point of view, the digital revolution will not only displace millions of workers, but will ultimately render many of our organizational systems obsolete in the next century.

Jenkins and Om-Ra-Seti also attract our attention to the legacy of black scientific achievement, which reminds me of Drs. Charles Drew, Percy Julian and Ernest Just from my student years at Howard University. Dr. Drew was a Howard medical school professor who pioneered the use of blood plasma, and created the first national blood banks. Dr. Just was a world class geneticist, and Dr. Julian was a chemist who not only created patented products, but industrial wealth through their manufacture. The authors want us to become very conscious about such black scientific and technological innovators, and to make the next generation of students aware that science and technology *are* black developments as well as rhythm and blues.

We are also admonished to understand the profound implications of breakthrough innovations, and to recognize a beginning period of new opportunities to solve medical, educational, societal and environmental problems. Because the world is not aware of the profound contributions that black scientific minds have had on world civilization, it tends to ignore any potential contributions we have yet to make.

What is radiantly clear in the thoughts of these two authors, is a message of hope and the ability of African Americans to master the science and technology of this current revolution. As we stand at the cross-roads of time, our choice must be for greater progress and development on a level we have not previously contemplated. In the minds of Jenkins and Om-Ra-Seti, we must either accept the historic mission of *KyberGenesis* or expect to wake up to a problem of nightmarish proportions shortly after the dawn of the 21st Century.

As such, this volume represents a first. Not only has it been made available in hard copy, but it is being published internationally - on-line. As such, it is simultaneously available domestically and throughout the world as the first electronically published book by African American authors via the Internet. I trust that this is the first, but not the last of such ambitious efforts by these two insightful authors. Their message is a wake-up call and something each of us should ponder very carefully as we approach the new millennium.

Andrew Young

Former Congressman, United States Ambassador to the United Nations, and Mayor of Atlanta. Author of *A Way Out Of No Way* and *An Easy Burden.*[3]

PREFACE

It has been said that the two great revolutions of this century are those of human rights and the explosion of technology. A major concern of this book is that these two revolutionary forces may be headed on a collision course, unless creative interventions are made to harmonize their potential capacity and positive energy. It's ironic that the same liberating potential that technology offers to free mankind from many aspects of routine drudgery, poses a parallel danger that it may simultaneously relegate those who gainfully performed such routine tasks in the past, to an idle future. Such a result is more than a personal tragedy for those so displaced, it also represents a fatal danger to the social and economic fabric of our nation.

While there have been many to decry these developments, very few have been the voices proposing alternative directions, particularly with regard to the African American community and the looming disaster inherent in this current technological revolution. Continued oblivion to the demands of technological literacy, not just for employment and economic advancement, but for self-determination and development, education, public expression, cultural enjoyment and a continuing sense of community, is similar to burying our heads in the sand. In part, this is attributable to the great divide between those who know and those who care.

As authors, we have made an effort to bridge the gap. We have been equally concerned to investigate the many creative ways in which the Information Revolution (accelerated by digital technology) offers opportunities that are, and shall continue to be, available not just to black people, but to many of the "dispossessed of all races" who have been unfairly denied access to information, economic participation and self-expression.

Accordingly, this book has been designed as a wake-up call to technicians and non-technicians alike, to become vitally concerned with the sweeping technological undercurrents radically and silently changing the demographics of the future. It is intended to raise important questions of public policy and corporate concerns. It is created as an understandable primer in the language of technology, to enable policy and opinion makers to speak in relevant terms to one another.

Also, embedded in our presentation is a clear assessment and declaration that outlines the many scientific and technological contributions that black people have made to usher in this new scientific millennium. Throughout the development of this project, we have been haunted by the historical facts (long obscured) that the world of scientific mastery is as much a part of the African Diaspora as its globally acknowledged rhythms and art. It has been our constant inspiration and conviction that the heritage of black people, which created the lunar calendar with which the world still marks its time, can create contemporary technological vehicles which can again benefit all of mankind. As analysts of the future, we hold high hopes for the innate potential genius of black people to uplift all of mankind, while at the same time we call attention to the potential disastrous downside of our situation, if it is left to spin out of control.

Further, we strongly stress that the new era requires a renewed commitment to intellectual and scientific pursuits; a new *spirit* to seize the opportunities embedded in the climate of this dynamic revolution. It requires monumental patience and qualitative *time; a* pulling together of various levels and dimensions of knowledge to orchestrate a plan and strategy for success. We must employ the patience of the pyramid builders, the dynamic energy and intellectual spirit of Moorish Spain, and maintain a commitment similar to the ancient ingenuity of the Dogon people in their celestial science. This is a time of *great change* and of *great sacrifices* if we are to succeed *as a* people *in* the 21st Century. It will require a dedication beyond the ordinary *and* a true sense of urgency to assist not only black people, but all of mankind to make this incredible adjustment and transition to the 21st Century. Indeed, there is an urgent need for the most talented black people to *get beyond* this present stage of complacency, otherwise the

Preface

light of knowledge and progress will be extinguished for millions of our brothers and sisters.

As such, we wanted to do something other than simply write an informative book, we want to provide a beginning blueprint of the ways in which the aspirations of our people can be advanced. This is not a mere intellectual escapade being suggested here; this is intended to be the seeds of a campaign not unlike that at the turn of the 20th Century known as the Niagara Movement led by intellectuals pledged to the social, economic, and political liberation of the masses as part of a newly industrialized society. Only this time, we suspect that the masses may well be ahead of their leaders in recognizing the importance of the great work to be done.

It is therefore important to look to grassroots organizational efforts aimed at mobilizing churches, unions, public housing units, boards of education, and students as the critical change agents. The need is for a massive bottom-up demand for inclusion rather than a trickle down system of benefits.

We are clear in our assessment that the journey we take in the 21st Century will bring us either to the brink of a major economic and technological collapse, or propel us on a course to unparalleled levels of progress. Black people must decide which *path* they will follow in the new millennium, a decision that must be made now!

By definition digital technology is mass technology rather than class technology. It has the potential for universal relevance to every living human being regardless of language, religion, race, geography, or economic circumstance. And it has the capacity to improve upon the model of current communication systems serving universal needs in education, medicine, information, culture, government and debate. But to accomplish this, one must be part of the design process that is still at work. This book is to help assure the inclusiveness of African Americans in that global design.

The Authors,
T.L.J and K.KO

PART ONE

THE IMPACT OF THE INFORMATION AGE REVOLUTION

Chapter One

FROM GATEKEEPERS TO GATECRASHERS

Timothy L. Jenkins

The Far Side of the Mountain

I t has been a source of amazement and alarm that, in spite of the roar of public attention surrounding the advent of the Information Age as the explosive successor to the industrial era, the leadership of the African American community has yet to broadly interpret the Age's far reaching implications for the vital interests of their constituents. The delinquency of their silence has been all the more profound, because of the palpable evidence that without major interventions, the utopian predictions of the Information Age for the society as a whole will paradoxically result in a doomsday scenario for the masses of black people. Alternatively, a clear understanding of the broad implications and susceptibilities of these tools of modern communications, coupled with information science, have the clear potential to foster unheard of strategies of liberation. The burden of this volume has been to articulate a new vision for African Americans in the Information Age.

3

The benefit and the burden of being black in America arise from the ability and the necessity to view the same things the rest of society sees differently. This difference is born of bitter experience, that popular propaganda is seldom predicated on the best interests of black people in particular or humanity in general. Moreover, black people harbor a justifiable skepticism that the larger society is equipped to interpret or even understand the best interests of those elements of the population it has excluded from so many of its inner sanctums. Ironically, by the very reason of such exclusion, the social perceptions black leaders hold sometimes allow them insights that are clearer and more reliable reflections of reality for the larger society as well. Contributing factors in the black/white leadership divide come from the material differences in their resources and power. In almost every sphere of life, the historic status of Blacks increases their vulnerability. Statistics affirm these differences in economics, education, health, social mobility, and even in certain areas of historical and philosophical aspirations.

Because of these increased vulnerabilities, many stresses which the majority easily survives, exceed the level of tolerance for Blacks. In this sense, observing the effects of certain conditions on Blacks may predict the later ramifications on the general public. Black people, suffering economically in the early stages of the Information Age, may be like the canary in a coal mine, forecasting climactic dangers before they become a general manifestation. Thus, as the euphoria sweeps the nation regarding the exciting expectations of the Information Age, African Americans must sound the alarm on the dangers of systematic exclusion.

On the surface, every reason exists to celebrate the proliferation of Information Age technologies. But it does not follow that information by itself can guarantee an improved quality of life or more secure democratic rights. Nor does the international migrations of information industries assure that the result will not be the lowest common denominator in wages and jobs. The propagandists insist that universally available information leads inexorably toward democracy, but they seldom acknowledge the mega-disparities that exist in the corporate versus citizens' ability to gather, manipulate, and interpret information in politically relevant ways.

Confronted by these pressing issues, black leaders must now move forward in a new role with specific agendas, promoting the development and advocacy of reform policies and programs that can wisely pick and choose among the probable social effects of the Information Age. The result could be an early wake up call for our nation, hopefully before the negative effects of tele-cybernetics become irreversible. By fulfilling their role, black leaders can move from being gatekeepers to gatecrashers, opening up new lines of thinking and new avenues of public policy. The beneficiaries of their interventions will not only be blacks, but workers of all races, ages, and their institutions. By the same token, if at the end of the day, technology will only provide an economic haven for the brightest and the best of us - regardless of race - then we will have cold and shallow comfort in the toll that this direction will have on our society. If those of us who care, exercise influence sufficient to force the agenda of our interest on the application of technology, then we should have our fortunes rise with the whole of mankind.

It is still too early to know which will be the predominant result. In the meantime, we must do all in our power to assure that we are technically aware of technology's positives and negatives, as each public decision is made in response to the rapidly changing world of *The Age of Light.* And woe be unto us if Marshall McLuhan was right when he said "the medium is the message," for most of us are likely to be left out of understanding or enjoying a vital economic connection with either.

In the final analysis, the essence of technology ought to be service. Judged from that perspective, it remains to be seen whether the interests of the black community are served or sacrificed. Absent purposeful leadership involvement, either could be true. The deciding factor will be the extent to which those who both understand and influence the direction of technology, take into account the peculiar interests of the black community as they may well harbinger society's interests in general. If its prime effect is to reduce the labor force to an absolute minimum in order to maximize profits or to allow jobs to follow tax breaks and the lowest wages wherever they might lead, then technology while benefiting some, will have failed us all!

Dedicated to the Future

This book is, therefore, dedicated to the future - not an inevitable future - but rather the future which we can design. Never before has there been a time when so much could be achieved in leveling the playing field of life through pluralistic imagination and commercial creativity, as modern computer-driven technological genius has now made possible. But we will first have to be open to a personal as well as an institutional *need to change*, before we can use technology to counteract social, economic, and intellectual inertia on the matters of race and ethnicity in America. Indeed, the refusal to open our minds to the discomfort of change may be the largest obstacle yet to our ultimate empowerment through technology.

In spite of its many positive potentials, the unfolding of the decade that closes the 20th Century and opens the 21st, is at best neutral. With equal facility, this epoch can irrevocably alter for good or ill the intellectual and economic disparities born of race, as well as spatial and social realities. The exercise of values in our allocation of relevant technological resources will be the critical challenge.

The factor that makes these next ten years so critical are both the unprecedented pace of emergent telecommunications and computer innovations, as well as the recognition that, unlike the agricultural and industrial revolutions, those who are left behind this time may never be able to catch up again. Moreover, the Information Age promises to impact monumentally on every area of human life, especially our social and commercial organizations, where the impact will be far-reaching and pervasive.

Emergent technologies will be the keys for determining economic and employment opportunity, freedom of expression, educational attainment and meaningful political participation; all of which are tantamount to deciding who will exercise predominant power for the next hundred years. As such, we stand on the threshold of the invention of what may well become a new worldwide class distinction, or technological caste system.

While the coming of this New Age is a matter of prolific study and investigation in all of these areas, ironically it has been left to the fringe elements of the nation's counterculture to examine its revolutionary implications for America's black, red, and brown minorities. Indeed, if one were to judge by mainstream portrayals of high-tech beneficiaries, it would be easy to conclude that cultural "homogeneity" is to be the uniform requirement of the next century, rather than an increase in diversity implicit in the national demographic shifts in which the minorities of today will become the population majority of tomorrow. Overwhelmingly, the computer icons, advertisements, spokespersons and media campaigns are standardized to look, feel and act like their industrial creators, resulting in their not being user-friendly to minorities or their unique cultural interests. We have not only seen the creation of the Information Age invisible man, but also the invisible interests and concerns of racial and ethnic diversity excluded from high-tech images. As a result, *Star Treks I & II* notwithstanding, we might be led subliminally to conclude that the future belongs to only the information industry's chosen few rather than the whole population.

Article 17 of the Universal Declaration of Human Rights asserts that access to technology is a fundamental entitlement, yet nowhere is such an "entitlement" given universal access. Accordingly, those of us who have been to a different mountain and seen a different promised land must now declare a different vision. Ours is a vision in which American society as well as world culture, through the marvels of technology, open themselves up to beneficial change based on a deeper and more intimate understanding of the creative differences of which they are comprised. With an appreciation for the enormity of the coming change in information access, this decade represents the last best hope to challenge the patterns of social exclusion from the past being extended and reinforced by technology into the future. The information and telecommunications revolution promises brand new games, which require that *we invent new rules* by which they can be played for life quality improvements rather than mere quantitative accelerations. Only then can the inherent power for change - implicit in high-technology communications - yield results that alleviate rather than further degrade our communities. In essence, we as black people must shape and mold the emergent Information Age revolution into our own image, and establish values and morals that are consistent with our historical traditions, to ultimately benefit the world. For example, it will not be appropriate to follow the pattern of mindlessly creating video games on CD-ROM that simply entertain people in the sport of killing the enemy. We need to rethink the possibilities of such tools, so they can help to produce a generation of enlightened people!

Alas, any hope of playing by a set of new rules, demands intellectual as well as behavioral modifications of today's leadership, not only on explicit matters of race and ethnicity in America, but the ingenuous ways in which seemingly neutral trends can help to perpetuate inequalities. In spite of the loudest protests to the contrary, minority group leaders and majority group power holders have both grown used to slow dancing with each other, while they are increasingly distanced from the growing economic and social insecurities that plague their constituents. Although it tends to be less frequently noted, educated white elites often display as little real appreciation for the material and emotional needs lying below them as certain mis-educated elite black escapees from the ghetto. Hence, the expressions of political and editorial surprise at the electoral revolts that have occurred throughout the nation in recent years, when blue collar constituencies have rejected predicted group behavior and voted with the opposition, or when opinion polls fly in the face of predictions from would-be pundits and opinion makers.

The establishment just doesn't get it; the majority of people feel betrayed by both their leaders and institutions. Almost nowhere, except in dark alleys, poorly lit parking lots or celebrated talk shows, does the world of most black leaders and white power holders come together with the alienated underclass and its seething social rebellion. These social and economic distances are seriously exacerbated by mainstream communication barriers that provide little or no ongoing dialogue. The heated debates regarding black rap lyrics as well as the librettos of white heavy metal ballads, vividly illustrate the symptoms of such class warfare.

For the first time, however, walking in another class' shoes is becoming feasible. On-line computer networks can offer a new town hall. Desk top publishing promises a new public forum. Civic teleconferencing can become a new vehicle for group dialogue. Distance learning will allow a classroom to be worldwide. No longer must music, art, and theater suffer an unnatural fence. The libraries and museums of the world can be available to the most remote corners of the earth for the first time in history. Diagnostic health care can now be distributed without regard to distance between patients and national hospital specialists. Soon, with everyone able to be his or her own publisher, the means for truth-telling as an everyday Internet exchange, rather than the occasional moment, can be at hand. While the uncensored picture that emanates from down under may not always be exactly pretty, it at least promises to be far more honest and realistic than the polished products of editorial middlemen with their own hidden agendas.

Few will deny that the instant presence of television has made a tremendous difference politically during the past thirty years, whether evidenced in the civil rights marches or the fall of the Berlin Wall. By way of parallel, the problem will now be assuring that unrestrained market forces alone are not the only forces left to determine individual and group access to knowledge or set the speed limits of the Information Superhighway. This calls for the development of enlightened public policies that balance the bargaining power among the players and provide a level playing field. On such a playing field the merits of an idea will be able to withstand the onslaught of superior economic power, and this can lead to a freer and more egalitarian society than the cash register alone is likely to foster.

But before we get euphoric over these grand *possibilities*, we need the sobering recognition that such progress is not a self-evident truth nor a historical imperative. On the contrary, if the old rules of means tests, class advantage, ethnicity and geographical preferences are applied to these new technologies, the result will not only be the perpetuation of existing disparities, but their indelible reinforcement. And based on emerging patterns to date, the perpetuation of the old rules are clearly at work. Low income children are half as likely to have access to computers at home or in school. Students at Historically Black Colleges and Universities are substantially less likely to have high-tech facilities, equipment, and technological programs of equal quality. Minority workers are disproportionately relegated to the tedious low end of automated systems, if they have any access at all. The geographical areas slated to enjoy entree to these marvelous new and costly communications systems are those least likely to include minority or low income households. In this regard, it is useful to be reminded that the majority of the world's population has yet to be able to place its first telephone call. In the United States population pockets exist that have actually lost ground in their access to telephones in the years from 1985 to 1995, and many of these are in the very cities which boast the most advanced forms of progress in telecommunications.

All of this suggests that this new information and communications revolution could easily bypass the minority communities of America just like the infamous interstate highways of old, providing few or no meaningful access ramps unless they are carefully designed into the plans taking shape now. Indeed it has been graphically suggested that, left to their own devices, minorities are most likely to be the major *road kill* of the Information Superhighway, with jobs flowing abroad, while those remaining in the country have unreachable high-tech entry requirements or offer a new form of house-bound peonage without hard-won worker fringe benefits or long-term job security. All of this makes the coming decade of pivotal importance, for the next ten years will determine who goes up and who goes down on the technology seesaw. Because we share a stake in the design of the future, we must exercise the option to modify these outcomes based on direct participation in the decision-making processes which are bringing about the construction of the new Information Superhighway. But to do this we must first reinvent our leaders.

One of the most astonishing discoveries we encountered was the private sector indifference shown by the various Fortune 500 computer hardware, software, and telecommunications companies; there is essentially a lack of concern not only toward the underserved information needs of black people in general, but also toward the $450 billion appeal of the African American market. Having participated in or been aware of efforts to induce such companies to expand their high-tech marketing outreach into minority consumer niches, with only three exceptions, we have witnessed a response that has been uniformly negative. When approached, such companies retort that either blacks aren't interested in high-tech telecommunication devices and computers, or those that are so inclined, can be readily reached through a generalized mainstream outreach.

This behavior flies in the face of the great weight of professional marketing in other areas which shows the importance of special niche market identification and promotion. Such indifference also underestimates the extent to which upper income black consumers not only exceed the general population in brand name loyalties, but also in the mainstream consumption of sophisticated electronic equipment. The consumer areas in question include CDs, hi-fi and stereo equipment buying, as well as VCRs and video cameras; all of which aggregated to a $6 billion electronic market among minorities in 1994, well above the comparable *per capita* expenditure of the general U.S. population. Indeed, the black market penetration of VCRs is greater than that for the household population as a whole. Consider what this might imply for CD-ROM products and other software capable of appealing to this same audience.

In a larger sense, this backward corporate attitude poses an additional threat to the long-term economic and social health of the nation based on technology diffusion. Corporate negativity toward the high-tech minority market suggests the specter of an ever increasing racial and ethnic divide in technology usage, due to ineffective promotion among minorities, leading to a permanently uneven computer and telecommunication diffusion throughout the population to the national detriment of a less competitive workforce and a less just society. All of this is to underscore the fact that, left to the traditional market forces of today, those *who know* and those *who know-not* will translate to a schism of those employable or unemployable along racial and ethnic lines comparable to a distinction of class or caste. One would have hoped for a more forward looking response from that very segment of the economy that prides itself most on its creative alliance with the future. But alas, even the industrial gatekeepers who stand to collect the tolls to the Information Superhighway have shown themselves unwilling to attract additional road traffic from the minority community. This only reinforces the urgency for the black community's internal mobilization to assure its access to the Information Superhighway and the policies that shape its path, as Malcolm X once said, "by any means necessary."

Looking Back to Move Forward

The Adinkra peoples of West Africa have a symbol called Sankofa, of a bird in full flight with its head turned backward. Sankofa signifies the truth that no people can know where it is going if it cannot look backward from whence it came. This may be the classic recognition of all culture. Visionary black leadership will be of critical importance in how we chart our future course. Therefore, we need to be reminded of some of the historic leadership strengths and weaknesses in our community to be able to discern the one from the other in the future. Because of the peculiar ways in which our traditions of leadership have been fashioned, such hegemony may itself represent a temporary impasse to the free flow of benefits from the info-revolution. Such an examination may also identify patterns and practices that are no longer affordable in the face of current requirements. At the same time, it can highlight unique strengths to which we must hold and carry forward for future progress.

From Colonial days to the present, black leadership has primarily been a matter of damage control or the juggling of crises. Limited to operating with inadequate resources against superior material odds, faced with an ever present urgency that defied long-term planning, and originally surrounded by a constituency with limited understanding, black leaders developed peculiar leadership styles. For most, day-to-day survival was the highest common denominator. Their coping with leadership responsibilities without any management tutelage was like having to learn to read without either a dictionary or the formal rules of grammar. Trial and error mixed with innate talent and personal fortitude often led to highly subjective, if not dogmatic, management styles.

Understandably, not only did the cult of personality sometimes become a problem, but also the requirement for self-reliance was frequently at war with democratic procedures. Moreover, the role of leadership carried with it the conflicting need to project one set of characteristics to black constituents and another to the hostile white world outside the community. Accordingly, it remained for black leaders historically to adapt to special balancing acts for survival.

The traditional procession of leaders has been first preachers, then teachers, and lastly doctors and lawyers. Each succeeding wave of such leaders has had to master the means of walking in two directions at once and the ability to "hit straight licks with crooked sticks" in order to meet the approval of two racially antagonistic audiences for their every act. Preachers were the first to be mutually acceptable in both worlds because they could disguise their temporal leadership as other-worldly guidance. Teachers became acceptable because they were usually controllable public employees. Lawyers and doctors were safe agents of change in the eyes of a dominant majority because of the constraints of their essentially conservative professional guilds. Along the way sprinkles of more radical writers, entrepreneurs or labor leaders have come to the fore, but for the most part, the traditional professions historically comprised the dominant leadership profiles within the black community. This is not to deny that sports, theater, and screen celebrities were briefly elevated to leadership roles, rather it is to recognize that the principal flow of direction associated with large scale membership and affinity groups with mass self-help agendas, has come from the same basic professional core, which for the most part had the credentials of higher education as the prerequisite for its status. Through the accident of such education passed on to their children, an almost hereditary leadership class developed which has benignly perpetuated itself from the employment differentiations of old until now, with the ever present potential for gradual estrangement from its constituency.

Such leadership has accordingly mastered those messianic arts and crafts required of them. Typically some measure of entrepreneurship and personal economic success, along with a mastery of oratory and audience appeal, were their principal instruments of influence. They exercised persuasion as charismatic spokespersons or grievance-brokers with power centers. Serving as middlemen and women between two worlds, the perpetuation of their own leadership roles was sometimes as subtle a goal as the objective improvement of their followers. This irony has been aptly described in such works as Carter G. Woodson's *The Mis-education of the Negro*, W. E. B. DuBois' early treatise, *The Philadelphia Negro*, E. Franklin Frazier's *Black Bourgeoisie,* and other analytic works that followed these pioneering publications.

Historically, this duality was maintained easily when the discriminations faced were palpable and universal both in law as well as in fact, as so vividly described in Gunnar Myrhdal's *American Dilemma.* But with the incremental and sometimes sweeping changes brought about by a steady march of victories over *de jure* segregation and discrimination born of civil rights protests, litigation and legislation, a new set of inequality challenges not easily addressed by the traditional leadership styles arose; the creation of a veritable *"Underclass"*, the name first given the phenomena by Douglas Glasgow in his seminal book of the same name. This signaled the demarcation of a new substrata of characteristics reinforcing the factor of race as a barrier to advancement such as welfare dependence, unemployability, and the alienation from middle class ideals, values, and aspirations.

With this metamorphosis has come a kind of leadership dislocation, whereby the alternate traditions of managed protest and accommodation (which had been the black leadership's hallmarks from precolonial days) are less certain or marginally applicable strategies. Now the issues are not petitioning for or even obtaining equality before the law, but obtaining equality *in fact.* With this bold reality has come the need for greater empowerment from within the black community, based on the mechanisms of self-reliance and self-improvement.

In spite of this need for a shift in emphasis, too often the traditional leadership in the black community has continued to emphasize *pro forma* legal remedies, which leave factual inequities beyond their reach. The cynical suggested that this resistance to change was more the result of conflicting interests between traditional leaders and those outside their social and economic class. But a more charitable view is that established leaders may have inadvertently either lost touch with the full weight of the social and economic forces newly confronting their constituents, or be at an intellectual loss for better strategies. The leadership's personal misperceptions may be further influenced by their own relatively stable economic circumstances, which are at stark variance with the increasing numbers of those for whom they would speak. These are problems easily addressed by honest dialogue and the reconsideration of the facts, but first they must be jointly acknowledged.

Because of the many bad experiences of hostile "divide and conquer" strategies as well as leadership assassinations (both real and figurative), a general reluctance to criticize or even challenge leadership figures from within the community has arisen. Those with the temerity to challenge such blind silence, frequently have become objects of criticism themselves, branded as disloyalists or worse, *agents provocateur* for sinister as well as invisible racist forces. Such conspiracy theories are all the more easily promoted when partisan, regional, and monetary considerations are part of the mix. The resulting differences have led to additional strains when both sides have resorted to name calling and mutual castigation of one another's motives, rather than addressing relevant issues objectively or collaboratively. This caused even further confusion, with the suggestion that many of the traditional civil rights remedies disproportionately benefit the traditional reformers rather than their down and out constituencies. Hence, we witness the pro and con affirmative action arguments addressed by Tony Brown in his book, *Black Lies White Lies,* as part of this ongoing dialogue. In addition, demagogues aplenty have practiced patterns of factual denial, which have made race and racial inequality the sole culprit for every conceivable social ill in the black community whether substance abuse, the high rates of crime, school dropout rates, low reading scores, teenage pregnancies, job unreadiness, and other social pathologies. These often radical voices have promoted a fatalistic generic excuse for failures, rather than their being attributed to personal inadequacies capable of reform and correction.

As if this were not sufficiently confusing, now comes a new breed of minstrel-like propagandists and politicians from the right, whose profession it is to heap self-blame on Blacks for each and every one of their social pathologies. For these neo-apologists, the *holocaust* of slavery either never existed, or if it did, it was primarily the fratricidal African's fault. Equally unfortunate, these distorted voices have been adopted by major political conservatives as their favorite Negroes and given talk shows, widespread media access, highly visible political appointments and the like. Throughout this process, the practice is to rely on the time-honored tools of hyperbolic rhetoric, *ad hominem*, and emotionalism, at the cost of clarity, precision, and objective debate on racial matters. Although thoughtful analysts, thinkers, and writers have existed in the black community throughout, these more measured voices have seldom had a platform off-campus or beyond the pages of scholarly journals and outside the covers of thick volumes in fine print.

Sadly, not enough of the existing cadre of brand-name leadership in the black community are describable in terms of the future analytic needs. Too often they are content with their select roles as middlemen and women within the power centers. Some are seduced with personal benefits or benefits for those who mirror themselves, without comparable attention to those below them economically and socially with different needs. They are too preoccupied with an assured leadership status throughout their lifetime to be concerned with development of a leadership transition system within their institutions, which prepares younger and equally capable leaders to take on leadership roles after their timely retirement.

Many among this current black leadership generation, like their role models before them, have little or no appreciation for the discipline of managing information in the work they pursue. To many, personal rather than institutional decisions are indistinguishable. Few of them consult quantitative data as a required tool for strategy development. Their preference is for speculation, intuition, subjective past experience, and anecdotal information. They are content to employ statistical data only for rhetorical effect, without ever documenting the factual basis for their citations. Take for example the frequently mouthed shibboleth that, "there are more black men in prisons than there are enrolled in higher education." To the contrary there are far more Blacks in colleges and universities and only a minority in confinement, but it is more dramatic to use shock rhetoric over the truth. An information-based scientific approach to leadership would prevent such excess.

A rigorous review of the institutions and organizations of the black community reveals a consistent absence of other systems controls common to modern institutional management. Typically this improvised approach has left key leadership figures open to willful charges of graft or financial irregularities, even when there can be no showing of criminal intent. From Marcus Garvey to the latest sensation of *laid back* approaches to financial accountability, these problems seem to be endemic to black institutions.

One finds similar disregard in personnel matters and staff planning. The functions of recruitment, hiring, evaluation, compensation, promotion, and dismissal in staff procedures cannot be assumed as a matter of formal routine. Typically, whatever exists in the way of written policies are rife with exceptions. All too frequently, nepotism, sexism, conflicts of interest, technical incompetence, and marginal productivity, are shown a blind eye in favor of personal loyalties, congenial personalities and all absolving "good intentions," reminiscent of Sterling Brown's indulgent encomium, "he mean good, even if he do so doggone po!" Because of the absence of planned maintenance, human resources and capital equipment are frequently consumed prematurely, rather than refurbished and scheduled for upgrading or timely replacement to maximize their useful lives. As a result, age-old crisis management is constantly required to meet what could be routine occurrences, leading to uncertainty, program disruptions, and recurring episodes of organizational disruption.

Similarly, local public agencies controlled by people who profess a commitment to high-minded service objectives, sometimes reflect the same shortcomings. These occasionally destabilized institutions include housing authorities, welfare agencies, churches, colleges and universities, labor unions, civic and social organizations, health centers, public school systems, business enterprises, professional organizations and a myriad of charitable activities. The ultimate price of this approach to management and operations is less effective organizations and institutions. It comes as no small wonder then that most of our leadership has been taken unawares by the revolutionary sweep of information systems and the managerial implications they generate. In large part, the crux of the problem is a lack of awareness of the necessary connection between valid information management and desired outcomes. While not universally applicable, having participated in all these activities for many years, we are embarrassed by the truth of this as well as the inveterate resistance to improvement by the very leaders who would benefit most from reform. Unless reformed from within, such leadership itself will be a principal impediment to community development and advancement. And unless reformed, such leadership will be unable to lead the black community into the Information Age.

Criticism of such practices should not be taken as personal attacks or forbidden in the name of aiding and abetting our enemies. Investigative journalism or oversight of leadership is just as indispensable within the black community as society at large. Writers must not be expected to play the ancient role of the African "praise singers," highlighting or magnifying accomplishments and following a code of silence on anything negative. The results will only be continued widespread organizational dysfunction in a community trapped in the denial of its procedural problems, given to a collective avoidance of the responsibility for internal reform, and prone to attributing any and all shortcomings on the single external cause of racism. Most importantly, denial will serve to stifle the diffusion of information systems throughout our institutions.

With the coming of program analysis, better communications, and information systems to the black community, many of these historic proclivities will be objectively challenged. Simple computer generated spreadsheets of comparative daily, weekly, monthly, quarterly, annual and biannual financial and performance results correlated to particular organizational units or individuals, will be able to objectify mission accomplishments alongside particularized costs. Structured reporting relationships and formal report dissemination, as well as documented peer reviews and quantitative evaluations as standard management procedures based on objective criteria and accountabilities, will go a long way to overcome subjective indulgences that cost productivity. The customary distribution of routine information to all appropriately interested parties will further enhance checks and balances on personal excesses and lead to greater confidence in the operations of the institutions we own and care about.

All of these management and information tools, while routine throughout the broader society, are still in their infancy in too many organizations and institutions within the black community. When these are newly introduced, they should not just come on the heels of a major scandal or after protracted litigation or bureaucratic guerrilla warfare. Instead, they should be routine assurances of willingly adopted group accountability consistent with modern management. In all of this, the tools of personal computers and telecommunications offer important improvements explained in detail throughout this book.

Furthermore, with the coming of the Information Age's instant media blend of news as entertainment, a heightened mischief will result from having community spokespersons and organizations which easily lend themselves to sit-com caricatures for managerial incompetence. Therefore, an urgent need exists to identify and promote a new paradigm in community leadership of those who can master the newly available information tools and the management capacities they offer. Moreover, given the increasing complexities of the economic, social, and political issues facing the community, we are compelled to seek and promote new voices which speak in factual, managerial, and quantitative terms as additional spokespersons. Existing leaders need to attract these new voices as valuable assets for their effectiveness.

Our leaders need to be aware of the new high-tech avenues through which to talk sense with the masses and to enable these new players to assist in that mission. Equally important are the means to simplify and present complex data and concepts through desk top publishing so that the man in the street can understand, as Marvin Gaye would say, "what's going on." The support of black technologists must be mobilized to combat the distortions of the right-wing on complex social, economic, and political issues. We need a different type of black talk show participant than those most frequently called upon now. Fiery sound bites need to be replaced with sober analysis of the kind that only information analysts can provide. While either possibility might not have been feasible with the gatekeeper controls of traditional media (with its inherently high costs and exclusivity due to scarcity), it is now highly possible with the technological explosion of multimedia outlets.

Revolutionary multimedia systems and state-of-art telecommunications technologies include the low costs for the production and distribution of videos, upscale publications, color coded graphs, CD-ROM presentations, animation, E-mail, on-line networks, teleconferencing as well as the rapid transmission of personal computer data and text. Using state-of-art Internet and World Wide Web electronic delivery techniques can mean less time and less censorship of these new voices. Described in greater detail later in our book, these are the new means by which the *old gatekeepers can be turned into gatecrashers.* All of this means that traditional leadership talent must now be enhanced by additional technology training and exposure, to be able to understand and relate to different, more analytic, and more quantitatively verifiable requirements with which to influence public policy as well as manage community institutions. Also, they need to seek out and work with those holding such technological training and talents as a matter of routine.

While the community might well be content with an evolutionary approach to making the managerial and system reforms discussed in this book, national political realities foreclose that genteel option. With the coming of the 104th Congress of the United States on November 6, 1994, many of the public policy assumptions in favor of continued external support for African American interests were turned upside down. For example, a public monopoly for primary and secondary education, which had been the mainstay for upward mobility, is no longer a foregone conclusion. Unending welfare support can no longer be the economic staple for one third of the black community. The expectation of affirmative action to address past inequities through access to higher education, jobs, and public procurement contracts seems to be on its deathbed. The steady increase in elective political power through national, state, and local office holders may be in jeopardy of a Second Reconstruction era.

The steady erosion of economic viability in our high density urban centers sounds parallel alarms. The aggravated tendency toward one-party politics within and without our communities poses a long-term threat of our political isolation. The loss of employment opportunities for unskilled, or even skilled labor as it has been known traditionally, promises a worldwide shift in unemployment and employability likely to be catastrophic to certain segments of the black workforce, and threatens permanent *Depression-like* conditions. These are the external factors that give added impetus to the need to reexamine the ways in which leadership is exhibited and exercised within the black community. With such broad-sweeping changes in required perspectives, traditional leadership types will need to undergo a radical metamorphosis to understand the rules of management, systems analysis, computer literacy, multimedia, and telecommunications, as well as their importance to understanding the domestic connection to worldwide labor and capital markets.

Hopefully, this will also call attention to the necessity for a more dedicated effort to recycle the purchasing power and economic resources within the black community to replace the diminished resources artificially supplied from outside sources. Indeed, the lessening of support from public spending, external philanthropy, and remedial public policy ought to now lead to the resurgence of long forgotten economic self-reliance which fell dormant when the walls of segregation began to crumble. While much of our leadership's energy has routinely made the case for greater external public and private support, too little emphasis has been devoted to recycling our own $450 billion in earnings and consumer power to provide the response to community self needs. Effecting this shift in emphasis away from external dependency to internal self help, will require a massive and deep reordering of leadership priorities.

Through C-Span, CNN and other twenty-four-hour vehicles of instant access to Congressional, and state and local legislative proceedings, the leadership role as information middlemen will naturally erode. As a result, only value-added interpreters who can build upon commonly known information with new and meaningful understandings and strategies, will be able to justify attention or a popular following.

With this proliferation of media outlets, even in the face of more highly concentrated ownership patterns devolving to a handful of international mega-corporations, there will undoubtedly emerge more cost-effective means through which diverse voices can be heard. This will be the inevitable result of media channel supply exceeding the demand for its use. But to succeed effectively in accessing these new modes of expression, will require higher sophistication than that commonly available among our traditional leaders.

Additional forms of leadership must arise to address the issues critical to the competitive interests of the black community. High-tech educators and entrepreneurs, finance brokers, as well as systems managers and planners, are needed in countless locations throughout black society. For the most part, these will be professionals and technicians who have grown up in the Information Age, learned state-of-art computer tools of work, and had an opportunity for hands-on experience within the belly of one of the major commercial structures which are at the center of the Information Age. These will be the very people least likely to have had leadership roles in the old paradigm.

This new generation of role models must see themselves as more than conspicuous consumers, with a recognition of the interaction of their material resources and skills with the security and well being of the black masses. Hopefully they will be more inclined to participate out of self interest in the social and economic uplift of that third of the population falling below the poverty-line, than many of their miseducated predecessors were typically willing to do. This new generation of *haves* will be the backbone for reform in public education as well as the invention of private means of education through alternative education systems, and will craft the paths by which black youth can be prepared for modern employment through applied forms of learning technology. The coming generation will see church resources as more than private holdings, and connect them with community renewal projects. They will also be able to negotiate better terms by which jobs and business opportunities are coupled with the grant of consumer patronage. Finally, this new generation must appreciate the age-old reality that one cannot take without giving back lest the source of the bounty not be renewable. In addition, this new generation leadership must be at pains to groom their own successors as soon as they assume office, lest the ruin of discontinuity undermine every new level of their accomplishments. The education of successors requires a role reversal for those who are the first to get in to racially restricted positions. Leaders must see themselves as pathfinders for others, instead of barring the door after themselves to assure their continued uniqueness and prestige.

Contrary to the doomsday predictions of some, black people can have confidence in the revitalization required by these changes in circumstances. Based on a bedrock of self esteem through accomplishments during the worst of times in yesteryear, our community has what it takes to reinvent its institutions and restore the ladders of hope that sustained past progress. Drug addiction and the other attendant pathologies are the symptoms not the disease. The disease is the despairing inability to fashion the realistic course of survival through self-controlled improvement. Too little has also been devoted to naming those who are the detractors within our ranks for their contribution to the plight of the village. Now this misdirected practice of silent indulgence must stop. It must stop now, not just because of the internal ethical appeals that have been heard for the past fifty years, but because of the imminent cutoff of prior support that was coming by external hands.

The challenge is to use this pivotal decade that spans the end of this century and the beginning of the next to replace the old style of gatekeeping with a new role of gatecrashers to the throughway to the future known as the Information Superhighway. It means retooling the educational engines of our communities. It means assuring internal economic benefits from the billions of dollars that mark the black community as the 12th largest economy in the world. It means zero tolerance for waste and dysfunctional self-seeking of select institutional leadership. It calls for a deeper celebration of self that is not predicated on a put down or even a protest against others, but calls for constructive criticism. It means a new message of concern and participation in educational development and communal parenting for our lost youth.

Fortunately the genius of modern day science and technology of the Information Age offers tools needed for this kind of broadsweeping change. The demand is that we step up and seize the opportunities inherent in the world reordering that will inevitably result through the communications revolution and the industrial, economic and social ripples resulting in its wake. We must replace rhetoric with analysis, mere opinions with factual documentation, speculation with studied probabilities, procrastination with real time initiatives, the historical with the futuristic, the haphazard with the calculated, the emotional with the deliberative and even representation must be replaced by the direct participation of the actual stakeholders themselves, through ongoing and direct means of communications. Our organizational behavior will not change, however, if the people at the top are not personally knowledgeable, committed, and actively given to the demonstration of modern managerial leadership. Simply giving lip service to the importance of computers in information and management sciences will simply generate lip service in response.

Equally important is the assurance that senior executives have the understanding and ability to manage others who are using these new tools. In learning what is and is not possible with personal computers, executives learn to gauge what they can expect from others. The great generals are those familiar with the perspective of the foot soldiers. The object is to make the tools of this complex new world an enhancement to intuition, not its denial. The reinvention of our leadership is a two way street; it will also introduce something new to the world of cybernetics, computational science, and enhanced multimedia applications. For too long such scientific innovations have simply been viewed in quantitative terms to make life faster and more materially profitable without improving goals, purposes or quality.

Because the historic strength of black leadership has been the advocacy of values, it should use this skill to refine the interpretation of cybernetics. By doing so, black people can give a voice and direction that goes beyond engineering for engineering's sake. In this way different and more people-oriented discussions can emerge to complement the language of science. Such a blend of sensitivity with knowledge is what much of the world of cybernetics has repeatedly shown to be lacking. It has known a great deal about how, but not enough about why. Black leadership is ideally positioned to add a *high-touch* to the world of high-tech. By high-touch we mean a personal and caring dimension that assures equal access, affordability, and applications for technology relevant to the disadvantaged elements of society.

In the following pages we make an effort to set forth, with minimal technical jargon, the vast array of factors that contribute to the heightened significance of the Information Revolution in the future lives of African Americans, and we suggest the means by which it may be harnessed to community objectives. To be sure of a common and all inclusive definition and understanding of the specific elements that comprise the information revolution, we examine the technical evolution of technologies leading to today's multimedia explosion. This dispels the notion that just because the subject is complex it has to be confusing. It is also intended to allow the non-technician to appreciate the distinction between what needs to be known and what does not in order to be able to understand and use the relevant technologies. In addition, we highlight the existence and major contributions of black scientific and technical minds in the evolution of various technologies and innovations. In our discussion of Information Age technologies, we give structural underpinnings to the nature of these developments and observe the trends in business and corporate reorganization that forecast a global synthesis to ever greater concentration of computer driven, multimedia, and communication power. The merger mania *sweep* of the 1990s, is the genesis of a major global movement to establish massive corporate power for the 21st Century.

Because of their central importance to our community, we address the educational and training applications of how the genie of computer enhanced telecommunications can be harnessed from the kindergarten through graduate school to enhance the lifelong learning of our community. Here we suggest new ways in which our real estate can become extensions of the classroom from churches to housing projects, and we call for taking our public school systems back. Then we turn to the black economics in information innovations to examine novel employment and the unparalleled entrepreneurial potentials that are, and will continue to become, available because of the Information Age, suggesting new ways in which we must position ourselves to take advantage of them. In this brave new world, we bring to light that creativity and ideas are foremost, offering opportunities that previously didn't exist.

Finally, we attempt the most ambitious of all undertakings in this world of technology analysis, and speak to the future paradigm of what can result from a disciplined community-wide effort by African Americans to weigh into the world of high-tech communications. The temerity for doing so, comes less from the arrogance to predict what the future will bring than the desire to help create the future. For those who may take umbrage at the tone of implied condemnation found in parts of this book, take heart. We, the authors, have included ourselves among those whom our words would condemn. For we all too readily recognize the insulation and isolation that our educational and economic circumstances have afforded, if not imposed, on us. And we fully recognize ourselves as the products and (not always) beneficiaries of the many systems of classification that distinguish the "haves" from the "have nots." If anything, ours is intended to be a work of "class traitorship" in order to awaken all of us in roles of leadership from the complacent drift and dream that technological knowledge and information can be expected to trickle down from us, throughout our community, without an active and assertive intervention on our part toward that end.

While writers with greater egos or insights than ours might seek to speak on a universal plane for society at large or all minority groups in general, regardless of their own uniquely biased orientations, we have consciously chosen not to imitate such expressions of cultural imperialism. Instead, what follows is a view of the historical, intellectual, social and economic change of the telecommunications and information revolution seen through informed eyes which are essentially those of the African American community. Indeed, we are obliged to so limit our perspectives, because this is the only way to remedy the long night of neglect that has obscured our community's unique technological needs, interests, and insights.

We would hope to be forgiven this expression of parochialism so that we can leave it to others of different backgrounds and persuasions to follow alternative paths. Our specially-focused work has afforded them the luxury of a broader social approach, now that the long silent interests of the black community in information technology has already been given a voice.

CHAPTER TWO

INFORMATION AGE TECHNOLOGIES

Khafra K Om-Ra-Seti

n the 1980s, microcomputers began a powerful ascent towards technological dominance in the marketplace. Mainframe computers of the 1970s and earlier generations began a period of slow but steady decline. By the mid-1980s, the explosive development and dynamic power of microcomputers began to truly shake the foundations of the modern world.

By 1987 CD-ROMs were capable of holding 550 megabytes (550 million bytes) of information, which could hold the contents of 1500 standard 5.25 inch floppy disks. From the prospective of the mainframe computer environment of the late 1970s and early 1980s, this development represented an incredible leap into the future: microprocessors as well as optoelectronics were generating a revolution in speed and capacity that would undoubtedly transform the entire computer industry. It was clear to see that digital technology was *The Wave of the Future*.

Throughout the Booming 1980s researchers and business enterprises developed new products and services at an alarming rate. The frenzied competition (on a global basis) helped to significantly promote one of the fastest periods of technological breakthroughs the world has ever known.[1] The integration of knowledge from various disciplines created new synergistic products and services, and set the stage for the 1990s' ascent towards the "Global Information Age Revolution".

The advances in science (particularly in physics and mathematics) in the 20th Century, have illustrated, in a most dramatic way, the profound significance of the unseen power of the universe and the creative discovery process. Our progressive understanding of the universe has dramatically shifted the relationship between man and nature. The technological and scientific revolution that is happening during the closing years of this millennium, marks an amazing milestone in the history of man's existence on the planet earth. This has been an absolutely incredible century, what African American physicist, Dr. Lloyd Quarterman identifies as, "an age of discovery," which dramatically illustrates that, "we live in the world of the unknown". From a physicist's point of view, the world that we as human beings experience is largely dominated by an unseen world, a world that mankind has struggled thousands of years to understand.

We are at the threshold of something so enormous as to shatter all illusions and false mythologies; in time it will be difficult to sustain a system of false beliefs and prejudices in the face of a preponderance of facts and revelations. The evolution of the scientific mind has brought us the reality of thermonuclear physics, laser technology, genetic engineering, and computers on a chip. We are not watching a science fiction movie or projecting some theoretical proposition; our science is now unveiling very critical realities about our universe.

This is the dawn of a New Age, the beginning of a dynamic era that will bring about whole new categories of jobs, industries, university training, and a major revolution in our systematic approach towards economics. This period is similar to the arrival of the Industrial Revolution that began in England in 1760, or the major scientific advances initiated and nurtured by the African Moors and Arabs in Spain and Portugal during the 12th and 13th Centuries: in each case there were major adjustments in economic and world affairs. The almost blinding pace of the evolution of technology will eliminate certain categories of jobs, and in some cases, entire industries, while new ones will emerge to take their place. Advances in robotics and artificial intelligence is shifting the production, assembly line, and basic factory job functions to the realm of intelligent machines. The proliferation of machines of many types will continue at a rapid pace, with machines making machines, as evolving technologies generate greater advances and highly intelligent systems. This is the wave of the future and we must either fully participate in it or be left behind.

Evolutionary developments in physics and mathematics in the 18th, 19th, and 20th Centuries gave birth to a materialistic/mechanistic worldview. In laboratories around the world, scientists unveiled the secrets of nature and the universe, and implemented mechanical and electrical systems to harness their energies. With the advent of the Industrial Revolution came the steam engine, assembly line production, rapid firing guns, the discovery of electricity, wireless communication systems, a profound knowledge of electromagnetic waves and the atom, and many other revolutionary developments.

COMPUTER TECHNOLOGY

The chaos of World War II opened up many fields of investigation, driven by the competitive need for faster computing machines, rocket engines, and greater power and speed in weapons and communication systems. The *atomic age* was born in the 1940s, along with the birth and expansion of commercial TV and computer technology. In 1948, the transistor was invented and it completely revolutionized the communication industries in a dramatic way. In time, the vacuum tube would be replaced by the much more efficient transistor. Progress in future decades brought further prosperity and technological wonders to the growing creativity of the scientific revolution of the 20th Century.

The first generation of American electronic computers was born around the time of the first atom bomb test that occurred in New Mexico in 1945. The first all-electric computer called the "Electric Numerical Integrator And Computer" (ENIAC), appeared in 1946. Consisting of approximately 18,000 vacuum tubes and enough electronic circuitry to fill an entire room, ENIAC was capable of only processing several hundred multiplications per minute and did not have operational programs electronically stored in its' memory. ENIAC also presented some operational challenges; its nearly 18,000 vacuum tubes generated a room temperature of 120 degrees, with many of its tubes burning out prematurely. The huge room-size machine cost less than $500,000 to build and was instrumental in solving many complex mathematical problems that previously required a large number of man-hours to compute. The computer revolution was born, which brought together the elements of digital processing and vacuum tube technology: the perfect merger of the physics world of electrons and the abstract world of mathematics. Thus, mathematics, science and technology would find one of its greatest expressions in the making of the computer. Built by physicist John W. Mauchly and engineer J. Presper Eckert, ENIAC would soon be superseded by Von Neumann's IAS Machine and further advances in the world of electronics.

Modern electronics experienced a major technological shift with the invention of the vacuum tube at the start of the 20th Century. With vacuum tubes, electric signals could be manipulated and amplified in order to generate strong and consistent signals, i.e. voice or music in the radio wave spectrum. The evolutionary transition from the vacuum tube to the transistor, brought about significant efficiencies in space, weight, power consumption, reliability and a considerable reduction in the cost of production. The transistor technology invented in 1948, during the initial stages of the baby boom generation, marked another important milestone in the history of science and technology.[2] The intensive research during the war years helped to stimulate the demand for these cost-effective powerful devices. With the efficiencies of the transistor, the computer moved on to incorporate greater computing and reasoning power, and rapid advances in speed of computer operations.

Similar to the multiplying and complexity of cells to create more complex biological organisms, the transistor represented a major evolutionary leap into the development of more complex computing machines. With the arrival of the integrated circuit in 1959, continued progress has consisted of placing a larger number of switches on a square centimeter of silicon. In 1970, Intel Corporation introduced the first DRAM chip (dynamic random access memory), and one year later (in 1971), the *microprocessor.* The introduction of large scale integrated (LSI) circuit technology and very large scale integrated (VLSI) circuits gave birth to the microprocessor, the CPU (Central Processing Unit) chip that is the basic brains of a computer. By 1985, more than 600,000 circuit elements could be assembled on one chip, and this was the beginning of a remarkable surge in scientific breakthroughs. *All of the full room-size circuitry of the ENIAC computer of 1946, could now be placed on one computer chip*: progress in several fields of science and technology brought about incredible changes in the computer industry over the past 45 years. The astounding projection for the year 2000 is that the power of today's supercomputer will be available in desktop models with a billion plus memory capacity.

The modern high-tech society that has evolved during the 20th Century could not have been accomplished without the rapid advances of the computer. From manufacturing to automation, database management, special effects in films and high-tech communication systems, computers are dominant throughout the broad spectrum of advanced societies. The computer has taken on an almost omnipresent significance; the ultimate mechanical *mind* and the crowning success and termination point of the Industrial Revolution.

SEMICONDUCTOR TECHNOLOGY

Computers consist of a very large collection of on and off switches which in some cases (supercomputers) are timed to a billionth of a second: the basic switch represents the heartbeat of all digital computers. Since the invention of integrated circuits in 1959, chip design and chip technology have made extraordinary leaps into dimensions of space and time. The brain power and speed of computers are driven by the rapid advances in computer chip technology.

Digital technology is the mathematical bloodstream of this era's scientific revolution. The binary mathematics of 0 and 1 serve as the basic machine language for computers. The memory and storage capacities of computers are measured in bytes, with each byte composed of 8 bits and each bit represented as a 0 or 1 in the logic and arithmetic of the system design. We have seen how computers are composed of a massive number of switches. In the binary system the number 1 equals an ON condition and 0 equals OFF. This digital operation is similar to a clock ticking away seconds that eventually adds up to hours, days, weeks, months, and so on. All of the processing is invisible and abstract. Under the binary system of ones and zeroes, the transistor's on-off conditions of true or false enables the computer to perform logical thinking. The natural number system consisting of the 10 digits 0 through 9, is the foundation of the binary system. It is often referred to as the *human number system*, since most of us have 10 digits (the ten fingers or toes). On the other hand, the binary system is considered a *machine number system*.

It is interesting to note that the *natural* number system that we use so extensively in our modern world, originated in India and was brought to Europe by the African Moors and Arabs during the Moorish occupation of Spain and Portugal that lasted for over 700 years (from roughly the 8th to the 15th centuries). The medieval scientific, mathematical and technological advancements of Moorish Spain were greatly enhanced by the *natural* number system. The Moors and Arabs made *algebra* an exact science, laid the foundation of analytical *geometry,* and were the founders of plane and spherical *trigonometry.*[3]

Thus the *binary* system, which is the mathematical heart of the computer, evolved out of the *natural* number system. The tiny electromechanical switches are timed to operate at unbelievable speeds; in some cases millionths and billionths of a second. Few of us can imagine what one billionth of a second is; the time it takes to begin imagining it, is not that fast. Computers essentially operate in astronomical time frames - the invisible microscopic world of electrons and photons, the mystical dance of physics and mathematics. Thus, an 8 bit byte that represents the letter K is processed instantly in computer time. The digital code of binary mathematics is a very interesting development.

In the digi-tech world of the 1990s, practically all media information will be brought together on a common platform, a common denominator facilitated by the digital revolution. Voice, text, images, music, video, complex calculations, and language translations can all be digitized (at blinding speeds) into ones and zeroes. Digital convergence, bringing about the merger of computers, TV, and telephones, is only the beginning of an explosion of *hybrid* media products. The entire foundation of the world will be revolutionized by this new digital reality. The universal languages of mathematics and physics have found their medium; everyone will have to do a reality check, for as Shaka Zulu stated in the film *Shaka,* "nothing will be the same ever again".

The semiconductor properties of silicon has made it one of the most widely used metalloid elements in computer chip manufacturing. Silicon is one of the most abundant elements on earth and constitutes about 28 percent of the crust of the planet. The element cannot be found in a free elemental state, but is retrieved in the form of silicon dioxide ($SiO2$ or Silica) and in the state of complex silicates. Silicon dioxide is a principle property of ordinary sand, and nearly 40 percent of all common minerals contain silicon. It is abundant, widespread, very cost-effective, and is really a perfect economical element for the complex production of silicon-base chips. Silicon can be found in so many different places that it is almost unlimited. Scientists tell us that one of the ways to process silicon is to prepare it as gray-black crystals.

As a conductor of electrical current, silicon has proven to be a very good semiconductor, achieving levels of efficiency near the best metal conductors such as aluminum, copper and silver. In the world of physics, we learn that if a physical property of matter conducts electrical current under the influence of voltage, it can play a very important role in the advancement of technologies in many different areas. Other chemical elements such as germanium, selenium, gallium arsenide, and zinc selenide are great semiconductors.[4] For instance, gallium arsenide, a synthetic by-product from aluminum/copper mining and lead refining, is the primary element used to conduct the flow of photon (light) energy. However, silicon is a much more abundant element and therefore cheaper to use. That's another reason why this technological revolution is going to transform so many different areas of advanced societies.

CHIP DESIGN PROCESS

Laser beam technology (a microscopic lithography technique), is used to etch chip designs onto silicon wafers. By the mid-1980s, many researchers were predicting that the physical limits of jamming additional circuits onto a silicon chip would be reached sometime in the 1990s. However, by 1994, the problem of physical limitations and concerns of switching to more costlier materials were resolved by greater advances in chip technology. Researchers at IBM, Bell Laboratories, NEC, Hitachi, Toshiba, and others concluded that the limit barriers for silicon chip density had been lifted. According to Paul M. Hom, IBM's director of silicon technology research, "there's no science limit for the next 30 years."[5] Thus, we can expect a continued increase in computer performance at low prices, thanks in part to the flexibility and abundance of silicon.

Physicist Gordon Moore, who is a cofounder of Intel Corporation, made an important observation back in the mid-1960s. He observed that chip manufacturers were able to double the number of circuits on a chip every year, which caused a dramatic exponential increase in power each time. As a result of this development, the actual cost of the circuit was cut in half. This became known as *Moore's Law* in the chip-making world, and chip designers used this axiom as a benchmark to increase the power of their designs. However, by 1977, the doubling effect had slowed to 18 months, and by the mid-1990s, began to run into new barriers, slowing further Moore's Law.

Microprocessors that incorporate all of the elements of a computer on one chip, will continue to undergo design changes, making them more complex and dynamic. VLSI circuitry (very large-scale integration) designs allow for many processors to be placed on one "CHIP," which will continue to expand the capability of the computer to perform intricate interrelationship programming. With computers operating at speeds of 400 mhz and higher by the year 2000, the potential for computer creativity in many areas will be phenomenal.

Chip density has reached unbelievable levels; as of 1995, manufacturers were able to cram more than 35 million transistors on a tiny silicon chip: 64-bit processors that operate at nearly the same speed as the 1986 IBM 3090 mainframe computer. Scientists will continue to press on to the ultimate limits of *quantum mechanics* physics that we spoke of earlier, reaching a point where the "solidity of an object" is impossible, and therefore cannot retain a form. Nevertheless, scientists and engineers were able to develop ULSI circuitry (ultra large-scale integration) that can house from 2,000,000 to 64,000,000 elements on a single chip, which clearly suggest that business and home-base computer systems of the future will have very dynamic brain power. Expectations are that by the year 2000, top of the line microprocessors will contain more than 100 million transistors, and that will represent an astounding accomplishment. NEC and Hitachi announced in February 1995, that they had developed a random access chip capable of storing more than one billion pieces of information. The so-called *gigabyte chip* for mass production, reached its prototype stage by the mid-1990s and will be commonplace by the year 2000. Desktop microcomputers in the home with one to two billion DRAM memories and five to ten billion byte hard disk with high-density storage capacities, will far surpass the performance of today's home systems: the cost will be around $5000. We are truly headed for *warp* speed!

Increased technological efficiency in etching more elements on silicon chips is dependent upon the type of laser beam used in the production process. During the early 1990s, ultraviolet light was the most commonly used laser beam in the manufacturing process. Researchers worldwide are now exploring the use of X-ray lasers (so-called blue light lasers) as etching tools that can produce shorter wavelengths, which means that greater densities are possible. Experimental designs using X-ray beams have created chips in laboratories with features at nearly .1 micron in size.[6] This is almost beyond comprehension, but the reality of these technologies will ultimately change our thinking about space and time. In late July 1994, IBM, AT&T Corp., Motorola Inc., and Loral Corporation announced their intention to form an alliance to jointly explore the full potential of the X-ray etching process. The proposed venture has an estimated budget of $100 million or more to bring into existence an economical solution to the next generation of chip making.[7]

Given these statistical factors of silicon economics and scientific technological efficiencies, we can see that future advances and progress will place very powerful computers in the hands of enterprising developers and consumers. In 1994, marketing research revealed that most of the 92 million households in America had TVs and telephones, and about 25 to 26 million of those households owned computers. As older generations of computers are discarded for the newer models, cheaper prices for the earlier versions will put the price of a computer in the reach of many more consumers. There are now far more computers on the planet than people, and this proliferation will continue uninterrupted in the 21st Century. Computer chip design and silicon wafers, along with other exciting technologies, will play a very important role in this period of astounding technological progress. Indeed, this is an incredible period to be a scientist or engineer: exploration into the invisible microscopic world of *quantum mechanics* is producing absolutely remarkable discoveries.

LASER BEAM TECHNOLOGY AND FIBER OPTICS

Laser beam technology represents another critical scientific breakthrough that is playing a tremendous role in the overall advances of the Information Age. A theoretical process for the stimulated emission of concentrated light was first proposed by Albert Einstein as far back as 1917. The invention of a gas discharge laser by Gordon Gould in 1959 (the year that his patent was filed) marks the real beginning of the practical application of laser power.[8] The semiconductor laser was invented in 1962 and its first successful mass market development came in the form of the Compact Disc audio player. Light amplification by stimulated emission of radiation (the acronym is LASER) has become the spotlight (literally) for several technological advances in such diverse fields as medicine, photography, communication, nuclear energy, manufacturing, the military, semiconductor processing, and basic scientific research.

Through the process known as *stimulated emission*, stored energy is released in the form of photons (in *quantum mechanics,* small units of light energy) and by a special technological process, light amplification is achieved. The wavelength of laser beams can be made to travel large distances at astronomical speeds into outer space. This is truly one of the most important developments during this period. As we have seen, sophisticated lasers are used in the microscopically detailed process of etching designs on computer chips. Without the magical power of lasers, this process could not be performed. Lasers are used to perform surgery, to blast plaque from clogged arteries, to bore holes in the skull, to vaporize lesions, as manufacturing and production tools, and in many other applications. Laser light is transforming a whole spectrum of things, and represents the next evolutionary phase up the technological ladder.

FIBER OPTICS AND LASERS

The combination of glass fibers and semiconductor laser technology is one of this era's greatest marvels. Scientific research discovered that a unique harmony existed between laser light and glass fibers, which allows the laser light to travel great distances through the fibers maintaining the speed of light (about 186,282 miles per second). However, the problem of light pulses fading as they travel through the fiber, required a corrective procedure to regenerate the transmission. About every 35 miles, as the light begins to fade, scientists developed devices that would convert the fading light back to electricity, amplify it again, and resend it as laser light. Further advances in fiber-optic transmissions resolved the problem of regenerating data every 35 miles. Emmanuel Desurvire, a researcher at Bell Labs, invented a device called an optical amplifier that essentially allows energy to be continually pumped through the fiber by an external laser. With that problem solved, the steady and continuous flow of "rivers of digital information" to all corners of the globe will be as relentless and persistent as the blood-flow in the human body. Each light pulse flowing through the fiber channels at astonishing speeds, represents voice, text, images, moving pictures, and other information sources.

Practically all communication software, from the written word to the most sophisticated motion picture, can be reduced to the digital machine language of computers (the 1 and 0 of the binary system), converted from electron signals into laser light, and sent flowing down glass fiber cable at the speed of light. Once the data reaches its destination, the pulses of light are reconverted to its electrical signals and presented in its original form, all in a matter of seconds in some cases. That's a real technological revolutionary feat, and it's going to dramatically change our world in ways that we have not yet imagined. This is not *Star Trek,* this technology is available in the 1990s. Fiber cable and laser light can transmit the entire contents of the *Encyclopedia Britannica* in one second. Engineers and scientists have come to recognize that fiber cable represents a 10,000-fold improvement over copper systems. Very high-speed telecommunication networks are being developed with this dynamic energy source.

With a single pair of fibers, we are now able to transmit over 3 billion bits of data per second. Before the year 2000, the transmission rate will be one trillion bits per second on the same single pair of fibers. This astronomical number is the equivalent of transmitting over 70 million simultaneous conversations. These are quantum leaps in technological advances and signal major *paradigm shifts* in worldwide communication.

OPTOELECTRONICS

With the increased use of laser technology in many areas throughout advanced societies, this new phenomena of *optoelectronics* (the marriage of light and electricity) has given rise to an entire new industry development. The basic characteristics of optoelectronics is the transformation of electricity to light and back again. As mentioned earlier, semiconductors such as gallium arsenide are engineered to emit light when electrical current passes through them. For the historic moment, it appears that gallium arsenide is the primary element capable of producing the light necessary for laser transmission. Gallium Arsenide is more expensive than silicon and scientists observe that it is a harder material to work with. However, researchers are hard at work trying to produce laser light from silicon, and when a method has been discovered (and we have reason to believe that it will happen), the ability to generate high-speed transmissions will become a lot cheaper.

In 1994, the U.S. Optoelectronics Industry Development Assn. (OIDA) reported that the component devices developed by the optoelectronic field, are responsible for roughly $50 billion in sales revenues in various product categories. Such devices as $2 lasers in CD players, bar-code scanners, flat-panel displays in laptop computers, optical sensors embedded in structures to detect stress, laser printers, optical sensors that monitor the engine in automobiles, light-emitting diodes (20 billion made per year), and fiber optic probes in the wings of planes are just some of the areas this new wave of sci-tech devices are moving into. In the future we can expect whole new categories of products to be built with the new revolutionary components created in this field. Entrepreneurs developing new product designs will have a wide range of choices in optoelectronic devices. One has only to imagine something, and it probably can be built!

Continuing research in this field is also moving towards the expansion of storage capacity in computer systems. The development of optical storage devices is an area of tremendous scientific concern. Researchers are exploring the possibilities of recording information as *holograms* and the potential of using blue lasers (short wavelength lasers) as part of a system to store vast quantities of data. Consider the scenario of storing 18 trillion bits of information on a 12-inch disk or holographic memories with multiple gigabyte capacities in the size of sugar cubes: these are some of the new technologies we will witness in the near future. If that seems startling, how about computers that operate entirely by thousands of tiny lasers-each one the size of a grain of salt-organized in patterns of integrated circuits, similar to integrated transistors. Consider also microprocessors that process data in *images* instead of bit by bit. The fact that one image could represent a million or billion bits of data makes this a truly remarkable statement. When we start moving images around the way we presently move bits, the unbelievable will clearly become reality: the word revolution will not even be appropriate here. As technology continues to improve, we can expect to see upwards to 100 gigabits of data per second flowing through fiber-optic channels. High-speed, low cost communication and computer systems will rapidly become a significant component of the emerging worldwide Information Superhighway.

Science fiction is becoming reality, for scientists are dreaming of *Quantum Computers*, computer systems that are driven completely by laser light. Such systems, says Seth Lloyd, physicist and nano-technologist, "would be...capable of running 100 million times as fast as a Pentium".[9] Mr. Lloyd and other scientists are imagining the infinite possibilities inherent in today's technological revolution. Each major technological breakthrough is setting the stage for even greater advancements. There are few limitations in this technological push for the 21st Century!

The competitive *rush* of these new technologies (and the competition is feverish) is bringing about a paradigm shift of profound significance: patterns of behavior, traditional ways of conducting business, and various industry frontiers will all experience radical changes in coming years. As one scientist has stated, "We are increasingly moving from the world of the electron to the world of the photon - the basic unit of light." The *Age of Light* is destined to reshape the world!

THE OPTICAL DISC MEDIUM

Optical disc technology represents part of the initial phase in the widespread use of optoelectronics. The first successful commercial use of the optical disc medium occurred in 1978 with the introduction of the *videodisc*. Videodisc players competed with "Home Video" systems for a piece of the rapidly expanding home entertainment market. Prerecorded movies released by Hollywood were the main driving force behind both systems. Home Video defeated the Videodisc player in the market the same way the VHS format in video clobbered Beta. The next major wave came in 1983 with the introduction of the CD-audio.

STANDARD FORMAT AND DESIGN

The information on a compact disc is represented by a spiral of small pits molded onto its surface. The surface of the disc is coated with a reflective metal layer which is then coated with a protective lacquer. This procedure helps to make the disc more durable and longer lasting than other storage mediums: it enjoys a longer shelf life and is highly useful for archival purposes. Tapes and film wear out under constant use and need to be replaced. A shiny underlayer of the disc stores the digital information. Data conversion from magnetic tape to the pits and lands of an optical disc is made possible by a *waveform* that transfers the encoded information to a modulator. The modulator controls a powerful shortwave length laser beam as it passes through a lens, forming an encoded image on a glass master disc. In order to read the material encoded on a disc, the laser beam is reflected off the surface of the disc onto a mirror that reflects the beams into a decoder. Thus, when we operate our CD players, beams of light representing the music are read and transmitted, the end result is the clear and undistorted sound of digital technology.

The optical disc has a far superior storage capacity than magnetic media: it is the most economical means ever invented of storing massive quantities of information in external packets. By using so-called blue lasers and other formatting techniques, scientists are working to extend the present storage capacity of compact discs.[10] The goal for CD-ROMs (whose previous capacity was 550 megabytes of information) is to vastly expand the capacity by the year 2000. The radial nature of compact discs allows for information to be stored in unique combinations and designs, making it a truly valuable tool for education, job training, and an excellent research system. The audio, visual, and access qualities of compact discs are clearly superior to many other types of media. The fact that we are dealing with digital imaging, is the basic reason for the greatly improved quality. By not being constrained to a traditional linear pattern, the flexible format of compact discs allows a user to access any point on the disc within a second. Since compact discs are replicated much like LP records, millions of copies can be stamped out from a single master for a very low cost per copy. It costs only $1.20 to manufacture a plastic disc, and this cost factor will continue to decline.[11]

CD-AUDIO

In 1983, Polygram organized the Compact Disc Group to unite the music industry behind a determined effort to move into the digital age. The traditional analog phonograph system Edison originated in 1878, had come a long way from the 33 1/3 RPM LP of 1948, to the birth of the high-fidelity industry of the late 40s, to the stereo phonograph record of 1958: this system remained dominant for nearly a century. But in 1983, digital technology made history. The Compact Disc Group was determined to develop a permanent recording medium rather than something similar to the existing disposable type. The ideal disc would have a long shelf life, and the system developed to play the medium would have a built-in tracking system based on sensors rather than the mechanical guidance system with needles that could cause scratching and persistent wear and tear. Music was recorded on 4.75 inch compact discs with approximately 74 minutes in playing time, and the market simply exploded. During the first year of introduction, 50,000 Americans bought the new invention at an average price of $750. Within the first four years, over four million units were sold. According to all observers of the industry, the compact disc audio player was the most successful consumer electronic introduction in history. The crystal clear sound of compact discs found a very receptive audience. Over 65 million compact discs were sold within the first few years of availability.

Aside from the fact that CD-audio has a fantastic sound quality, the primary reason for its remarkable success in the marketplace was due to the unified efforts of industry leaders to *standardize* the product. Under this umbrella, only one CD system was ever marketed. With just one basic format to concentrate on, manufacturers focused on developing a single class of product, which led to greater market efficiencies and lower prices for the hardware.

By 1987, compact disc players could be purchased for less than $200 and music discs were commonly sold at prices between $13 and $16. In 1994, a five-disc carousel player could be purchased for less than $135, however the discs were still selling for $13 to $16. The hardware got cheaper, but the software remained relativity expensive. This hardware/software scenario will be repeated in other arenas as newer digital markets are opened. The fundamental economics of the digital age favor greater profit margins in the software arena, rather than in hardware production. By the year 2000, robots will be making a lot of products at much lower production costs. The creative ability in software will be an important area of concentration, particularly for independent entrepreneurs.

As for phonograph records, as one author has stated, "Phonograph records went the way of the eight-track tape." The rapid rise of compact discs and CD players meant the demise of phonograph turntables and vinyl records. Consumer electronic manufacturers are basically unconcerned with the old turntable market; they devote no time and effort towards improving the record format or the basic turntable. What we are witnessing in the 1990s is the end of a product life cycle in vinyl analog records. Many of us old-timers will continue to hold on to our turntables and classic LPs, realizing that these items are now beginning their first phase of becoming antiques. The phonograph record and turntable is one of the early victims of the *digital onslaught/juggernaut*. In time, traditional mainframe computers and others will bite the dust. In fact any industry, business entity, political or social organization that resembles or possesses characteristics of a *dinosaur* will have their technological judgment day before the digital onslaught/juggernaut. This is one of the most interesting scientific revolutions in history, it represents the crowning achievement of the past 1000 years of scientific, mathematical and technological contributions by many cultures the world over. The digital onslaught/juggernaut is bringing about scientific revelations and a scientific enlightenment.

CD-ROM

Compact disc read-only memory (ROM) is based on the same technology as the audio CD, differing only in its storage format and playback device. It's a direct descendant of CD-audio and was designed to serve as a microcomputer disk drive. The massive storage capacity of CD-ROMs generated a great deal of attention during its introduction in the 1980s. Like the audio CD, CD-ROM discs are inexpensive to replicate in mass quantities, (injection-molded from a single master) making them the data storage medium of the future.

The Dutch company Philips, developed the basic design for CD-ROMs in the early 1970s, with a specific goal of producing a product for data storage and delivery. During the mid to late 1980s, Bill Gates and Microsoft began a serious campaign and conference series to build support for the emerging CD-ROM industry. Bill Gates' commitment in this arena was critical, for he understood the long-term value of creating an *industry foundation* wherein everyone would benefit. Thus, his initial interest was to create a market in which many could prosper by helping to build an expanding software and hardware foundation. This cooperative spirit and atmosphere in the early stages of the CD-ROM industry development, is an excellent example of what can be done when industry leaders come together for a common cause, in this case, the creation of an entire new industry.[12]

What really makes CD-ROM look so attractive is that it's positioned with low-cost processing power, low-cost random access memory, low-cost hard disc capacity, and low-cost improved display technology. Multimedia systems for home use are equipped with sound cards and speaker systems that produce CD quality sounds from CD-ROM devices, all for less than $1700 (1996 prices). Given the flexibility of presentation, rapid access time (any point on the disc can be accessed in a second), and overall ease of use, whole new ranges of information products are being developed and many more envisioned for the future. The PC's evolution to greater functionality beyond the spreadsheet, word-processing, and database management tasks, has begun in full swing with CD-ROM. It has created a whole new realm of use for the PC: the distribution and individual access to large bodies of information.

Based on the 550 megabyte format of the 1980s, each CD-ROM disc was capable of holding:

(1) The textual contents of 280,000 printed pages.
(2) The contents of 1500 double-sided, double-density magnetic floppy disks.
(3) Nearly 100 minutes of video (not of the best quality).
(4) A crisp color picture and 10 seconds of narration for each of 3000 segments of an educational or reference program (almost 8 hours of content).
(5) 600 full-screen color photos.
(6) Large bodies of information represented digitally in any combination, in any proportion and order, of any of the above categories.

In early 1995, Philips and Sony announced that they would bring to the market a 7.4 gigabyte CD-ROM format capable of playing a 4 1/2-hour movie.[13] The so-called high density CD-ROM (HDCD), in read only format, became available in early 1997. This new multi-gigabyte CD is specifically geared for the movie/video market. The implication and industry prediction is that digitized CD-ROMs will replace the videocassette and VCR format within the next five to ten years. The much better picture and sound quality will ultimately win the global marketplace the way CD audio overcame vinyl records and the turntable. But don't stop there, this multi-gigabyte development will ultimately have a tremendous impact on the *VideoGame* arena, transforming that entire multi-billion dollar market with the intrusion of an avalanche of videogame titles in CD-ROM format.

By December 1995, another milestone was reached in establishing standards for the compact disc industry. Two groups of industry leaders composed of Sony and Philips in one camp, and Toshiba, Time-Warner, and five other electronics and movie companies in the other, agreed to (once again) establish one standard for a new super

capacity disc called *Digital Versatile Disc* (DVD). Thus, DVD became the final collective version of the multi-gigabyte high density
CD-ROM that Sony and Philips were preparing to bring to the market in 1997. With super density technology, theater quality sound
effects, picture quality better than laser disc, and megabyte capacity
far exceeding the first generation of CD-ROMs, this new standard
will be elevated as the global standard, taking the compact disc revolution to the next level.

By taking advantage of a new generation of lasers, engineers have
developed innovative designs to further the capacity of digitized discs,
that will ultimately become the standard platform medium for CD-
disc for film and the VideoGame arenas. Single-sided DVD formats
will be capable of storing 4.7 gigabytes of data; the so-called Single-
sided Dual Layer disc will hold 8.5 gigabytes; and the Doubleside:
Dual Layer discs will be capable of storing a massive 17 gigabytes of
information![14] These new formats and new hardware systems will be
introduced to the market in 1997 and will be the next explosive development of this era. The new capacities will overshadow the
original CD-ROM format, which translates to manipulation of greater
quantities of information.

With the rapid adoption of the Motion Picture Expert Group
(MPEG) standards for the transmission and storage of motion video
signals, the overall quality and presentation value of CD-ROM has
increased dramatically. In essence, the new standards are providing
the best quality digital video (the images are smooth, clear and very
professional) and digitized theater-quality sound. A key hardware
development that will escalate the digital onslaught/juggernaut to
transform the videocassette and videogame arenas, is the incorpora-
tion of the MPEG standard as a major feature of new microcomputer
systems. By late 1996, practically all new personal computers systems (with built-in CD-ROM drives) sold, included the new MPEG
standard.[15] This represented a major step towards positioning the home

entertainment market for widespread digitized software for the 21st Century.

Another factor in this digital equation is the rapid adoption of CD-ROM recorders (CD-R), which is a read and write digital system for home use. Approximately 25,000 units were shipped in 1994, however, by 1996, total shipments exceeded 1.8 million units. Again, the price of the hardware is moving this revolutionary equipment to center stage, which will have a dramatic impact on making the CD-ROM a preferred medium by consumer markets.[16] One of the main reasons the videocassette captured the small format, home entertainment market in the 1970s, was due to the recordable feature of the medium. If consumers are able to record on CD-ROMs the way they currently record on videocassette, then there is no question that this will be a major wave in the 21st Century. Given the introduction of blank Double Side: Dual Layer discs (which can hold 17 gigabytes of data), additional disc capacity for the personal computer will take a quantum leap into the future. This single development will bring enormous savings to many people, particularly developers and small businesses struggling to lower the costs of their operations. Industry analysts predict that by 1998, CD-Rs will sell for around $300 and will be a prime candidate to replace many of the millions of installed read-only CD-ROM drives

According to Dataquest Inc. (a company based in San Jose, California that compiles statistical information on computer technology) approximately 3.6 million households had multimedia/CD-ROM systems by the end of 1994.[17] With roughly 26 to 27 million households that own computers in the United States, the market for CD-ROMs is still relatively young. However, the growth curve has been phenomenal in recent years. The year 1993 was the turning point: the sale of computer systems pre-configured with CD-ROM drives, grew by 1800 percent worldwide. This momentum continued in 1994, and by 1995 the industry standard for most PC systems included CD-ROM drives. With the hardware expansion campaign putting more CD-

ROM drives in the home market, the rush to develop software began to snowball in many directions. Thus, as we headed into 1995, the market for CD-ROMs was considered poised for a major growth cycle.

In December 1986, there were approximately 53 consumer-oriented CD-ROMs on the market.[18] By April of 1988, the total number of titles had grown to 230. The number of titles for CD-ROMs experienced a tremendous increase during the first three to four years of the 1990s. In 1993, over 70% of all CD-ROMs produced in the world were made in North America (with most of the action occurring in the United States). About 25% of worldwide CD-ROM production for that period was produced in Europe. The rest of the world's involvement was very minimal or nonexistent.

By 1994, nearly 8000 titles of CD-ROM information products were available. In both the years 1988 and 1994, the majority of CD-ROM products that hit the marketplace were developed in the United States. Clearly, the U.S. has been at the forefront in spearheading the growth of CD-ROM products on a worldwide basis. Most of the production and consumer markets for CD-ROMs were centered in America and Canada.

However, for many of the early pioneer developers, the CD-ROM market has not been a pot of gold. One of the reasons for the low sales figures centered around the hardware issue: the number of installed-based systems in consumer households and other locations is estimated to be less than six million in America.[19] In addition to stiff competition (8000 titles fighting for shelf space) and production costs, the benefits and profits for the early pioneers are yet to be realized. In a *Business Week* article in May 1994, Dataquest Incorporated provided these observations:

> ... one-third of all CD content companies have revenues of less than $50,000 a year, half of them pull in less than $125,000 and 5% make $1 million or more...The cost of de-

veloping the more novel interactive content is rising along with the quality.[20]

Other problems associated with certain types of productions, deal with the difficulties of securing "licensed rights" for various segments required for a proposed project. CD-ROM producers are acknowledging that for contemporary projects, "There are perhaps 1,000 or more sources of licensed rights that will wind up in a fully developed CD-ROM."[21] However, despite these numbers and obstacles, the future looks very promising for CD-ROM products. During the 1993 Christmas season, CD-ROM software generated $102 million in sales revenue, an impressive figure over previous years. Industry analysts are projecting that by 1997, 37 million software units will be shipped in a rapidly expanding worldwide market. If CD-ROMs follow the same J-curve of CD-audios, then we can expect phenomenal growth in future years, particularly for more sophisticated, specialized products with more creative features.

In the foreseeable future, perhaps the only real challenge to CD-ROM popularity and growth (as single units) will come from multimedia services flowing over phone and cable lines. Repositories of huge database file servers distributed over high-speed fiber-optic cable or satellites, may divide the market for these types of information mediums. But like so many of the perplexing issues of the Information Age, there is no clear picture of how this market will ultimately be structured: many people may still desire to have their own archival CD-ROM libraries of specialized information in the same way they collect and store CD-audios. It will all boil down to what the consumer desires, and this market will ultimately have to consider the global consumer.

As we entered the 1990s, a larger variety of CD-ROM titles were produced, as opposed to the earlier areas of concentration. For instance, most of the titles of CD-ROMs produced in 1988 were concentrated in a few general categories that catered to limited audiences. Of the 230 commercially available CD-ROMs in 1988, most were focused on the archival, statistical and librarian markets. Some of the product areas consisted of the following:

(1) Medical, pharmacological and veterinary products, (20 titles).
(2) Book and serial reference data CD ROMs (approximately 21 titles).
(3) Bibliographic references and abstracts of literature, (20 titles).
(4) Scientific and engineering reference and bibliographic products, including many scientific encyclopedias.
(5) Finance and business products, which experienced a significant growth curve starting in 1987. Areas of concentration included financial news, economic and industry statistics, business directories, and prices of stocks and bonds.[22]

By 1994, the range of titles of CD-ROMs had experienced tremendous expansion, from encyclopedias to Tarot card games. Expanded use by all segments of society has generated greater awareness concerning the full potential of the medium. The CD-ROM market is wide open and growing, and that growth will continue as the Information Age becomes more entrenched and acceptable by millions of people in societies throughout the world. For African American entrepreneurs and producers, the field is wide open to enormous possibilities, particularly in education, history, science, music and an endless number of other areas of interest. Most of the 8000 commercially available titles of CD-ROMs in 1994 did not feature African Americans, or if they did, the presentations and images were of the traditional recipe. For black people to have strong, positive images of their culture and history represented in CD-ROMs, they will have to develop these new, dynamic products themselves![23]

We have identified this unprecedented period of opportunities and development, as it relates to the *black experience,* as *KyberGenesis! KyberGenesis* is the futuristic beginning of a major industry movement for scientific and technological development in the *black* world. If black people are to be successful and prosper in the 21st Century, there has to be a major movement to harness the dynamic power of science and technology on a level similar to the Moorish dynasties in Spain and Portugal during the 8th to 14th Centuries. A serious lack of unity and a well-defined *vision* and *mission* are the roadblocks to this critical development. This new and dynamic era is a major door of opportunity that should not be bypassed by those who are fully aware of "what time it is."

DIGITAL TECHNOLOGY AND THE FILM INDUSTRY

Some major far-reaching decisions will be made in the near future regarding the basic production and distribution systems of the film industry. The digital juggernaut is moving toward redefining the industry and creating new opportunities and a broader base of market participation. Hollywood has been the dominant force in the film-making world for nearly 80 years; how the industry leaders respond to the challenges of the digital age will determine their role and position in future periods. In 1994, we entered a period of chaos and there were no clear definitions, boundaries or technological architectures that were certain to prevail in the future marketplace. Two of the critical issues facing the film industry in coming periods are cost of production and distribution.

DISTRIBUTION

Digital technology will redefine the channels of distribution for films. Since the Home Video and Cable revolutions of the 1970s and early 1980s, the distribution system or the route that most first-run feature length films will follow are:

(1) Theater exhibition
(2) Home Video
(3) Pay-per-view (Cable)
(4) Pay TV services like HBO and Showtime.
(5) Basic Cable
(6) Network (free) TV
(7) Independent TV
(8) Foreign markets (with specially scheduled releases
   for theater, video and cable).

One of the main goals of Information Age industry developers is the creation of a massive system to rapidly distribute films directly to home subscribers via fiber optic networks and associated technologies (movies-by-demand). The decision of whether to distribute first-run feature films via this new network, bypassing the theater exhibition channel, is a hotly debated issue during this chaotic transition period. Theater chains and the Home Video markets might be in a desperate struggle for survival by the year 2000, if the decision is to circumvent these channels. However, the decision certainly is not a simple one. Total revenues of the Home Video market were $13.2 billion in 1993. For many Hollywood films, as much as 45% of their revenues are derived from the Home Video market. Analysts also point out that nearly 57 million people visit video stores each week. The sheer magnitude of these numbers are not to be taken lightly by anyone performing budget and projected sales analysis on future periods. Nevertheless, dramatic changes will take place due to the power of the digital onslaught/juggernaut.

For the theater system of the future, greater changes are predicted to take place. George Lucas, the trend-setter film maker and creator of the *Star Wars* and *Indiana Jones* film trilogies, offers these observations on the issue of theater exhibition:

Older theaters will be gone. I think today's multiplexes are going to expand and become larger entertainment centers that also have IMAX theaters and maybe 3-D theaters. There are going to be bigger, higher-quality images and better sound. There will be a much higher quality of presentation. Things like our THX sound system in theaters will add to that.[24]

A couple of key decisions may decide the structure of a new distribution system: the potential profit margins of a newly proposed digital channel of distribution (greed), and the issue of developing industry standards and a unified position backing specific technological and distribution architectures. Industry leaders are in a position of tremendous power to declare a major revolution in the film distribution arena.

COST OF PRODUCTION

Digital and computer technology will gradually bring about a dramatic shift in the actual cost of producing major motion pictures. The special effects wizard, George Lucas, has focused much of his time and energy toward merging the creative advances of high-technology with that of filmmaking. Since the extraordinary success of his first *Star Wars* film in 1977, Lucas has channeled most of his profits and resources into Lucasfilm Ltd. and several related high-tech companies. Feeling that Hollywood was too slow for his thinking and out-of-touch with the rapid advances of the current technological age, Lucas set up shop in Northern California (near Silicon Valley and the San Francisco Bay Area) and began his independent, high-tech movement in filmmaking. Time and the microcomputer revolution of the 1980s has proven that Lucas was right about his fundamental shift in film development. High-technology has brought about a major shift in film production, as digital imaging transformed the special effects and content development of film.

Using state-of-the-art techniques and computer workstations made by Mountain View-based Silicon Graphics, Lucas has remained focused on making exciting high-risk films, with excellent quality at a low cost. In an interview session with the *Wall Street Journal* regarding the issues of how emerging technologies will affect movie-making and entertainment, Lucas revealed the budget numbers associated with *The Young Indiana Jones Chronicles* production:

> We did a shot in the TV series for $1,500 that would have cost a studio $30,000 if they were doing the same shot for a feature film. We're inventing new technology that I feel confident will allow us to cut that cost in half again. Within the next couple of years, we'll be able to take what was a $30,000 shot and do it on the big screen in full resolution for $6,000 or $7, 000.[25]

By using new computer/digital technologies, Lucas and company have been able to make crowd scenes with just a handful of actors, and elaborate background period scenes that were completely computer generated. At his Industrial Light and Magic company, the real-life looking dinosaurs that were featured in *Jurassic Park* were developed using these new emerging technologies. The technology of *Computer Generated Images* (CGI) will only get better with time. If the dinosaurs in *Jurassic Park* are forerunners of a new era in special effects, then we can safely assume that we are about to take a quantum leap into the unknown: the cinematic motion picture will become a much more powerful medium.

Given the explosive technological developments (we outlined in earlier sections) predicted for the remaining years of the 1990s, we can expect that the production quality of films will continue to rapidly improve. Lucas is clear on this issue as he tells us, "I think we may have reached a level here where we have actually created reality, which of course is what we've been trying to do all along."[26]

The excitement and rapid advances in the film industry are reminiscent of the *roaring* atmosphere of the 1920s that included the birth of the *sound era.*

Digital Matte Painting has moved to the forefront of film imagery in studios that are now focused on the power of new technologies. The impact of this move is both significant and scientifically revolutionary. In traditional matte painting for film, a mask covers part of a frame (or many frames), thereby replacing areas of live action film footage of actors on location or in film studios. The combination of matte paintings and action film footage provide the illusion of a director's vision for a particular scene. The scene could be on a distant planet in outer space, with matte paintings helping to create the atmosphere and environment. In the early days of cinema, paintings on glass were positioned in front of a camera lens; the painting and the movie set behind it, were simultaneously captured on film. Many innovative designs and images could ultimately be incorporated in a film by using these techniques.

The 1990s matte artists have a much larger array of technological devices and systems to use for filmmaking. By employing optical printers, scanners, sophisticated software packages (such as *Adobe Photoshop)* and computer systems, today's *special effects* artist is capable of designing and creating some very imaginative digitized scenes for film. With the emergence of these new technologies, developing "period scenes" on small budgets can be readily accomplished. And as memories and storage capacities in computers approach the billion and trillion byte marks (respectively) in the not to distant future, this area of filmmaking will explode in many different directions. Combine this fact with the emerging technologies of virtual reality, holographic imagery and other breakthroughs in special effects, and we can readily see how the entire industry of filmmaking will experience an enormous technological revolution. It is very important for black people to understand this, and not simply on some intellectual level, but on a level of mastering these new technologies as they arrive on the scene: this is the message of *KyberGenesis*!

Equipped with Mac computers and the *Adobe Photoshop* program, many of these early pioneers in digital matte painting are learning to reconstruct realities and to make them come alive in film. It is a comparatively low-cost process and will in time play a significant role in the majority of filmmaking endeavors. This represents a major opportunity to make high-quality *period* films with low budgets. Black entrepreneurs and filmmakers need to take full advantage of these new state-of-the-art techniques that are emerging out of the digital revolution. Black filmmakers need to broaden their perspective and explore a wider range of options: set up special effects departments in their organizations, purchase land and buildings and start their own studios and distribution networks. This is not pie-in-the sky or some unrealistic dream: Hollywood was started during a period of technological revolution and by those who were bold enough to seize that defining moment in history.

We need *period* films on the life and times of black scientists and great thinkers, and the great cultural and scientific traditions of ancient African Civilizations. These images and stories will inspire our children and the world. It may be historically accurate and well-meaning to portray the evils and horrors of the black slave era on the silver screen, however after nearly a *century* of those stories, we feel that this message has been driven home. It is *time* to use our resources and talents to explore the rich and varied history of thousands of years of African history: we have been locked in this 400 year room of history long enough. There is an urgent need to inspire our children and the world with a much broader vision of the African universe.

GLOBAL INFORMATION INFRASTRUCTURE

Emerging out of the telecommunication and digital revolution of the 1990s, is the grand concept and global vision of an *Information Super-*

highway. With the United States as the leading exponent and global apostle of the Information Age, trend-setting images and symbols are moving this nation further to the forefront of a major global communications revolution. The centerpiece of this new superhighway is a computer network called "Internet," which was built by the Pentagon in 1969 as a backup military option in the event of a nuclear war paralyzing world communication systems. Thus, Internet, a mass of interconnected computer networks, was strategically positioned to be the surviving communications system in the event of a holocaust. Over 30 years later the system is now the main artery of a major effort to link additional networks to an ever-expanding web of communications developments on a global basis.

On January 11, 1994, Vice President Al Gore delivered a speech at UCLA in Los Angeles, outlining the goals, objectives and future plans by the Clinton Administration to further the technological designs of a national *superhighway.* Since that speech, Al Gore became the national guru for the telecommunications revolution. The term and concept of the *Information Superhighway* has generated grand visions of a vast superstructure of some type. Author John Naisbitt decries the terminology *superhighway*, as the descriptor of the coming new age. Instead, he sees a different technological reality; a *network of networks*, linking the entire nation and the world in a grand global communications system.

The fact that millions or even billions of people will be communicating to one another through a global system of interconnected computer networks, is a very powerful social, political, economic, financial and technological movement. It is estimated that by the year 2000, over one billion people will be using the vast Internet system. What we are witnessing is the development of a *Global Information Infrastructure,* promoted and sponsored throughout the world by a very vibrant free enterprise movement. Regional and worldwide conferences and summits are focused on expanding the building blocks of this movement on a global basis. Thus, the universal imperatives of the Global Information Infrastructure are: competition, open access, private investment, universal service, and deregulation or flexible regulations. When fully implemented by the majority of the world's nations, these global principles will define a new competitive marketplace for the 21st Century and beyond.

With nearly one million people joining the worldwide web each month, this movement is shaping up to be the fastest growing tele-communications revolution in history. It is certainly unprecedented and will bring about global changes that no one can possibly predict at this time. The magnitude and vast potentials for cultural, scientific and technological interchange is beyond mind-boggling. Fully aware, market-driven economies and societies will reshape our world in astonishing ways.

Given the explosive growth of the worldwide Internet system, it certainly behooves specialized interest groups with significant data-bases of information, to establish their own dynamic networks. These networks would then have the option to link up to the grand design or to operate independently. The grand design in the Information Age, favors important industry developments that can lift a small interest group of players to global prominence. African Americans need to pay very close attention to the full significance of these earth-shaking developments.

EXPANDING THE MEDIA UNIVERSE

The 500 channel future is another popular concept floating around in the media gossip. Digital compression technology that can raise the ca-pacity of existing cable channels tenfold, was the basic platform from which the media moguls built the 500 channel universe. Whether this is an accu-rate number of channels or not, one thing is for certain; there will be a much larger base of viewing options in the future. Many of these new channels will cater to specific niche interests, provide valuable educational and cultural information, and create opportunities for new entrepreneurial endeavors. In addition, we expect to be provided with more home shop-ping options in a rapidly expanding cashless society, access to electronic libraries, interactive pay-per-view events and concerts, specialized data services, and televised classroom sessions.

Rapid expansion of information technologies and the need for a much broader range of educational and training experiences by the general population, will accelerate a movement toward the use of TV for greater intellectual use, rather than today's mundane, addictive TV slop-drama. By necessity, people from all walks of life will need to *know* more and be better educated. Wasting valuable time watching useless TV dramas and slapstick comedy will be called into question by an urgent awareness that perhaps that time can be used more wisely, particularly if economic benefits are possible; training for a new job or expanding one's intellectual interests in a highly competitive global environment. Increasingly, it will truly be recognized that the "future belongs to those who prepare for it." There is hope that the technological medium of TV will finally be used for much greater purposes than selling soap and mindless programming.

It is interesting to note that African Americans have *not* taken full advantage (as a group) or have been ruthlessly excluded from the various communication revolutions that have taken place throughout the 20th Century. For instance, the Independent Black Film movement that developed between 1910-1953, did not result in the building of a major industry foundation. The birth of TV in the late 1940s and early 1950s, the Home Video and Cable revolutions of the 1970s, and the Microcomputer revolution of the 1980s, have all witnessed no major industry developments by African Americans. If no major industry construction emerges out of the 1990s telecommunication and digital revolution, it will represent one of the most profound tragedies of this period.

The rebirth of *Buckwheat* and the *Little Rascals* in 1994 was just the beginning of the massive image distortions that can proliferate on the worldwide *Information Superhighway* of the future. Images are important. I was reminded of this by Mai-Ling-Sue (a five-year old Chinese girl) while we were looking at pictures together in a car magazine. As she turned each page, she would ask me if I liked certain cars featured in the polished advertisements. When we got to a page that featured a large advertisement of a black man smoking a cigarette, Mai-Ling looked at the photo, and without missing a beat, pointed to me and said, "that's you, that's you." She then started pointing at the cigarette the man was holding (in the pose of a smoker) and wanted to know if I liked cigarettes. I tried to explain to her that I did not smoke and do not approve of cigarette smoking. But she was puzzled, for clearly the man in the picture (a symbolic representation of me, a black man) was enjoying his cigarette, so something was not right. Now take that same encounter and expand the scenario to include an *overabundance* of media images depicting basketball players, boxers, rap artists, criminals, and clownish images of black people on TV and in film, and we get the development of a concentrated image distortion. All black men do not play basketball or are comedians; some of us are lawyers, doctors, scientists, computer programmers, airline pilots and mechanics, stock brokers, bankers and many other types of professionals. But young minds pick up images very quickly. If we want 1.2 billion Chinese people to view African Americans as an intellectually aware group of people and important contributors to the American civilization, then there must be a concerted effort to get that message out in the new age. It is our hope that black people will work together to change the negative images in the Information Age, so that the Mai-Lings of the world will receive positive and dynamic images of our people and culture. If we are not involved in the total process of developing CD-ROMs, the new digital age movie-making process, database and file-server developments, and many other industry activities, then the future image distortions will very likely generate powerful negative statements and symbols that will shape the minds of billions of people the world over.

ROBOTICS, AI AND EXPERT SYSTEMS

THE JAPANESE CONNECTION

With the start of the 1980s, the technological push to develop high-level intelligent machines took a dramatic shift in world affairs. In 1981, Japan announced its intention to formerly initiate the development of the Fifth Generation of Computers. The so-called *Fifth Generation Project* grew to encompass the basic mission of Artificial Intelligence (AI) research, which includes expert systems, image processing, speech and other types of knowledge-based computer applications and systems. Fifth generation scientists dreamed of producing machines that could learn from their mistakes; developing complex systems capable of processing information in concepts, images and ideas, building machines with vast repositories of knowledge that would be able to solve highly complex problems; and computers that design and program other computers. This was the early 1980s, and as we move into the later 1990s, we can readily observe how all of this can come together by the year 2000. The technological *vision* of the Fifth Generation is fast becoming a reality.

Computer science and technology took a bold leap into the future, and in the 1990s we are witnessing the results of the extraordinary developments that have led us to the birth of an era of truly intelligent machines. Given the advances of science and technology that will arrive by the year 2000, we can clearly predict that robotic mechanisms that incorporate high-level AI systems will be a permanent part of our 21st Century world. The computer advances chronicled in the earlier part of this chapter represent very hi-tech technological breakthroughs, the kind that can give intelligent thinking and sophisticated electronic (or optic) brain power to robotic mechanisms. Much of what has previously been considered science fiction, will soon become part of our basic reality.

Japan's strategic technological shift in the 1970s was one of this century's major innovative periods, similar to the birth of television or the telecommunication era. Japan seized the *historical moment* and dramatically shifted gears for the advent of the Information Age and the 21st Century. During the 1970s, Japanese thinkers and writers flooded the general public with books, newspaper and magazine articles, television programs and other media sources, proudly proclaiming the promises and benefits of the coming new age.[27] Japan's decision-makers and business leaders embraced the concept of the end of the smokestack industrialism age, and gave total support and resources to move their society to the forefront of a global technological revolution. As a result of Japan's intense focus on the 21st Century (at that moment in history; and this is a lesson), they were able to collectively build a large population of sophisticated robots and manufacturing systems that were heavily dependent on computers and information. Superior products were produced, along with major production and economic efficiencies. America was slow to respond to the Japanese global shift.

When the 1980s hit the scene the robot was fast becoming a major fixture in the manufacturing and production arenas in both Japan and America. The 1980s increased the momentum for technological innovation. Computerized manufacturing facilities, robotics, CAD-CAM systems, and new custom-designed automotive systems revolutionized whole industries in the space of one decade. Many types of job functions and routine tasks were automated, wiping out thousands of jobs in the process. Many American workers experienced job displacement and problems of retraining which became critical for both rural and metropolitan America. As we move further into the 1990s, millions of jobs once held by people will no longer exist as paid positions. The unmanned and totally automated factories - run by computers and robots - is a major global trend of the future. High-tech competitive battles will speed up this process, generating destabilizing situations.[28]

ROBOTICS

The concept of robotic mechanisms is an ancient one, but the practical application and evolution of the automated worker began to take shape during the Industrial Revolution and the start of assembly line production. The basic term *robot* comes from the Czech word robota, which means compulsory labor. Rooted in the automation movement, the robot is considered a subcategory of automated devices.

The dream of building a realistic robot could not be realized until the invention of the computer in the 1940s. A field of study known as *Cybernetics,* born during this period, is based on interdisciplinary science focused on communication and control systems in machines, organizations and living organisms. The study of feedback mechanisms (the fundamental principle of automation) led to the development of electronic brains and programming systems designed to simulate human movements in mechanical devices. One of the first true robots to appear on the scene was called *Shakey,* and was designed and built by researchers at Stanford Research Institute in the late 1960s. By the 1970s, a serious effort began to take root for the mass production of robotic mechanisms.

Japanese involvement in the science of robotics is significant. The robot factory and assembly line is a reality in today's world. A Toyota Motor Company plant located in Toyohashi, Japan, represents a prime example of this new system. This plant operates 640 intricately designed robots with a computer system capable of producing 100 variations of three models of their cars. The Victor Company of Japan (JVC) employs 64 robots at one of its plants. These robots can fully assemble a camcorder. They perform 150 assembly and inspection tasks that prior to 1987 required 150 people. Robots are involved in the production of everything from VCRs to customized computer chips, and the Japanese have become the acknowledged experts in utilizing robots in solving practical problems in everyday life. Robotic technology has become synonymous with lower labor costs, around the clock operation, precision and speed, and the most reliable work force on the planet. By 1988, Japan used two-thirds of all robots in the industrialized world. The goal for the 21st Century is to rapidly expand this horizon by having one or more robots in the home. America was the first to invent the industrial robot, and began licensing this technology to Japan in the 1960s.[29]

ROBOTIC EXPLORERS

In July 1994, an important technological event was given widespread media coverage. A robot by the name of Dante II debuted in cyberspace and gave the world a glimpse of the role many robots will play in our future high-tech society. Dante II (a spider-like, eight-legged robot, standing 10 feet high and weighing 1700 pounds) was involved in a mission of research and data analysis on Mount Spurr, a volcano located about 80 miles west of Anchorage, Alaska. The robotic system was equipped with 1000-volt electric power/fiber-optic cables, eight video cameras, a laser range-finder, chemical sensors, and a sophisticated electronic brain with AI programming that was critical in guiding Dante II through difficult terrain consisting of deep mud and snow, and dangerous crater gases.

Dante II was able to move three feet per minute and had a 1000- foot hookup with a generator and satellite transmitter that allowed scientists, engineers, and Internet users to observe the entire operation via cyberspace. Built by John Bares and colleagues at the Robotics Institute of Carnegie Mellon University in Pittsburgh, PA, Dante II was heralded as the forerunner of robotic devices that will be used as explorers to other planets, involved in deep oceanic research, and used in dangerous industrial environments. Dante's exploratory experiment represents the beginning of a period of scientific adventures by robotic mechanisms, some of which will take Internet users (or a similar communication system) electronically on visits to the Moon, Mars and other destinations in space. By collectively experiencing the journey through the robot's electronic senses, mankind will truly go "where no man has gone before".

ARTIFICIAL INTELLIGENCE (AI)

At the core of the development of AI is the human desire to replicate the thought processes and related activities of the human mind. Advances in parallel processing in computer designs will continue the drive for smarter machines. Author Richard Jenkins provides insight on some of the early premises of AI developmental research:

> Studies of the human brain determined that its neurons, numbering in the tens of billions, work together in parallel to create intelligence. By copying some of the brain's processing strategies, researchers hope to build computers capable not only of solving large scientific problems but also of reproducing human intellect.[30]

AI attempts to bring about a linkage between words, ideas, and associations. The two major approaches that AI has taken are the physiological and psychological; the study and development of high-tech computing systems and penetrating research into the nature of human thought. With so many unknown complex thought processes going on in the human mind, the ultimate goal of AI, which is to create humanlike electromechanical *androids*, may never be fully realized.[31] However, advances in the near future will produce some very interesting and remarkable robotic devices.

EXPERT SYSTEMS

The most practical application for narrow fields of specialized knowledge has been the development of expert systems. These computerized systems are designed to behave like human experts on particular subjects. They consist of a collection of facts and rules that can provide educated guesses about problems in a variety of fields. Many of these programs can also estimate the probability of their conclusion being correct and present a line of reasoning. For instance, an expert system in medicine designed to assist in patient diagnosis, will analyze a patient's laboratory test results, review the medical history and examine disease symptoms, and then provide a physician with a set of recommendations based on the analysis.

Thus, what's contained in these programs is the expert knowledge of a professional or group of professionals in some specific area of expertise. All expert systems permit users to query them about the reasoning behind their decisions; this characteristic is important in the interactive training environment.[32] Expert systems will continue to evolve with various hardware and software advances, and will contain a greater number of modular programs designed to increase the depth and intelligence of a specific subject. The continued development in high-level software languages will be the main source for providing stronger reasoning and intelligent capabilities for many optical disc systems of the future. The ability of expert systems to automatically write conventional computer programs is just one aspect of this movement. Optical-disc systems have begun to incorporate these new designs in order to enhance the overall potential of providing a truly creative interactive environment.

SATELLITE COMMUNICATION SYSTEMS

The period of technological chaos that we have entered in the 1990s, will witness the rise and rapid deployment of another communication wonder of this age: *artificial satellites.* As the global telecommunications industry struggles to redefine and reconstruct the world for the 21st Century, the most dynamic and intense scientific and technological struggle in history will bring about extraordinary developments and possibly some amazing opportunities. The wireless revolution of the 1980s and '90s, along with digital age technologies, has corporate planners and research scientists pursuing various paths in search for the ultimate and most efficient technological communication system of the future. This is definitely a period of *cautious optimism*, particularly for the industry leaders who must decide where to invest billions of dollars on projects that may or may not be the winning system. Multiple trillion dollar global markets are at stake, and everyone knows that a wrong move or decision could bring about a collapse in a major business entity or industry. There are bound to be some *dinosaurs*, as revolutionary technologies transform entire societies the world over.

The satellite option features some interesting characteristics: it's wireless, it has a wide range of possibilities and potential uses, and digital technology now gives it greater power and flexibility. A brief historical review of satellites will help to put these issues in proper perspective.

HISTORICAL REVIEW

The first artificial satellite to orbit the planet earth was *Sputnik 1*, which was sent into orbit October, 1957 by the Soviet Union. This event accelerated the race-for-space movement between the United States and its Cold War adversary, the Soviet Union. On November 3, 1957, the Soviets launched *Sputnik 2* which stayed in orbit for 112 days. On January 31, 1958, the United States launched its first satellite, *Explorer 1,* and became the second major global player to put a satellite in orbit. As the decades rolled by, over 3000 satellites and many space missions continued the quest for space exploration and man's ability to learn more about the universe we live in.

Many of the earlier satellite missions were scientific in nature and provided invaluable information about the electromagnetic spectrum and "radiation belts" surrounding our planet. Measurements of magnetic fields, cosmic rays, solar radiation, the density, temperature and ionization of the upper atmosphere, and examination of space phenomena have opened entire new fields of study and are responsible for various types of industry developments in many fields. Satellites equipped with astronomical instruments made observations of various phenomena that was impossible to examine from earth stations due to the radiation absorption in the atmosphere. A wider range of X-ray sources were discovered in the 1960s and '70s. Scientific observations through satellite eyes unveiled the mysteries of gamma rays and ultraviolet radiation, and revolutionized the study of physics in these areas.

Thus space exploration has been of practical use to the daily functioning of society. Many spin-off benefits that are completely unrelated to space, have and will continue to revolutionize our daily existence. Greater knowledge of the universe we live in is a fascination shared by millions of people the world over. The enormous popularity of the *Star Trek* series, the *X-Files* and the *Star Wars* movies have certainly proven that there is an intense interest and concern for "what's out there". The all-seeing eyes of space satellites circling our globe, are providing us with valuable information about the earth's mineral resources, and will eventually produce greater knowledge about space matter and new sources of energy on other planets. As we uncover more information about our planet, solar system and galaxy, mankind will most likely discover the ways and means of unlocking the vast treasure chest of an unlimited store of energy resources.

The Dawn of the Golden Age of Astronomy: 1995

The science of astronomy began to explode in 1995 with the use of sharper and more efficient hi-tech telescopes. With better telescopic eyes to peer into our universe, scientists began reporting some very remarkable discoveries. One of the new tools that helped to revolutionize this scientific arena is *infrared imaging*, which enables telescopic vision through the dust and glare of neighboring stars. This work and specialty was pioneered by Dr. George R. Carruthers, an African American.[33] From observatories such as the Lick Observatory on Mount Hamilton, scientists reported the discovery of planet-like objects orbiting stars like our sun, the existence of new galaxies, the birthplace of comets, a second black hole in our galaxy and other mysterious phenomena. High-tech telescopes and other information age technologies will continue to broaden our *vision* of the universe in ways we have explored in science fiction. "Space, the final frontier" (as the *Star Trek* series reminds us), will play a much greater role in the 21st Century in our conscious development as a species on the planet earth.

The discovery in 1995 of a planet orbiting a star similar to our sun, is a very interesting development. As reported by astronomers Geoffrey Marcy and Paul Butler of UC Berkeley at Lick Observatory, this planet is orbiting the star 51 Pegasi in the constellation Pegasus: the distance from earth is approximately 45 light-years. Other mystery objects with planet-like characteristics, are making their dramatic appearances under the telescopic vision of our new hi-tech telescopes. NASA unveiled its plan in 1996 to initiate a program called "Origin Project," that will build a new generation of telescopes to seek out new planets in the cosmos. Astronomers like Marcy and Butler are now actively searching for distant worlds and intelligent life in our galaxy. The 21st Century will witness a very intense interest and growing support for this area of space science.

The Dogon Mystery Star

The Dogon people of Mali, a black ethnic group now living in West Africa, have maintained and preserved, for countless generations (over 700 year tradition), a body of ancient astronomical scientific knowledge that has completely baffled the modern world.[34] Scientists do not understand how these people can possess the knowledge they have about the universe, without the benefit of modern technology. Painted on the walls in the caves and hills of modern Mali, is the Dogon celestial science that renders an accurate assessment of our solar system, planetary movements, star formations, galactic space and the existence of an unseen mystery star scientists call Sirius B (the Dark Star). The Dogon have accurately plotted the orbits of stars circling the giant star Sirius (called *sigi tolo*). In 1950, American astronomers confirmed the existence of the Dark Star which orbits the massive Sirius. Dogon ancient science states that Sirius B is the smallest star and has the most density of any star in our galaxy. Modern science has confirmed that Sirius B is a *White Dwarf*, a star that has literally consumed its nuclear energy - burning out - and is in a state of cooling off for billions of years until it is as heatless as outer space.

According to the Dogon, the complete orbit around the giant Sirius takes 60 years, and this has been calculated and confirmed by modern day astronomers. The Dogon mystery system has taught for countless generations the 60 year cycle of Sirius B. According to their science, the Dark Star (called *po tolo* and which cannot be seen by the unaided eye) "is the most important star in the sky." In their over 700 year tradition, the 60 year cycle is sacred, and at the end of this cycle the earth, the giant star Sirius, and the Dark Star will be in perfect alignment. Thus, every 60 years the Dogon celebrate the *Sigui,* the time when this celestial alignment takes place. The last Sigui was held in 1937; the next scheduled alignment will take place in 1997, and this event will very likely be monitored by scientists all over the globe. There is much to be learned from ancient African science, and African Americans should dig deep into many of the mysteries of African Civilizations.

SATELLITE ORBIT

Geosynchronous Orbit is the operational cycle that has now become the standard in the space industry. NASA launched Syncom 2 (the first satellite to follow this orbital path) in 1963 and established an important milestone for satellite science. In geosynchronous orbit, a satellite is launched into a circular orbit over the equator at an altitude of 22,300 miles. In physics we learn that an object placed in a circular orbit will travel at a constant speed. Scientists discovered that the higher the altitude of an object (satellite), the lower or less speed it will have relative to the surface of the earth. Thus, by placing a satellite at an altitude of 22,300 miles (35,800 km) over the equator, the result is a geostationary orbit, because at that point the satellite is moving at the same speed as the earth, rotating once every 24 hours. Hence, it's scientifically possible to place a satellite in orbit that can have a fixed position over some specific spot on the equator. Combine this scientific reality with advanced digital technologies (reviewed in earlier sections) and we can fully appreciate the enormous possibilities inherent in this type of communication network.

The greatest expense and risks in this type of communication venture are the up-front development costs of the satellite, and the transportation or rocket expense in launching the satellite in orbit. However, if the satellite is successfully placed into geostationary orbit over the equator at the designated altitude of 22,300 miles, technically the system would be able to orbit in the vacuum of space indefinitely without any rocket or propulsive power. If its entire orbital cycle is maintained and no part of it passes through the earth's atmosphere, the satellite may continue to enjoy an orbital life for a very long period of time. It's a high-risk venture, but it's fascinating and can be very profitable in the long run. Loaded down with the most advanced technologies of the 1990s, new satellite ventures will have an expanded list of features over and above what previous satellites could offer.

TELEDESIC CORP., IRIDUIM, and others

Given the enormous technological potentials (and the end of the Cold War), the race for space is no longer a contest between superpower governments. The new global reality has initiated a movement that may flood the equatorial belt with perhaps thousands of hi-tech satellites by the year 2000. Perhaps the most sensational announcement of planned satellite network systems, came from an alliance formed by McCaw Cellular Communications, Inc and Bill Gates' Microsoft Corporation, to establish an independent company called Teledesic Corporation. Revealed in March 1994, the new business entity plans to establish a network system of 840 satellites that will circle the globe in low orbit, offering a large array of services. An article appearing in the *Wall Street Journal* cited the following:

> A ... plan to launch a $9 billion satellite network is being
> derided as the next Star Wars - as in the failed defense
> strategy,...By the year 2001, Teledesic plans to have its net-
> work of 840 satellites circling the Earth in a low orbit, offer-

ing a broad array of interactive voice, data and video services at prices similar to conventional wired services.[35]

Other companies such as Motorola Inc., Communications Satellite Corp., Loral Corporation, and Westinghouse Electric Corporation are actively pursuing projects that will offer wireless phone, data and fax services to global customers. Motorola has a 34% stake in Iridium Inc., an international consortium that plans to spend $3.37 billion to develop a 66 satellite global network system.

These and other satellite projects from Japan, Europe and elsewhere will steadily divide the concentration and power of the global telecommunications industry in the 21st Century. AT&T's $12.6 billion acquisition of McCaw Cellular, tells you something about their strategy for the future: the handwriting is on the wall and they don't intend to be a relic of the past. The satellite revolution of the 1990s will play a key role in the development of the new wireless industrial power base of the 21st Century.

THE 21st CENTURY

Holographic imagery (three dimensional photographic images), virtual reality (computer simulated environments and models), the science of superconductivity (the flow of electrical current experiencing no resistance, will deliver high-speed levitated trains and ships) and hypersonic air travel (air travel at two to three thousand miles per hour) will all be part of the dynamic 21st Century world. The decade of the 1990s represents the transition period that will organize the foundation and standards for our next century. Black people need to understand that this is clearly the *time* to make dramatic changes in response to the enormous implications of these expected future developments. This new paradigm shift should be studied very closely and given top priority by black organizations, governments, and think tanks throughout the world. It's important to develop strategic plans, hold conferences, and strongly consider reengineering many of our current organizations in order to fully participate in what we consider to be a period of incredible change.

CHAPTER THREE

BLACK SCIENTIFIC LEGACY

Khafra K Om-Ra-Seti

THE KYBERGENESIS CONNECTION

Without a carefully defined master plan and collective *vision* for the 21st Century, the black world is essentially rudderless in an ocean of endless possibilities and suspended in the permanent postponement of Dr. King's *Dream* of a utopian society. The *KyberGenesis Connection* is a call to action; a significant revolution of the spirit and creative mind-set of the black world to redefine itself in the midst of the momentous Information Age Revolution.

We are in the initial stages of the birth of a new age and a revolution in paradigms for continued scientific progress. This requires a transformation in consciousness and values, with significant attention given to establishing a proper base of priorities. We need not wait for validation or certification from the rest of the world to begin this movement. *KyberGenesis* is a collective unconscious revolution of the spirit that is focused on mastering the science and technology of this era.

For the black world, the mission of science and technology is an urgent matter. A major technological renaissance movement is required to revitalize the economic and technical stagnation that permeates far too many segments of our communities. A vast number of black people will be left behind in the wake of this current technological revolution if no significant movement is initiated. Far too many black people (in particular our young people) are locked out of the American Dream and the technological wave of the 21st Century: complacency at this moment in history only means that a huge disaster awaits us in a few short years. This is no time for day dreaming, giving a few motivational speeches or passing out a few scholarships to only our brightest; the message of *KyberGenesis* is to start a deeply entrenched scientific and technological movement for the survival and success of generations to come. *There is an urgent need to do something about our future now!*

Black people need to give this movement the same kind of spirit and energy that focused around Dr. King and the Civil Rights Movement. Many of our best scientific minds need to focus on building and sustaining a peaceful but brilliant revolution of profound significance. In addition, this movement needs to be given the kind of financial and economic support necessary to place it on a fast track of success and superior development.

We explored in Chapter Two the historical significance (in the early 1980s) of Japan's strategic technological shift to initiate, on a grand scale, the development of the *Fifth Generation of Computers*. Starting in the 1970s, the bold visionary leaders of Japan began a program for active mobilization and support of a master plan for their people and the 21st Century. We stated that, "During the 1970s, Japanese thinkers and writers flooded the general public with books, newspaper and magazine articles, television programs and other media sources, proudly proclaiming the promises and benefits of the new age. Japan's decision-makers and business leaders embraced the concept of the end of the smokestack industrialism age, and gave total support and resources to move their society to the forefront of a global technological revolution." This is a lesson and a vivid example in this century of the collective will of a people.

A model similar to this should be adopted by African Americans to promote broad-sweeping reforms in the educational system, revolutionary rehabilitative programs for the prison system, collective action on the business and economic fronts, and the propagation of *KyberGenesis* in all forms of media at our disposal. *KyberGenesis* seeks to bring into consciousness a higher level of respect and commitment for knowledge, technical expertise and education in the black world. Many of the genius and creative minds of our people are trapped in a vicious spiderweb of poverty, hopelessness, mis-education, violence, drugs, and a host of other social pathologies. We must harness the power of these new technologies in the war to help liberate many people from these vicious cycles of aimless lives that have no substantial long-range goals.

KyberGenesis is a call to use our knowledge, historical genius and resources to develop a new scientific imperative and paradigm for the black world: it's a call to participate in one of the most dramatic scientific revolutions in world history. In the 1990s, the black world is at a perilous crossroads, and science and technology are important pillars for our future survival.

BLACK SCIENTISTS and ENGINEERS EXPANDING our TECHNOLOGICAL UNIVERSE

The complete story of black scientific development must be told and fully understood by black people and the world. Like so many areas of black achievement, this important historical legacy has been nearly submerged in the generalized thinking of Western Civilization. We are constantly reminded of the social pathologies and failures of black society, but rarely does the media and educational system focus on the brilliant accomplishments and success stories of black pioneers, great innovators, and other positive developments. It's a sad commentary, and black people must not allow this to continue in the 21st Century; our children and the children of the world must know the truth: *From the Truth will emerge enlightenment and a new reality!*

There is a serious need for black historians to do an in-depth analysis of the overall impact of African Americans on the scientific and techno- logical advancements of the Industrial Revolution. At present, we are only scratching the surface of this very exciting field of study. Also, present- day black scientists and engineers need to *write* about their discoveries so that we may have a larger database of well documented information.

One of the greatest assumptions in the western mythological system regarding black people, is that we have not been involved in the scientific and technological revolution of the past two centuries, that black people have made no meaningful contributions to science and technology! While this glaring omission continues in colleges and universities throughout Western Civilization, black scientists, engineers, mathematicians, physi- cists, and other brilliant minds, are quietly recruited by some of the most prestigious research and business organizations in the world. For the most part, their contributions to science and technology may never be known, such as the black scientists that worked on the *Atom Bomb* project dur- ing World War II.

There is a serious need to get African Americans excited about Information Age technologies and the exciting potential opportuni- ties that lay ahead. Our point in this brief discussion on some of the scientific achievements of black people, is that we need to pay closer attention to the sci-tech developments in the world; what inventions and scientific breakthroughs black people have initiated, and the significance of all technological breakthroughs. When a new technological era is born, great opportunities and economic developments are presented that were not available before: there are greater advantages to developing a new venture at the beginning of a major scientific revolution.

For example, it is important to understand the broad-sweeping impli- cations of Lewis Latimer's (1848-1928) work in perfecting the light bulb.

His patent design (recorded in January 1882 under the title, *Process for Manufacturing Carbons)* of the black dense carbon skeleton that constitutes the electric light filament, gave the world a cost-efficient, longer lasting lighting system. We should have films and television shows highlighting the important achievements of the early black pioneers who participated in the Industrial Revolution at the turn of the 20th Century against heavy odds, and despite the absence of what author Russell L. Adams cite as "freedom from full-time pressures for personal survival, and a stimulating cultural environment?"

Black scientific minds produced railway switches (W.H. Jackson, 1897), rotary engines (A.J. Beard, 1892), refrigerators (J. Standard, 1891), electric railways (W.B. Purvis, 1894) the Graphite Lubricator (Elijah J. McCoy, 1843-1929, *"Is it the real McCoy")* and many other inventions. These were major contributions to the advancement of the Industrial Revolution and yet, even in the 1990s, we are still bearing witness to the writings of those who are attempting to use science to support their claims of a false notion of black inferiority. Black people need to present the complete history of black scientific and technological achievements in ancient, medieval, and modern times on an unprecedented level in this new age reality.

COMMUNICATION SYSTEMS

Rapid advancements in communication systems brought tremendous progress to all levels of advanced societies. Throughout history various methods were employed to facilitate long-distance communication such as smoke signals, the drum, sun-reflecting mirrors, fire, water, homing pigeons, paper, and the pony express. With the coming of the Industrial Revolution, the world was reshaped, redefined and conditioned to the surging pace of the scientific and technological revolution.

Practical application of communication by electricity came in 1837 with Samuel F.B. Morse's invention of the telegraph system in the United States. The Morse method of dots and dashes enabled messages to be sent letter by letter through the new revolutionary medium. The system was universally adopted and developed into a major industry. The next major technological advance for wire communication systems was voice communication. Voice transmissions, or telephone, was invented by Alexander Graham Bell in 1876. The technological advantages and superior services of telephone over the Morse code received rapid approval from the commercial markets. Telephone evolved into a major monopolistic industry in America during most of the 20th Century.[1]

GRANVILLE T. WOODS (1856-1910)

Many people referred to him as the "Black Edison," for Granville T. Woods was a brilliant inventor in the field of electronics. Granville's electromechanical genius produced over 50 patents in his lifetime, many of which were highly significant in furthering the technological evolution of the Industrial Age. His love of the mysteries of electricity remained a burning passion throughout his professional career. The Woods Electric Company of Cincinnati controlled the many patents and inventions that came from his fertile imagination. Beginning in 1884 Granville's reputation as a great inventor grew, as many of America's largest corporations came to him for use of his patents. Westinghouse, American Bell Telephone, General Electric, American Engineering and others found need of the unique and brilliant electrical designs that Granville produced. Patent number 315,368 (April 7, 1885) was a remarkable invention that could be used to transmit messages by electricity using voice signals rather than the Morse Code. This invention was eventually purchased by Bell Telephone. In his description to the United States Patent Office, Granville brings out the superior qualities of his new innovative system:

> My system (called by me "Telegraphony") entirely overcomes
> the failings of the ordinary key and sounder...the sounder at

the receiving station will cause the air to vibrate in unison
with the electric pulsations that traverse the line-wire. The
person at the receiving-station will thus receive the message
as articulate speech.[2]

One of Granville's other great inventions was the *Induction Telegraph,* a system designed to facilitate communication between two
moving trains. Modern civilization owes a great round of applause to
Granville T. Woods and many of the other black inventors that came
before and after this great man. But because this civilization fails to
recognize black achievement, they are not given the same respect as
Edison or Ford.

Despite the massive legacy of slavery, black people were very excited
about the enormous possibilities of the Industrial Age. As a black man,
Granville T. Woods lived through one of the worst periods in African
American history. In his patent entitled *Telegraphony,* Granville was clearly
describing a unique system for voice communication. It is extremely unfortunate that he was unable to expand the Woods Electric Company into
a major telephone and telegraph company prior to the turn of the century.
Westinghouse, General Electric, American Engineering, and most importantly, Bell Telephone were all standing at Granville's door eager to purchase his inventions. Granville was inventing voice communication devices within the same time frame that the telephone was introduced to the
world. Black historians need to examine more closely the enormous impact of Granville T. Woods and his historic legacy.

There is a lesson here, which is the close connection between the introduction of an important innovation and the development of an
entire industry. Granville was clearly at the forefront of the emerging
telecommunications industry in America, and perhaps some other
major technological developments. The 50 patents he was awarded
in his lifetime, were significant contributions to the advancement of
communication technologies and other fields of electronics. Unlike
Bell, Edison and others, Granville did not achieve the enormous fame and

fortune of his peers, or a prominent place in American history books. His contribution to telecommunication and inventions by others, helped to give Bell Telephone the technological edge to dominate the telecommunications industry in America.

The arrival of the telephone was a phenomenal success, it was a far superior technology than the dit-dit, dah-dahs of the Morse Code, banging out letter by letter the written word. Voice communication over long distances brought about a whole new range of possibilities and revolutionized the industrial economic infrastructure of many countries the world over. Phone communication sped up business transactions, brought about greater efficiencies and smoother integration in large corporations and governmental organizations, provided an economic boom for world commerce and capital markets, and provided convenience and prosperity to a broad area of everyday life. The business *deal*, and the day-to-day communication needs of the average person had evolved to a much more personal level, bringing people closer together. The advent of the telephone was one of the most important events of the Industrial Revolution, and like the computer of the Information Age, it reorganized many things.

The creativity and resourcefulness of African Americans were very much alive after the destructive period of the Civil War. There was a tremendous growth in industry during this period, and despite the hardships and nearly universal suppression, by the year 1913 black inventors had patented an estimated one thousand inventions. Their creative genius was felt in such diverse fields as electrical equipment, industrial machinery, rapid transportation, chemical compounds, and throughout many other areas of the industrial arts. These black pioneers were pressing forward with the zeal and excitement of the new era.

THEORETICAL   PHYSICS

British physicist James Clerk Maxwell advanced the theory of the electromagnetic nature of light in 1873 in his thesis *Treatise on Electric-*

ity and Magnetism. Expanding on this thesis, Heinrich Rudolf Hertz discovered electromagnetic waves in 1887, which led to the development of wireless communication and the commercial success of radio in the 1920s. By 1900, many scientists were focused on unveiling the secrets of the *electromagnetic spectrum* that included light, heat, and radio waves.

Early pioneering black scientists were also eager to expand the knowledge of this spectrum of energy sources. The first African American to receive his Ph.D. was Edward A. Bouchet (Yale University, 1876) and his concentration was in physics. Dr. Elmer Samuel Imes (a brilliant African American physicist) received his Ph.D. in Physics from the University of Michigan in 1918. Dr. Imes' contribution in advancing the examination of theoretical physics is significant. Historian and economist, James G. Spady elaborates on this point as he writes:

> Elmer S. Imes ... established definitely that the quantum theory could be extended to include rotational states of molecules. His doctoral dissertation, one of two known publications by Imes, appeared in the *Astrophysical Journal, 1919. Measurements of the Near Infrared Absorption Spectra of Some Diatomic Molecules* initiated the field of high-resolution spectral studies. This alone earned for Imes a lasting place in both theoretical and industrial physics.[3]

DR. CHEIKH ANTA DIOP

Albert Einstein, the best known scientist of the 20th Century, began publishing his theoretical papers in 1905. His third major paper in 1905, *The Special Theory of Relativity,* left many scientists scratching their heads; in general, the mainstream scientific community did not understand or agree with his thesis. The principle of relativity and the principle of the invariance of the speed of light (the speed of light in a vacuum is a universal constant) were the two main postulates of this revolutionary theory. His most famous theorem, $E=MC^2$ (energy is equal to mass times the speed of light squared) is a symbolic reminder of his legacy and impact on the 20th Century. James G. Spady's comments on Dr. Cheikh Anta Diop's (1923-1986: the Senegalese physicist and African-Egyptologist, and a brilliant linguist, anthropologist, archeologist, historian and political activist) interest in Einstein's theories is fascinating.[4] He tells us that, "At a time when only a handful of people in the world understood Einstein's relativity theory, Diop translated a major portion of it into Wolof, the language of his people." During a period of his scientific career, Dr. Diop worked in one of the most distinguished nuclear research centers in France. This particular center was established by Frederick Joliot-Curie, "son-in-law of Marie Curie who, with her husband Pierre, won the Nobel Prize for the discovery of radium."

As a *Black African Futurist,* Diop believed that as the world's oil reserves are depleted, nuclear fusion (thermonuclear), solar and other energy sources would be the best replacements. He envisioned the replacement of gasoline-fueled automobiles by hydrogen-fueled vehicles, a process that is being examined in research laboratories around the world. Diop felt that the continent of Africa has enormous natural potential for generating many forms of energy sources. In his book, *Black Africa,* he explored a number of possibilities for continental growth, unity and development.

Advances in *Quantum Mechanics* in the decades preceding the beginning of World War II, gave the world a mathematical foundation for describing the physical phenomena of electromagnetic waves and atoms. Further advances led to new fields of study in physics: elementary particle physics, superconductivity, nuclear physics, condensed matter physics and other specially defined areas.

BLACK NUCLEAR SCIENTISTS AND THE MANHATTAN PROJECT

Near the close of the war, both the United States and Germany were in a race against time to develop the world's most destructive weapon in history; the *atom bomb*. In America, the people and institutions involved this project were under tight security. Scientists working on the Manhattan Project (code name for the atom bomb project) were under oaths of secrecy not to reveal its development. There was real concern in President Truman's Administration that the Germans might have been the first to develop this weapon. Thus, billions of dollars were secretly earmarked for this top secret undertaking. Some of the best nuclear minds in the world were focused on this project. The more popular and well known physicists associated with the Manhattan Project were J. Robert Oppenheimer, head of the Los Alamos Laboratory (the place where the bomb was being assembled), Ernest O. Lawrence of the Radiation Laboratory at the University of California at Berkeley; and Enrico Fermi and Arthur H. Compton of the University of Chicago.

Dr. LLOYD QUARTERMAN

In recent years the world has come to learn that there were many black scientists that also worked on the Manhattan Project. Dr. Lloyd Quarterman of Columbia University, one of the black nuclear scientists that worked on the atom bomb, was specifically cited by the U.S. Secretary of War for "work essential to the production of the Atomic Bomb, thereby contributing to the successful conclusion of World War II." In a rare interview session with Professor Ivan Van Sertima in 1979, Dr. Quarterman revealed some little known facts regarding his life's work and the other black scientists that worked on the Manhattan Project and other research activities. In his words, "...the world's first nuclear reactor, which used the atomic splitting process in a peaceful way, was set up here in Chicago. It was under an Italian scientist, Enrico Fermi.

In 1948 I did all my quantum mechanics under him."

In addition to Quarterman, over 12 black scientists worked on the Manhattan Project. Dr. Ernest J. Wilkins and Dr. William J. Knox, who like Quarterman, played leading roles in helping to solve the riddle of the atom. The other scientists included Sidney Thompson, George W. Reed, Clarence Turner, Dr. Moddie Taylor, Robert J. Omohundro, Sherman Carter, Jasper Jeffries, Benjamin Scott, Ralph Gardner, Harold Evans and Clyde Dillard.[5]

As one of the leading black scientists on the Manhattan Project, Dr. Quarterman's brilliant career included a period of time working with Einstein at Columbia University, and a period of critical research at the Argonne National Laboratory, which he joined in 1946. At Argonne, major research and development of nuclear reactors took place. The team of scientists that Dr. Quarterman worked with developed the first nuclear reactor for *the Nautilus,* an atomic powered submarine.

DR. HENRY T. SAMPSON

African American contributions in the area of nuclear physics have been substantial in the 20th Century. Many of these scientists have labored in research laboratories around the world, receiving little or no recognition for their significant inventions, penetrating research and creative ideas. While researching this area, it was our good fortune to have made contact with Dr. Henry T. Sampson, the inventor of the *Gamma-Electric Cell.* Dr. Sampson received his BS degree from Purdue University, his MsC from UCLA, and a MsC and Ph.D. from the University of Illinois. For many years he was the Director of Mission Development and Operations, Space Test Program at the Aerospace Corporation in El Segundo, California, where a great deal of his pioneering work was developed. Continuing in the scientific tradition similar to Drs. Quarterman, Knox, Diop and others,

Sampson's Gamma-Electric Cell device converts nuclear radiation from reactors or isotopes, directly into electricity without going through a heat cycle. The device was awarded patent number 3,591,860 on July 6, 1971. In the nuclear fission process, which involves the splitting of the atom, radioactive materials emit ionizing radiation that can cause serious damage to living tissues. Constructive methods to convert these powerful radiating energies into practical and safe energy sources, is the fundamental philosophy behind the development of Sampson's Gamma-Electric Cell. His device represents one of the peaceful solutions towards the use of nuclear fissionable products.[6]

In a completely different arena, Dr. Henry T. Sampson is best known as one of the most important black writers of this century. Sampson's area of concentration in this field has been the black presence in the film and entertainment industries. His extensive writings in this area are widely recognized as important source material for anyone researching this long neglected area of American history. In his now classic book entitled *Blacks in Black and White: A SourceBook on Black Films* (now in a newly revised and expanded 2nd Ed., 749 pp.), Sampson traces the history of the black film industry from its beginnings around 1910 to its demise in 1950, chronicling the activities of pioneer black filmmakers and performers who have been virtually ignored by film historians.

DR. SHIRLEY A. JACKSON

Following in the tradition of black scientists in physics, Dr. Shirley A. Jackson received her doctorate from MIT in theoretical physics. From 1976 until 1991, Dr. Jackson conducted research in solid state and quantum physics, theoretical physics and optical physics at AT&T Bell Laboratories. Since July 1, 1995, she has held the Chairmanship of the U.S. Nuclear Regulatory Commission.

BLACK PEOPLE and SPACE SCIENCE

Many African Americans have made very significant contributions to the space program throughout its nearly four decade existence. Colonel Guy Bluford, Dr. George R. Carruthers, Patricia Cowings, Christine Darden, Isaac Gillam IV, Colonel Frederick D.Gregory, Dr. Mae Jeminson, Dr. Ronald E. McNair, and Robert E. Shurney, are just some of the people who have made remarkable contributions to several branches of space science. It would take an entire book to describe their achievements, and we certainly cannot do that here. However, we would like to mention the significant work of some of these space pioneers.

- ◆ **Colonel Guion S. Bluford:** Colonel Bluford was the first black astronaut to journey into outer space. His maiden voyage took place on August 30, 1983.

- ◆ **Brigadier General Charles F. Bolden Jr., United States Marine Corps:** Prior to his current assignment, Bolden was mission commander and space shuttle pilot for four space shuttle missions, including the deployment of the Hubble Space Telescope in 1990. He has been one of the leading astronauts of this century.

- ◆ **Dr. George R. Carruthers:** Dr. Carruthers is a black astrophysicist and inventor of the *Far Ultraviolet Camera/Spectrograph.* Dr. Carruthers is one of America's most brilliant minds in the area of astrophysics and space science. He has written well over 60 articles for various scientific publications *(Astrophysical Journal, Science, Instrumentation in Astronomy, The Interstellar Medium,* and others) and was awarded patent number 3,478,216 on November 11, 1969 while he was still in his early twenties. The title of the patent was *Image Converter For Detecting Electromagnetic Radiation Especially In Short Wave Lengths,* which clearly points to Carruthers burning interest in the electromagnetic spectrum. His extensive research and his development of the ultraviolet camera/telescope, broadened the scope and vision of the science of astrophysics.[7]

◆ **Dr. Patricia Cowings:** Dr. Cowings is a NASA scientist and researcher, specializing in Aerospace Medicine, Human Vestibular Physiology, Bioastronautics, and Psychophysiological Biological problems of long duration space travel. In her work at Ames Research Center (at Moffett Fields, California), Dr. Cowings developed the Autogenic Feedback Training Exercise (AFTE) that includes the Autogenic Clinical Lab and biomedical monitoring system. In 1997, Dr. Cowings was recognized as one of the top 30 African Americans in science and technology in America.

◆ **Christine M. Darden, D.Sc.:** Dr. Darden is a NASA aeronautics scientist and one of the leading thinkers working to solve the *sonic boom factor*, which one day will allow planes to fly at hypersonic speeds (about two to three thousand miles an hour). From 1989 to 1994, Dr. Darden was group leader of the Sonic Boom Group at NASA Langley's Systems Analysis Division.

◆ **Colonel Frederick D. Gregory:** Colonel Gregory is one of the first black astronauts, and as a test pilot of more than 40 different aircraft, he has played a major role in America's Space program. He helped to design the *micro-wave instrumentation landing system* and has redesigned the cockpit for space shuttles in the 1980s.

♦ **Dr. Mae Jeminson:** Dr. Jeminson was the first black woman to make a historic journey into outer space. In recalling her experience aboard the Space Shuttle *Endeavor* in 1992, Dr. Jeminson stated that, "I felt a part of the universe, as much as a planet or the moon. That's what I remember most. Since then, I've always felt very comfortable wherever I was." A medical doctor and engineer, Jeminson had a double major in African American Studies and chemical engineering at Stanford University. After leaving NASA in 1993, she started Jeminson Group Inc. in Houston, Texas, a research organization that focuses on advance technologies, particularly those suitable and practical for developing countries.

♦ **Dr. Irene Long:** Dr. Long is the director of the Biomedical Operations and Research Office at the Kennedy Space Center.

♦ **Dr. Ron McNair:** Dr. McNair was a physicist and astronaut, and internationally known as a leader in laser physics technology. A man of many talents, Ron was also a fifth-degree black belt karate instructor and a jazz musician. Ron died aboard the Space Shuttle *Challenger* (in the company of six other astronauts) when it exploded in midair on January 28, 1986, one minute and thirteen seconds after lifting off from Kennedy Space Center.

♦ **Benjamin F. Peery, Ph.D.:** Dr. Peery is professor emeritus in astronomy at Howard University. His areas of research include the physics of stellar structure, evolution and nucleosynthesis, and the physics of interacting binary stars.

In the 21st Century there will be an enormous push to explore the vast potentials of our universe. The "Outer Space Connection," with its infinite possibilities, has long been a subject of interest by black people the world over. From ancient African Civilizations, to the Dogon Cosmological System, to Benjamin Banneker of the 18th Century, to modern day astronomers and scientists such as, Benjamin Peery, the black mind has been pondering the mysteries of the universe. A great deal of excitement will be generated in the field of space science in the 21st Century, particularly as new discoveries are made and space travel becomes a practical experience through the telescopic eyes of unmanned space vehicles.

BLACK INFORMATION AGE PIONEERS

Black scientists and engineers have made significant contributions to the astounding technological advances of the 1990s. During the 1980s microcomputer revolution, many African Americans were on the frontlines, initiating major breakthroughs in the areas of semiconductor technology, laser system designs, fiber optics, telecommunication system designs, and other related communication and scientific developments. Bell Laboratories, one of the largest research and development organizations in the world, provided the scientific workbench and employment for many of these innovative thinkers. In its staff of over 23,000 scientists, engineers and other types of technology experts, Bell has incorporated some of the most brilliant African Americans in these fields. Many of the approximately one to two thousand black innovators and researchers are involved in developing new scientific breakthroughs, while others concentrate on exploring the ways and means of applying the new scientific knowledge. The following is a brief chronicle of some of the leading black scientists and innovators in this arena:[8]

♦ **David Blackwell, Ph.D:** Dr. Blackwell is professor emeritus in mathematics at the University of California at Berkeley. His life's work has literally been in mathematics, and he is internationally recognized and honored for his work in statistical analysis.

◆ **Brian Jackson:** Jackson represents one of the most creative minds in the continuing development of semiconductor technology. Working out of the Advanced Large Scale Integration Development Laboratory at Murray Hill (the place where the transistor was born) during the 1980s, Jackson was one of the first scientists to experiment with using the X-ray lithographic technique to create designs for semiconductors. He specially designed and built a computer to automatically perform the semiconductor inscription task, and creatively used mathematical and programming methods to fine tune the operation.

◆ **Carolyn W. Meyers, Ph.D.:** Dr. Meyers' primary research concentration is on structured property relationships in metals, ceramics and their composites. She is the associate dean for research and interdisciplinary programs for the College of Engineering at the Georgia Institute of Technology and associate professor of mechanical engineering. Prior to her work at Georgia Tech, Meyers was the director of the Center for Professional Success for the SUCCEED Coalition, which consists of eight engineering programs in the Southeast focused on developing engineering curricula. She is considered one of the most important professors in her field.

◆ **Bartholomew 0. Nnaji, Ph.D.:** Dr. Nnaji is a professor of industrial and Mechanical Engineering at the University of Massachusetts at Amherst. His many responsibilities include his post as director of the Automation and Robotics Laboratory at UMASS; founder and director of NEMESIS, The National Center for Computer-Aided Medical Imaging and Devices for Diagnosis and Surgical Intervention Systems; founder and chairman of Geometric Machines Corporation; and editor-in-chief of the *International Journal of Design* *and Manufacturing.* Originally from Nigeria, Dr. Nnaji is an internationally recognized expert and consultant on robotics and automation. As a robotics researcher, Dr. Nnaji has worked to develop robots that perform precision manufacturing with great efficiency. He is at the cutting edge of a revolution in robotics that is destined to fundamentally change the working environment in the 21st Century.

♦ **William R. Northover:** A brilliant chemist, Northover's pioneering work at Bell Labs (from the 1960s to the 1980s) gave birth to some of the most important developments in *fiber optics* research. During a period of eight years of intense research, Northover and colleagues focused on the science of *glass fiber lightguides* that could transmit digitally coded information. In the 1990s, this technology is generally known as fiber optics, one of the most astounding scientific developments of the 20th Century. Further advances in fiber optics have lead to some of this century's most incredible inventions, with the impact on the telecommunication industry being the most dramatic. Fiber optic laser systems are completely revolutionizing communication networks all over the world. The glass fiber lightguides that Northover helped to pioneer have expanded the entire breadth and width of the communications universe.

♦ **Jesse E. Russell, Sr.:** Mr. Russell's expertise and in-depth knowledge of *microprocessors* was applied to the telecommunications industry in the 1970s. While working at Bell Labs in Columbus, Ohio, Russell designed a *smart* data terminal using Intel's first commercial microprocessor. As an innovative engineer, Russell came up with a new design for data terminals to monitor the frequency of phone call connections and similar types of network problems.

- ◆ **Earl D. Shaw:** Shaw is a pioneer in laser technology and is recognized by some history books as one of the early developers in his field. He is known as the co-inventor of the spin flip Ramon laser, "an important demonstration of lightwave turnability used for air pollution and other molecular measurements." Shaw's research developed a design to expand the range and complexity of laser technology.

- ◆ **James E. West:** Mr. West is a physicist and co-inventor of the foil electret, a device used to convert sound into electrical signals in hearing aids, portable tape recorders and lapel microphones. Most of West's research has been conducted at the Bell Labs Murray Hill research center.

Throughout the 20th Century, the creative genius of black scientists, engineers and other technological professionals have played a major role in helping to define and invent the industrial and information age society. They have labored against enormous odds with infinite determination and perseverance to translate their dreams into reality. Despite the legacy of institutionalized racism, black scientists have remained committed to a firm belief in their ability to rise above the barriers and misinformation that would stop their progress. Superior knowledge has torn down the false images and presented a truthful reality: black scientists are very important in the struggle for overcoming the massive racism that exists in Western Civilization.

As we move steadily towards the 21st Century, let us be conscious of the need of raising up a generation of *New Age* black scientists that are committed to the truth and will help to ultimately work for a better tomorrow. We must encourage our young people to take on the challenge of science and technology, and to prepare themselves for the growing demands of the Information Age Revolution and the broad sweeping changes of the 21st Century. As we state many times throughout this publication, we are at one of those pivotal points in history when massive changes will sweep across the entire world and redefine how we work, play, study and interact with nature. If indeed mankind is on a collision course with nature (as some scientists have warned), then future black scientists may need to master their disciplines to not only help their people in the struggle to be successful in the new age, but also to save our world! Substantial participation by black people in the current scientific revolution will help to define the new paradigm and overall mission of science and technology in the 21st Century and beyond.

PART TWO

PREPARATION FOR THE 21ST CENTURY GLOBAL AGE

CHAPTER FOUR

EDUCATION AND TRAINING WITH MULTIMEDIA

Timothy L. Jenkins

A Leon Higginbotham, former chief judge of the U.S. Court of Appeals for the Third Circuit, noted in his volume, *In the Matter of Color: Race and The American Legal Process*, that the antebellum South made it a crime to teach a Negro to read and the same criminal codes doubled the penalty for teaching him to write.

Yet in spite of these historic discouragements, literacy and education have always been a highly prized individual attainment. Understandably, after emancipation all forms of education and training continued to be central strategies for group advancement by African Americans. For the same reason, those opposed to their advancement have continued to make the denial of educational opportunity a principal means for assuring black economic and political disability. The Federal Courts have long been the source of relief in such matters, with a string of cases stretching from professional schools to elementary schools, both in the South and the North; the *de jure* denials of State-provided educational opportunities have been successfully challenged through Civil Rights litigation.

After the doctrine of separate and unequal education on the basis of race was formally struck down by the Supreme Court's 1954 ruling in *Brown vs. The Board of Education of Topeka*, the public schools faced a national challenge of providing *de facto* equal educational opportunity. At the center of such controversy have always been the continuing disparities in the public educational investments provided. Those investments not only include physical plant and facilities, they also include properly trained staff and comparable ratios between students and teachers as well as operating budgets.

As recently as 1995, however, the Southern Education Foundation was still able to conclude that 40 years after *Brown* and more than two decades after the judicial, legislative and executive branches of the Federal Government insisted that dual systems be dismantled, the enforcement of educational opportunity throughout the nation remains "restricted, fragmented and uneven." Similar conclusions apply in all regions of the country at the primary, secondary, and higher educational levels alike. In addition to the traditional requirements of education, we now have the matter of computer literacy as a central element in the preparation for future jobs and professions.

The U.S. Labor Department statistics declare that 70% of the jobs of the 21st Century will be computer related; and those jobs will carry a thirty percent premium in wages. Against this backdrop the U.S. Census Bureau reports that minority and low income children, especially those in central cities and rural areas, are far less likely to have access to computers either in their school or their homes. Beyond the access to a computer *per se* comes the requirement of a modem, the hardware attachments needed to enable a computer to access remote on-line data and information networks. Here too, income and location demonstrate a racial imbalance in modem access. Inner city African Americans and Hispanics as well as rural African Americans, Hispanics, and Native Americans are behind the general population in access to on-line networks, by three to fivefold. Soon the standard aptitude tests for admissions to college will only be given through personal computers. And an ever growing number of colleges and universities are establishing on-line computer connections for their admissions processes and enrollment actions.

Clearly the lack of computer and on-line access most black youngsters suffer, points to a major problem that is likely to scar the face of America throughout the next century, unless successful interventions are made now.

Fortunately, the technology for educational advancement, and even catching up for those with deficits, is already well advanced. The problem is making it both accessible and affordable as well as user-inviting on a racially evenhanded basis. Numerous examples show that when exposed to state-of-the-art equipment, black youngsters are not only able to compete as equals, but excel in their mastery of technology. Performance and a given aptitude is not confined to the mastery of electronic games; it includes computational skills, desktop publishing, multimedia production and artistic portfolio development. Across the country a rising tide of social activists have come to focus on computers in the classroom and in public libraries as the principal educational requirement of our time. Increasingly, when computers have not been provided as part of the school curricula, innovative efforts are being made to create after school access that looks to available sites from churches to national guard armories.

From coast to coast *guerrilla* technology projects have grown up to reach minority youngsters with the enlightenment of computer and telecommunications technology. In some instances these have been tied to churches, civic centers, and public housing programs. In other cases they have been inspired as free standing private tax exempt training organizations with the support of in-kind and financial inputs from private industry. In several cases substantially funded efforts have been launched as an inter-state joint venture between a major corporation and a single non-profit sponsor with multiple access points nationally. A giant step was recently taken by the leadership of the eight national "black churches," with the endorsement of the idea for the creation of a national super network aimed at the entire black community coast to coast in collaboration with a black enterprise, Unlimited Visions, Inc., located in Washington D.C. Through the Commerce Department and the National Science Foundation, the federal government has provided small sums as planning and operating grants for certain innovations. These are initiatives which are badly in need of collective orchestration, replication and expansion with cooperative public, community, and corporate leadership to exploit the uniqueness of the educational and training capabilities computers and on-line networks allow.

The whole purpose of education and training has always been to prepare the participant to function on his own according to the principles of instruction. The inherent understanding is that the student/trainee must adapt and apply those principles in ever changing empirical circumstances on his or her own. But a minimal educational process requires that the principles of learning be taught uniformly. The emerging recognition is that very few advanced educational objectives can be uniformly realized without applied technology. Curricula cannot be fully improved without technology. Teachers cannot be fully prepared to improve the management of their class load without technology. Improvement in school administration also requires technology. And without technology, the student learning to apply learning principles cannot reach optimal efficiency.

Increasingly the political discussions, both at the national and local levels, have focused on education as a major area of concern in making the United States as well as its lesser jurisdictions economically competitive. But within the broad margins of the question looms an even greater urgency, for black and other minority students are falling further and further behind. Lamenting the quality of the student being produced is not enough, we must do something about it. Especially acute is the need for action by and within the black community. Parents, community and business leaders alike need to engender public concern for better education of black youngsters as the only realistically long-ranged anti-poverty strategy. This carries with it the recognition that fixing the problem of education requires a new element of dynamism among

Blacks nationally as well as at the local level.

Sure the federal government can help by setting proper policies. But policies without practice will continue to miss the point. The need is for a popular awakening that *memory learning* is at best secondary to *learning to think*. We need to teach our children how to think, how to plan and how to implement a given strategy. In addition, we should consider the ancient African system of education, which was based on the premise that the university is within the individual and needs to be awakend! Innovative information systems and designs uniquely tailored to the needs of the black community, can play a major role in bringing about psychological awakenings for educational excellence. As a result, marketing educational technology in our communities is required in such a way that the case can be made as to why higher technology in education is less expensive in the long run even for the green eyeshade bean-counters; why it produces better results for the pragmatist; and why it is more fun for those who seek painless intellectual growth.

Consequently, a whole new set of promotions are required to make learning competitive with other discretionary uses of time for black youngsters. This requires access to attention-catching demonstration units to get parents and kids hooked before they decide to buy some other piece of high-cost electronic equipment. This means pro-educational technology propaganda. This means enlisting the support of celebrities and local opinion makers for educational endorsements. And most of all it means a thoughtful leadership taking back the control of school boards to assure that they not just serve as stepping stones to higher political offices, but contribute to restructuring education in innovative and result-oriented ways for the new age.

In the black community as well as the white, education is the building block for economic development as well as cultural enrichment. Therefore, the type of education provided must also be crafted to meet both the employment and professional needs of the market place as well as establish a sense of self in the broader society. To assure a proper fit, employers need to play a role in curriculum review alongside professional educators. It also requires those in the arts to enter the school houses as well. Such participation is of particular value in avoiding stale approaches long discarded as state-of-art primary and secondary school teaching.

Given the rate of change in the fields of technology where professional access to information quadruples every eighteen months, academicians cannot be the last to learn new applications. Therefore programs for constant contact between the school house, the culture centers, and the workplace are indispensable for teachers as well as students, because increasingly the distinction between education, entertainment, and training is not only likely to become blurred, but the role reversals of teachers and students indistinguishable as well. Ultimately, we will have to face reality, that when it comes to the full exploitation of computer technology, many of us from the old school just don't get it: sometimes it takes a ten-year old to show us how.

Because each participant varies as to his/her preparation at the start, individual assessments are an important part of the initial process. A wide variety of applicable diagnostic software programs are on the market that not only determine achievement levels, but the best selection of learning media as well. Through the use of these systems a training program can be individually tailored to each participant. A number of factors should be considered in developing an effective training process:

(1) The participants are likely to come with varied levels of preparation.

(2) Each individual will have unique abilities for learning.

(3) Each person will have somewhat different means for applying their learning.

(4) Each student will have varied amounts of time available for the learning process.

(5) Finally, they will need varied amounts of follow-up reinforcement after the study process is over.

More than ninety years ago, W.E.B. DuBois wrote that "education and work" were "the levers to uplift a people." While he may not have considered it at the time, for most Americans the educational environment is in a state of flux. Increasingly, preparation for the work experience requires on-the-job training rather than traditional classroom instruction; the requirements of the workplace are in a state of rapid change. Through the electronic use of visual images, the arts also become powerful teaching tools, facilitating the use of film clips, animation, diagrams, and free-hand sketches. Multimedia learning systems provide a unique response to each of these demands that will in time change the face of structured educational/training processes, from teaching basic numeracy and literacy to the high level skills required of a surgeon. Through multimedia, the course content is simultaneously supported by images, text and sound for saturation learning.

The capacity for individualized training would never have been possible in the traditional classroom, given the limitations of a single teacher. But with the advent of software operating independently on separate personal computers (PCs), the effect is to multiply the instructors. These types of computer-tutorials are another set of tools to provide remedial work for those who need it, without wasting the time of those who do not. The typically overcrowded environment in which education is offered to most young blacks, makes it of utmost importance that the technology exists to compensate for scarcity of teaching personnel. Also in this overcrowded environment, it is all too likely that the gifted black student will be overlooked or considered a restless problem-child simply because the material (as offered) fails to engage his/her interest.

Within the thousands of educational software products on the market, most are positioned based on the following four categories:

♦ **Drills:** These are the rote learning or practice programs useful for skill reinforcement, but not capable of creative instruction. More in the nature of a game, any learning that may occur is incidental. All too often when computers are made available to black youngsters, drills are the only programming of which these obsolete machines are capable of performing without sufficient memory or speed to execute complicated functions.

♦ **Simulations:** These call upon participants to role-play in imaginary situations. Using historically or geographically accurate settings, these literary devices invite the participant to become a scriptwriter for the development of story scenarios incorporating an individual's imagination. Simulations build experience, as well as, improved reaction times with pre-programmed decision trees. Almost nowhere is there a substantial body of courseware that makes use of the black experience to exploit simulation programming. On the other hand, through simulation software, students of all types can learn to design make-believe cities, governments, or businesses that go a long way in teaching the basic principles of thought.

♦ **Reference Materials:** These are not only the electronic equivalents to hard copy encyclopedias and reference books, but include the added features of multimedia for still and moving pictures, sound and animation with texts that branch off from a series of visual icons displayed on a PC screen. Combining a curriculum that provides an educational strategy, heightens the prospect that novel learning can occur at a pace of the student and in the direction of his/her curiosity. A small sample of programming exists which is built upon an Afrocentric perspective to assure it being especially inviting to black youngsters. But from this small keyhole a tremendous archway could result. Innovative software developers have not only fashioned visual images that connote color and feature differences, but have blended in names, gestures, music, and interests that have affinities with the black experience. As a result, such courseware has succeeded where all others have failed to get black youngsters at all age levels promptly engaged in intellectual pursuits. Once exposed to such software, students and teachers alike have clamored for more. As a result, the classes in which it was used soon became overly subscribed, with students waiting in the halls to participate in changing shifts.

♦ **Personal Study:** These are software tutorials that force-feed information at a pace controlled by the participant. While widely varied, these range from the least desirable elements of the old programmed learning systems - linear, rigid and with limited participant engagement - to intriguing duels of mind against machine to assure a full challenge to a participant equal to his/her unique level of ability.

Creatively approached, any one of these four systems can be used to tailor course content to trigger new levels of engagement by minority students, such as ethnically familiar computer icons, locations and names with instant recognition, and situational analogies drawn from real life inner-city experiences and black historical settings. An enormous potential exists for the development of a wide range of products. However, practically no software developers have heretofore vigorously adopted these affinity approaches to black youngsters. Instead, the superficial response has been the random re-pigmentation indifferently given to animated icons that occasionally suggest a token black presence in cyberspace.

A major challenge exists here for black educators and the educators of blacks. Before the educational software industry follows completely in the footsteps of the textbook publishers, innovative approaches are called for to design electronic material that is not only more inclusive in its content but also in its presentation. African Americans need to have a total presence in the software development field, particularly in education, the sciences, mathematics and many other technical fields and subjects. The discussion should not be Afrocentrism versus Eurocentrism, the issue should be real world education versus fairyland education. Unless our youngsters see themselves and their realities in the teaching materials offered, it is understandable that many of them will tune out on education as a form of *myth-information*. It is timely therefore that efforts be made to bring together the abundant teaching of musical and graphic art talent in the black community to electronically reinvent the teaching curriculum.

A previous generation can remember the *Negro History Bulletins*, published during the 1940s, '50s, and '60s and distributed in the mail by Carter G. Woodson's Association for the Study of African American Life and History. In its pages the periodic journal presented school level text and images of the black diaspora left out of the standard textbooks. These same materials and many more, generated in the interim, offer a wealth of content for electronic courseware in language, arts, science, history, geography, anthropology, and fine arts. Through the electronic presentation of such materials, master teachers can collaborate and share their successful experiences to create world class curricula. Using the combined deliveries of cable, online networks or even the VCR, these materials would go a long way in making education not only more relevant to black student interests, but more accessible as well.

If the relevant ethnic and racial content cannot be readily absorbed into the official curriculum, through after school and weekend classes offered at churches and other available facilities in the black community, ethnic-based material can be presented as academic and cultural reinforcements. The importance of such an initiative is heightened by the fact that black educators represent a minuscule percentage of public school curriculum developers, in spite of the enormous percentage they comprise of the public school student and teacher populations.

Increasingly, software developers are finding ways to stimulate learning through the vehicle of electronic games, which incorporate computer chips that allow programs to be interactive as well as contain vast memory banks. Such electronic games fall into three major classifications: (1) *arcade*; (2) *adventure*; and (3) *storytelling*. The typical *arcade game* tests rapid motor skills and coordination with minimal requirements for information retention or recall. The market penetration of arcade games among African American youth is quite dramatic, with statistics showing that 80% of black high schoolers are acquainted with the rules of such games. Unfortunately, these are the only computer-type games most black youngsters know or have played. The violent content of most arcade games leaves a lot to be desired as well.

The *adventure games* represent the next level of complexity. These call for the player to respond to programmed challenges through reasoned alternatives and choices to reach a given objective. Following the pattern of fairy tales or mystery stories, adventure games allow the player to match wits with the machine in an effort to win or reach the next level of complexity. Increasingly, efforts are being made to employ the techniques of adventure gaming to training and educational purposes to teach such skills as complex as electronic assembly and repair.

In the *story-telling* format, the intent of the game is to leave the process sufficiently open-ended to allow the individual playing to shape the final outcome. Unlike the adventure game, storytelling does not presuppose right and wrong answers *per se*, but simply accommodate a variety of possible directions. Games of this type lend themselves to creative writing skills, problem solving and issue analysis.

As the use of technology expands throughout education, such games will provide a means to engage black youth in both the procedures of computers as well as imaginative content reflective of the kind of experiences they encounter in life. It is also our belief that our youth will begin to expand their horizons if they *see* themselves reflected in their educational materials.

Through the use of computers and on-line courseware, the additional flexibility exists to allow the training to occur at varied times most convenient for each trainee, including pre-dawn and after midnight hours. And of course, all classroom courseware delivery can be video recorded for personal viewing at any time during or after the course duration. Among the core attributes of interactive computer- based training, is its ability to allow each student to advance at a pace uniquely configured to him/herself. For instance the teaching modules can be designed only to allow those using them to move on to the next grade of complexity, after the lower order of required knowledge has been demonstrably mastered. It also can replace the standard forms of examination to certify proficiency, allowing the completion of courses by some when others are only halfway along in the process. Consequently, the gifted or the intellectually challenged will not have to experience any dull moments in the learning process.

Another advantage is the ready access to multimedia excitement allowed by computer- assisted learning, both as a diagnostic and teaching tool. Not only is it capable of painlessly identifying those learning strengths peculiar to each student, it can also vary the approach to select the teaching style likely to work best for a particular learner. For example some retain information best by reading, others by hearing and still others by visual demonstration or animation. Through multimedia techniques, a selection of teaching methods can be identified which best matches student aptitudes. This looms large as an enhancement for black students, who tend to have a disproportionate exposure to television and an affinity for processing such forms of information that renders the classroom a very

pale competitor for attention. Not all "attention deficit disorders" are attributable to the students, some of them are brought on by the anti-
quated quality of teaching as well as the monotony of the materials and
teaching-disabled schools.

A further attribute of state-of-art multimedia, is its ability to be presented in CD-ROM formats capable for use in off-site homework assignments as well as in the class or laboratory. Because of the vast information
storage capacities of the CD-ROM, (see Chapter Two) it is capable of
providing a large volume of standby, supplementary information for reference branch-offs or detailed explanatory excursions at the click of the
finger and an equally facile return to the main path.

Distance Learning

Depending on the desired degree of sophistication, training technology can also be used to enhance traditional classroom instruction
through point to multi-point distance learning. A single teacher or
teaching presentation can then be simultaneously received in more
than one location hundreds to thousands of miles away from each
other, with resulting economies in personnel and travel costs. Such
techniques may be coupled with optional return audio and/or visual
feedback. Such visual feedback may be teacher or student controlled
or both. It may operate over telephone lines, local wireless systems,
cable or long ranged satellite delivery systems. It is capable of split
screens for up to sixteen or more simultaneous pictures.

Because the term distance learning has become a catchall desig-
nation for any system using one or more technologies in telecommunication, it would be useful to examine several applications in a bit
more detail. The learner may be an individual or a group, either in one
facility or many. The exchange may be one-way transmission of voice,
video, and/or data, or it may involve a two-way process.

In 1988, Congress initiated legislation to develop the Star School program for state-of-the-art telecommunication activities to improve learning for students in small schools, rural and urban settings, as required to reach under-served populations. As a result black student populations have been major participants in the Star program. The resulting Star School program was to be managed by the U.S. Department of Education to encourage innovation, collaboration, and exploration of new teaching styles and services for student and teaching professionals. Since its inception the Star Program has reached all 50 states, the District of Columbia, Puerto Rico, and the Virgin Islands. Various organizations have served as service providers, including the Black College Satellite Network. Many of these providers received Star funding to produce programs and expand the use of distance learning technologies. These have resulted in classroom instructional modules, cultural enrichment activities, and video field trips. Complete courses have been offered for credits along with in-service training and staff development programming. Through Star, the Philadelphia school system has developed a number of programs that highlight African American culture and art from various museums for nationwide distributions.

Satellite and cable distribution are the most commonly used distance learning technologies as well as the ones through which the greatest volume of programming is available. Using the same techniques that distribute most broadcast and cable TV signals, satellite-based distance learning services can efficiently reach hundreds or thousands of receiving sites located all over the United States.

Satellites travel in a geosynchronous orbit, which means they travel around the Earth at the same speed as the Earth's rotation. At 22,300 miles above the equator, the satellites appear to be stationary. Earth stations *uplink* the signal to the satellite, which is then *downlinked* to a concave receiving dish pointed in the signal's direction. The cost of transmitting a satellite signal to one location or a thousand locations is the same. Such a system would be a highly cost effective mechanism for reaching the entire span of the black community without the exorbitant cost of commercial broadcasts. While most satellite transmissions are one way, a variety of telephone and similar technologies can make satellite programming interactive by adding two-way audio, allowing for interactive exchange between distance learners and the source for feedback and clarification. This type of program is usually referred to as teleconferencing.

Using light waves sent through the thin glass strands called fiber optic cable, video and digital information (which use a fraction of the space and energy required by conventional copper cable) represents another delivery system. Because it is expensive, fiber optic cable is currently only available in densely populated areas. However, several states are building fiber optics as the backbone to networks that will serve schools, hospitals and government institutions.

Most of us are familiar with cable as the source for dozens of video channels available on home television sets. These same services are also available to many schools. Some cable companies have developed special services targeted to educators and students. As digital video technologies develop, cable is likely to serve as a transmission route for a wide range of interactive video services for both schools and homes. Cable can also serve as a "final mile" connection between a school and a fiber optic network or a satellite downlink system.

Microwave and instructional television fixed service (ITFS) systems are regional video distribution systems. They are used by a number of states and large school districts to distribute distance learning programming. These systems operate like a low-powered television station, distributing video signals to locations equipped with proper reception antennas to which they have line-of-sight access. Since the microwave signal travels in a straight line, the transmission range of these systems is limited to a radius of thirty to fifty miles. The FCC has set aside such licenses in cities all across America for the designated use of local school districts.

Educators with access to a computer, modem and the Internet also have access to an increasingly large selection of on-line data resources, dial up bulletin boards, and worldwide web images. These services offer electronic mail, research databases, information forums and discussion groups for a variety of special interests. On-line services typically charge some combination of a monthly fee, a per minute connection fee, and surcharges for access to specific information sources. In most cases the initial access is offered as a local telephone call, avoiding the cost of long distance rates. These same technologies can be used in combination with one another. For instance, an ITFS system might be used to feed a satellite signal from a centralized receiver to a number of locations. Similarly, a satellite program may use a computer system for electronic mail and the distribution of printed materials between points. Many educational users today are finding ways to share such resources.

Distance learning can be just as effective for providing new training information to other professionals as it is for the student. The interactive nature of its many services mirrors the collegial peer to peer exchanges. Thus it can prove a natural and effective way to share new information, upgrade skills and continue one's education without leaving office, home, or workshop.

The advantages of distance learning give it just as many applications in the community as among educators. For instance, it is an ideal means for civic education, community mobilization as well as issue dialogue with panels of experts on an infinite range of topics. For the black community, such methods could be improved conferencing without the necessity of costly travel, accommodations or loss of valuable time. Accordingly, teachers with a gifted way of presenting their materials can enjoy a class of thousands rather than a confined classroom. Similarly, the lecture notes developed can be shared with countless other teachers of the same subject matter, complete with visual supports and references. Consequently, new forms of instructional collaboration could evolve with teaching peers commenting on each others' work regardless of distance.

With the current pressures on teachers to prepare their materials for six hours of delivery some 180 days per year, distance collaboration could prove invaluable. Through such an interstate system of dialogue, levels of education might be lifted to a higher common denominator without the laborious approval process implied by national standardization efforts. Furthermore, the process of reaching beyond the confines of the classroom will allow interested parents to get into the mix. Not only will they be better prepared to assist with homework assignments, but offer suggestions for effective teaching as well, without the type of confrontations that typically occur during structured parent/teacher visits with lots of onlookers. In California the local telephone company has contributed a novel system called Parent Link, which allows telephone mailboxes between teachers and parents on a 24-hour basis.

Bill Gates in his 1995 book, *The Road Ahead*, cited a novel experiment in a Middle School in Union City, New Jersey. It illustrated how a PC network linkage between teachers/parents as well as classrooms/homes led to rapid improvements that allowed students falling well behind state norms to pole-vault three years ahead of their peers within two years. Along the way, drop out rates and absenteeism zeroed out. Such improvements have been duplicated in countless other cities where similar public/private investments were made.

Still, a further refinement of education and training can be provided that approaches the level of hands-on technical assistance. Through the device of a small camera mounted at the eyeglass level of the trainee, the instructor can see exactly how the student is performing an exercise in order to offer coaching advice throughout the demonstration exercise. Using combined CD-ROM and touch-screen technology, the trainee is able to finger point on a monitor to get collateral information on every step in a training exercise. Thus an automobile mechanic, paramedic, or would-be jumbo jet pilot can be talked through the required procedures either by simulation of actual problem solving or as "a help" activity (on-call during actual operations) for a seamless working and learning experience.

A case in point has an army tank crew respond to lifelike emergencies through a training exercise which exactly duplicates the sights, sounds, and instruments required on the battlefield. The same system can be installed in the control tower to talk an air traffic controller through a near collision crisis. Obviously, training conducted so realistically is likely to be infinitely more effective than one dimensional instruction could ever be, but cost may reserve its most advanced applications to a limited set of circumstances that can justify such expenditures. Simultaneously, it must be noted that costs are adjusted drastically based on the volume of the units of production. Therefore, the costs will be greatly reduced by the extent to which particular software packages are in widespread demand. For the X-generation of young blacks who seem to be totally bored or intellectually turned-off, such approaches may offer the last best hope for academic or training retrieval.

Some time may elapse before the cost-effective production systems and sale ratios, allow sophisticated simulation as well as expensive interactive CD-ROM courseware to become the rule rather than the exception. But for primary and secondary teaching systems faced with serious personnel shortages as well as escalating labor costs for essentially repetitive instructional requirements, interactive learning packages may be the most economical short-run solution. Needless to say, the development of such products carries with it a new set of interstate accreditation requirements which as yet are largely unknown. This process also presupposes the means for training the teacher/trainers to learn how to be facilitators in their proper application. The timing of the introduction of such techniques may also become, if not a political question, at least a labor policy issue, i.e. teacher "union rights" questions being of considerable importance. Because of these complexities it will be critically important that parents, as very interested parties, become sufficiently informed to provide citizen oversight to what public school systems decide upon as the new equal opportunity in education. Therefore, the recommendation is for a proactive national black leadership, which reaches out to local PTA groups with suggested courses of action and curriculum development to make use of technology as a matter of right.

Indeed, the question of access to any type of computer and telecommunications assisted instruction may be the next Civil Rights front, because inner cities and remote rural school districts are least likely to benefit from the new educational wave, absent an affirmative expression of public policy. Beyond the basic educational requirements of computer literacy in the context of typical public school curricula, a variety of enrichment applications exist when computers are used to access the world of educational data bases.

In 1994, the National Telecommunications and Information Administration commissioned the United States Department of Commerce and Bureau of the Census to collect data on household computer ownership in the United States. The Census conducted an extensive survey, interviewing over 54,000 households nationwide. In brief, the Census found that the likelihood that a U.S. household has a computer is directly related to the household's level of income, racial characteristics, and educational attainment. The greater the income and educational attainment, the greater the likelihood that the household has acquired a computer.

Among distinct racial groups, Asian and Pacific Islanders collectively have the greatest likelihood of owning a computer, followed by white households. Even among those groups with the greatest likelihood, however, household computer ownership does not reach 50 percent. Among racial groups for which there are data, black households are the least likely to own a computer. When the data is viewed by family income, fewer than 9 percent of families with income below $15,000 have a computer; up to 21 percent of families with incomes below $35,000 have a computer, and a little over a third of families with incomes up to $50,000 have a computer. It is not until family income exceeds $75,000 that more than half of the families have a computer. While the problem is most acute in inner cities and remote rural areas, the numbers show that when accessible, such facilities have even greater use than among the general population. Especially high rates of usage apply to free training materials and job search information.

The Census data documents that, until the level of education of the heads of the household includes graduate work, the percent of computer ownership does not exceed 50 percent. Less than a third of families where the heads of household completed 1-3 years of college have a computer. Less than five percent of the households headed by a person with less than a high school education have a computer. The level of modem ownership for outside connectivity on-line likewise increases directly with the level of education.

The data also documents that households headed by persons with at least a college degree are almost eleven times more likely to own a computer than households headed by a person who did not complete high school; white households with incomes above $75,000 are three times more likely to own a computer than white households with income between $25,000-$30,000; African American households with incomes above $75,000 are four times more likely to own a computer than African American households with incomes between $25,000-$30,000; and Hispanic households with incomes above $75,000 are five times more likely to own a computer than Hispanic households with incomes between $25,000-$30,000.

Finally, looking at the age of the heads of households, the data indicates that fewer than 40 percent of households overall have computers; less than one-third of families where the heads of household are in the 30-40 or the 50-60 age brackets have computers; there are computers in fewer than one-fourth of families where the heads of household are between the ages of 20 and 29, and in fewer than one-fifth of families where the heads of household are over 50 or below 20 years of age.

But state-of-the-art training and education are more than technical matters, they run to deeper levels of basic values as well. High among these values is a respect for learning itself. Negative peer pressure away from learning must be confronted as part of the process of reinforcing educational awareness. Here it is important to combat the suggestion that studying is not a *black thing*, so dangerously common among African American youngsters. Tragic inferences have resulted from such thinking that intellectual activities and interests are "white" or indigenous to Asians and therefore off limits to African Americans, with predictably disastrous effects on our survival as a people. Warning against such a danger, Dr. Jawanza Kunjufu suggests, "This may be the first generation of African American youth who will not exceed their parents in academic achievement." The collapse of many black communities in America is imminent if this tragic trend is *not* reversed. The untapped genius of an entire generation will wallow in the mud of despair and hopelessness if the *light* of regeneration does not activate the collective mind. Should experience prove this to be true, it will not be the fault of our children, it will be ours. For it will mean that in spite of the vast arsenal of high-tech tools available to make the learning process both exciting and personally relevant to black youngsters, we failed to make good use of them. Not only are black people at the crossroads, we have reached a point where a new road and a new beginning is required.

Starting with such basics as self-esteem and pride of heritage, magnificent software can be developed. Using the simple tools of PC-generated clip art, animation, video inserts and text, teaching youngsters the way educational software can be generated would be the equivalent of rolling together our storytelling traditions and love of games. The same multimedia PC techniques of integrating sounds and sights along with text, could foster imaginative courseware that addresses black-on-black homicide, teen pregnancy, substance abuse, health risks and other relevant social and cultural issues.

To date, slight interest has been shown by the mainstream software developers in niche educational materials. But the need to be self-reliant requires that the black community not wait for others to solve its problems. It already has possession of the necessary skills to create these new age products. Collaboration is required to bring educators, clinicians, techies, and moral leadership together with the goal for innovative curriculum development.

Although the first applications of computers were in mathematics, general education was soon to become one of its major expressions. From programmed learning of the '60s, we've come to think of computers as teaching machines. Early computers were too cumbersome and costly to be practical for educational purposes, but when microcomputers came along in the '70s, it suddenly became feasible. Now that personal computers are becoming ever more powerful and less expensive, teaching programs and software are evolving rapidly.

While a lot of educational software is on the market, very little can be said to be revolutionary or even very good. And almost none of it has been addressed to the particular needs of African American students, in spite of the fact that they constitute almost half of the student populations of the largest 100 school districts in America. Similarly, other than on the matter of English language instruction, precious little in the way of instructional software has been addressed to the other ethnic minorities. When taken together, these minorities with blacks constitute some 75 percent of the big city school districts nationwide.

According to statistics from the Children's Defense Fund, the educational system is scarcely succeeding, with one out of every four black eighth graders obliged to repeat at least one grade, and the reading, science, and math levels of black 17 year-olds are nearly the same as those of white 13 year olds. The average SAT scores for black students were lower than for any other racial or ethnic group. The rate of black youngsters going to college has fallen, and by recent counts, very few African Americans earned a Ph.D. in science and only a handful earned doctorates in engineering. In part, this is the product of the low expectation of black students by the nation's public school teachers, some of whom are themselves black!

All of this points to the need for interventions both in the school systems and beyond. Clearly the levels of public investment in high-tech training should be made equal, but beyond that, new private supplemental initiatives are required in the form of after school enrichment programs focused on computer literacy. In addition, we need computer programs for math and science as well as social science studies that recognize the African American presence and contributions. Such high-tech schools could be introduced in church facilities from coast to coast. Through the use of computer networks, common programs could be developed. Satellite linked Direct Television and PCs also offer solutions for reaching those facilities on-line which may not otherwise be connected to a telephone or cable system.

But the educational infrastructure will also determine the success of such innovations. School buildings must not only be water tight, but enjoy the physical security to keep costly equipment from casualties and theft. At the same time, electrical current and telephone access must be provided to schools at a much improved level.

Surroundings Count Too

The chairman of the Federal Communications Commission, Reed Hundt, is quoted as saying, "There are thousands of buildings in this country with millions of people in them who have no telephones, no cable television, and no reasonable prospect of broadband service ... They are called schools." As dark as such humor may be, the other reality is that were we able to provide the latest in video disc players, electronic scanners, computers with big screen projectors and overheads, etc., the aged physical plant of most schools could make little use of them. For that reason, another aspect of educational reform for African Americans, calls for the rethinking and redesign of the school house on a vast scale, particularly in light of new multimedia educational technology. Modular class scheduling, maximizing the use of high cost equipment, the increased use of films, television, tapes, slides as learning tools, staff reorganization and methodology changes, have many implications for the school's physical plant as a factor in providing quality education.

While the expansion of instructional aids, media, and interchangeable small and large group sessions have been in development for some time, only recently have the spaces within which these techniques are employed, been broadly revisited. Except in a few cases, the spaces being used were not planned for such purposes. While a large number of new schools or training adjuncts to churches are being built, most of the spatial adaptations to technology will have to result from retrofitting of existing structures. The learning situations will be varied and so will the methods for storage and calling up information, using vintage structures.

Three types of interrelated facilities are required: spaces for learning, spaces for production, and spaces for storage and retrieval. When audiovisual teaching aids were in their infancy, these three functions suggested three distinct activity zones, i.e. a classroom, a production studio, and a library. With the computer's sophistication these functions and spaces can more or less merge.

There may not be a reason to distinguish seminar rooms from laboratories or lecture halls. Indeed multiple rooms can be electronically linked as though they were one big auditorium, while still allowing the intimate feel unique to small settings. With desk top surfaces, the same room can be designed to provide individual work stations for multimedia production, with low rise partitions to contain noise and lessen distractions. As for data storage, cabling will allow networks to access files and file servers from any number of points and from any required distance, including Internet.

New thinking is suggested on the modular use of space to accommodate more than one function. Considerations should include the desired atmosphere through attention to shape, proportion, materials, lighting, color, and acoustics. Here the inputs of faculty and student users can be valuable, along with an appreciation of their psychological reactions toward a particular interior design. Wherever possible, the relationships with surrounding and connected space deserves consideration. Lobby and waiting areas, traffic patterns in and out, rear versus front entry are all relevant especially when large screen projectors or non-projected displays are required. Visibility and comfort, as well as lighting choices and acoustics, are frequently only given negative attention through complaints after the fact. Such postponed attention can be costly, requiring that systems once installed be re-configured later. The better approach is for full and careful planning from the beginning.

To be fully effective, the technological teaching apparatus introduced, should consider temperature control, ventilation, seating arrangements, and other relevant factors to minimize unwanted side effects. Economies of space, materials durability, ease of cleaning, appearances and costs, should all play a part in the selection process.

While all of this may be obvious on its face, the record is replete with failures. Thus, it's important to consider such elements in a timely fashion; concern is needed on the probable result of participant discomfort; for the avoidance or need for constant corrective interventions. Such atmospherics are particularly critical to communicating subliminally the value and importance attached to the work expected to take place in the space provided.

Teaching the Teachers

One of the contributing factors inhibiting the successful diffusion of teaching technology throughout public education, is the relative indifference shown toward the preparation of teachers. At the heart of the matter, teachers must be adequately trained and retrained as the technology changes. Providing such training, with the specific mission of computer training or science, is required. The teaching technology available has applications to the Social Sciences, History, and Geography, as well as Civics and Government. And with the universal budget retrenchments in Music Education and Arts, multimedia may well be the primary means to keep such subjects in the curriculum. But the use of new technology is far from self-evident, and careful introductory training is required. The average age of teachers has been shown to exceed that of workers and managers in the general workplace. It should not be surprising, then, that most of them grew up and started careers long before the advent of PCs and state-of-the-art telecommunications. Consequently, special attention is required to assure that teachers understand how they can benefit from computers and communications systems in their particular area. It is also necessary to lessen their anxiety of technological encroachments on their professional turf.

It is all too often the case that new technology introductions are presented with little or no proper teacher training or clear explanations, which means there is little promise of success. Teachers may also be given no on-duty hours to acquire newly needed skills, nor be provided with expert help to address their follow-up questions when they encounter bumps in the road. For a training program to be successful, there must be in place a carefully designed training system.

The predictable results of such inadequate planning for teachers is either confusion or rejection of the technologies offered. Equally undesirable, PCs often become the property of a faculty clique, without ever having across-the-board impact felt throughout the curriculum. If this is a general phenomena in public education, it is particularly striking in minority school environments where teachers are taxed to do far more than prepare lesson plans, and for greater numbers of students with often deficient facilities.

Parent appreciation for teaching technology is vitally important, lest the perception emerge that computers are being used as a substitute for teachers, which may be perceived as a further dehumanizing element of education. Minority group parents might be particularly susceptible to such an impression, absent explanations to the contrary. Indeed both parents and teachers need to appreciate the positive possibilities technology offers in humanizing the classroom environment. Not only are students given the challenge of collaboration in teams, but teachers can learn to be less defensive about learning from each other as well as from their students. Accordingly, the overall result of properly introduced technology is the reinforcement of learning as a truly humane, collaborative and investigative process.

Another beneficial result of the introduction of computers and software to the classroom, can be a diminished reliance on anxiety-causing exams. Unlike the classroom of old, computer learning allows for constant verification of the learning process at every stage in the form of questions and answers along the way on any of the preceding courseware. As a consequence, students can get used to the confidence building process of giving correct answers as well as the confidence of knowing that incorrect answers will not result in scorn, but rather private explanations of the error with tutorial material for future problem avoidance.

Equally important, minority group youngsters need the reassuring experience of being treated fairly for once in their lives, before they can get beyond thinking of themselves as victims of race and social circumstances. They must also be able to experience success or failure, knowing that the outcome is solely based on their merits, rather than irrelevant factors over which they have no control.

The world of computer-based learning offers an important new means by which to succeed or fail beyond the reach of race or social circumstances. Based on logic rather than subjectivity, the human interface with computers can be free of unnecessary social anxiety and tension. It offers a level playing field in which the mind is king.

It offers the best learning opportunity yet to enable African American youngsters to escape the baggage put on them by society at large for being violent, uncreative, unmotivated or not capable of being educated. Also, the mastery of this brave new world offers an independent foundation from which to move the world. Through its instant global access, it allows the user to have his or her ideas seen and assessed without the necessity of being personal, unless it's necessary. Conversely, the value added to intellectual technology is that it removes the scapegoat of discrimination as the claimed basis for failure. Simply put, the machine will neither perform or fail to perform based on anything other than the proper instructions.

Through the escape to the world of cybernetics, one can enter into a neutral environment away from race and gender. As such, it can become a wholly new vehicle for personal empowerment, intellectual growth, economic capacity and social access for what might otherwise be a wholly lost generation.

CHAPTER FIVE

BLACK ECONOMICS WITHIN INFORMATION INNOVATIONS

Timothy L. Jenkins

Technological innovation has several stages: first, the creative stage when the idea is given theoretical expression; second, the demonstrative stage when the feasibility of a theory is shown to be implementable as predicted; third, the applications stage when an identified human need is satisfied in an improved way through the use of the innovation; and finally the diffusion stage when the first tier applications are made part of second and third tiers of applications serving a broader family of human needs beyond those initially contemplated at the first invention.

Throughout the process, innovation plays back and forth with the dynamics of economic determinism. At the creative end, the economics of technological innovation determine whether an inventor has the discretionary time to think through ideas systematically and reduce them to writing or experiment, not to mention the antecedent requirements for study time and collaborative access to acquire the knowledge of the principles from which theoretical invention can spring. While it continues to be true now, as it has been historically, important innovations also occur in informal settings without formal preparation and study. However, in today's world these are the exceptions rather than the rule. Most technological innovations are now the products of disciplined research undertaken in circumstances carefully contrived to facilitate systematic thought and collaboration through large-scale resource concentrations.

The increasing formality of large organizations in the pursuit of purely creative research, still fails nevertheless to guarantee all of the discoveries that smaller less formal settings and procedures allow. Indeed, abundant examples of superior discoveries from smaller and more modestly funded efforts in parallel investigations of common questions are frequent headlines. In all of these matters, the role of imagination by inherent genius defies the laws of pure economics. Therefore, while there are no African American controlled research institutions which enjoy the depth of financial support known to major corporate America and predominantly white academia, nonetheless ample examples of ground breaking discoveries exist. Some of these were discussed in earlier chapters, others are at work on the campuses of Historically Black Colleges and Universities (HBCUs) throughout the country.

Precisely because necessity is often the mother of invention, the differences in the necessities of the black community promise different inventive directions. The following suggests the impact of such differences. Where money is scarce, lower cost solutions become priorities. In a community with a greater percentage of nonreaders, the use of icons and touch screens for computer commands have greater necessities. Where the student attention span is less sustained, more attention holding mechanisms of information delivery are required. Where individual ownership of personal computers is likely to be infrequent, group use applications and alternative kiosk access in public spaces may predominate over single user approaches that presume private ownership or individual workstations.

Such socioeconomic considerations unmask the commonly accepted mantra that the processes of technological invention are *race neutral*. On the contrary, because most invention is driven by the search for a solution to a given problem, the choice of problems requiring solution controls the direction of one's research. Comparable realities have already come home in health related research. Both women and minorities have begun to protest the imbalance in medical research areas toward those ailments peculiar to white males, simply because these are the predominant decision-makers in the selection of the problems for solution.

The same is true in the field of information technology. Areas in which the most aggressive research occurs are driven by the decision-makers' priorities, leaving it to counterculture research to look in other directions. Social bias may be involved in the first instance by the definition of one's constituency. Most computer specialists define information science to mean the manipulation of data needed to facilitate large, complex organizations. Hence these are the problems given priority. In their eyes, only airline schedules and reservations, weather reports, stock quotations and trades, government intelligence, and opinion polls are large and highly perishable informational commodities worthy of state-of-the-art attention.

The development of systems to handle, gather, and present such data, however, may be wholly different from those required to meet a different set of social or economic needs. Here, what is ostensibly race neutral may be infected with an overall bias too pervasive for detection. Hence, it becomes important for those engaged in information systems to come from the alternative communities that need research inputs. Accordingly, HBCUs can play a leading role in pointing out Information Age applications which might otherwise be neglected. Contrast the dirth of consumer-accessible health care data and information, to that available on retail sales data. Compare the state of cultural information retrieval that is European versus that available on the rest of the world. Where is there any research on the relevance of solar energy for computer applications and telephony as contrasted with that describing the myriad of wiring options available on the telephone exchanges? To combat this trend, there is a need for an aggressive thrust by black scientists, technicians and research entrepreneurs in the 21st Century.

Throughout, keep in mind that while each stage of technological innovation represents potential profit centers, rarely will creative/research elements or the feasibility/testing elements (standing alone) represent major economic opportunities. Instead, the economic value of such activity derives primarily from the connection with the later applications or diffusion stages, for only the latter represent measurable profit and job producing market penetrations. By that yardstick, black entrepreneurs have numerous points of entry into the high-tech commercial flows from computers, telecommunication, and information transfer. In most cases the resulting opportunities are capital intensive, with competitive success predetermined by the comparisons among the investment pockets of the players.

Increasingly, this means that only Fortune 500 companies (and those smaller companies allied with them) can expect to be winners at the applications and dissemination stages of technology. Except in such fields as web page designers, small scale content publishers, and systems operators, the financial cost of entry for black entrepreneurs could well become insurmountable; therefore, they may have to invent new game rules before they can play. One of the new games Blacks must play is the pooling of resources to buy out well managed and profitable high-tech firms. Another well defined strategy is to enter an industry and market during its formative stages, when there is less of a competitive struggle to survive. Companies concerned with the sale and distribution of high-tech products, as well as those for installations and repairs, must be included. Many of these opportunities will come on the market in the near future from the Fortune 500 firms seeking to outsource all but their core operations.

Precisely because of the interplay of economics with technological innovation, careful attention is required to try to assure equal economic access throughout the process. The same is true in the area of technologically defined employment as well as entrepreneurship. Consider the previously stated prediction that in the 21st Century 70 percent of all jobs in the U.S. economy will relate to computer technology. Couple that pronouncement with the forecast that computer-related employment will result in wages that average 25 to 30% more than those that require no such skills. Factor in the ways in which state-of-art telecommunications has altered the meaning of distance and national frontiers, and the result is an economic revolution, rife with racial and other socio-economic overtones.

Alvin and Heidi Toffler in their little book, *Creating A New Civilization: The Politics of the Third Wave*, celebrate the current and coming economic migration from the smoke stack industries to those of the Information Age. They argue that the dominant sectors of the economy are no longer the manufacture of big steel, automotive and locomotive works or textile mills and the like; but rather the clean rooms of microprocessing, telecommunication stations, software development laboratories, and other related high-tech centers. For them, the economic migration is both evolutionary as well as necessary for commercial efficiencies and profitability. The new order suggests small will mean better. In their thinking, these shifts will require more house-bound employment, less institutional job security and a greater employment leveling of workers across international boundaries. What they fail to emphasize is that these very shifts will carry with them enormous social and political implications along racial lines. Indeed, in the earlier Toffler 561-page work, *Future Shock*, which has had such a profound effect as a wake-up call for the dawning of a new cybernetic era, there are fewer than a dozen references to the factor of race or ethnicity as ingredients in the radically altered future. And race, exacerbated by technology, may very well be the fault line that ultimately cracks America in two mutually antagonistic societies.

Consider the fact that in 1938 it was estimated that better than 90% of the black male work force was gainfully employed. Today that figure has eroded to 75% and is still falling. And in some geographic pockets the percentages are even reversed. Given the fact that a disproportionate segment of that black workforce was engaged in manual activity (and still is), the implications of the Toffler paradigm looms large in the prediction of a *shocking* economic dislocation of the African American population. This is coupled with the parallel changes that lessen the leveling role of unions, complicate the governmental enforcement of nondiscriminatory selection of workers, and defy the unifying standards of centralized salaries and fringe benefits. The dynamics of the labor market will be further convulsed in the Information Age by the pervasive loss of job security. Unlike the industrial era, workers can no longer expect to spend an entire career with one employer or even necessarily in one vocation. A lifelong cycle of learning requirements, quite unlike the patterns of yesteryear, is called for. As a result, the institutions of training take on new and varied roles in the market place. Under the influence of technology, the delivery means for such training must be substantially different than before.

In other words, the dynamic implications of robotic replacement of workers, the international migration of jobs, and the atomizing of the workplace could well spell disaster for black workers unless we institute massive training and reinvestment interventions to upgrade their skills, as well as massive interventions to assure job-related information access and connectivity to the population pockets in which black people find themselves. It is also essential that the plants that offer high-tech employment be accessible to black workers, their cities, and their neighborhoods.

Unfortunately every mega-trend to date appears to be headed in the opposite direction. These untoward trends call for an urgent initiative to see to it that black workers have the kind of job training and job access that will qualify them for Information Age employment. Having said that, it is equally important to appreciate the differences between the cybernetic jobs which are still essentially mechanical as opposed to those requiring creative high-tech skills. For example, the checkout clerk who wields a bar code reader may be engaged in a computer related function, yet the service function performed is essentially mechanical and is exactly the type of task that is being eliminated most quickly through automation. Low skilled jobs are distinguished from those with a high skill requirement to understand and interact with the cybernetic functions involved: e.g. a skilled word processor, at the uncomplicated end, to the population simulator of certain health risks, at the high end.

In spite of obvious linkages between technology, training, and employability, there seems to be no comparable public policy linkage designed to alter the course of inertia within which technology, training, and employability drift. In fact, judging from legislative trends of the Federal government, fewer public resources will be available for job training, while the private training investments will be reserved for those already employed. This is an especially ironic development, when all *welfare reform* initiatives are predicated on the recipient's ability to find work before the cutoff occurs of public benefits.

While the prediction of economic directions born of technological change always encounter elements of surprise (given the uncertainty of inventions), we feel that certain forecasts promise considerable reliability. For example, we know that a vast number of routine labor-intensive jobs now held by minorities, will be relegated to machines. The pace and extent of the process can and will be affected by applied science as well as management decisions. The considerable degree to which a disproportionate percentage of the black labor market has been concentrated in manual sectors calls for the development of policy and management options that have social and political sensitivities. As a necessary consequence, the processes of expanded automation and robotics, with their disproportionate dislocations among black wage earners, cries out for the invention of systematic means for reaching the black population with training and reinvestment strategies. Not a matter of compensatory justice alone, it is the only enlightened way to enable the body politic to function and adapt without cataclysmic upheavals.

In microcosm, we have already witnessed the widespread effects of automated telephony on workers directly. Soon, we will see the ripple effects on the managers associated with such workers. This is a prime example of an industry in which blacks have enjoyed considerable success with high wages and stability afforded by widespread unionized contracts. While highly visible and concentrated in the telephone industry, more subtle examples of black displacement exist throughout the realms of construction, food processing, manufacturing, maintenance, data entry, printing, graphic design and other industries.

Importantly, with the highly intelligent applications of computer systems, the employment displacement is simultaneously at work at the higher skilled Masters Degree and Ph.D. levels previously immune to the computer driven mechanization process. With the volume and speed of super computers as well as workaday PCs, many human intellectual functions are themselves becoming redundant due to new applications of artificial intelligence. This will have the devastating potential of marginalizing the very leadership class in the black community with the know how and talent to shape positive civic directions. Such losses cannot be easily accommodated in the national body politic so desperately in need of grass roots leadership.

But it is not our function to detail these macroeconomic matters, since that is clinically done in countless other works. Our mission here is to draw attention to the peculiar *racial* twists hidden within such otherwise colorblind statistical reports associated with the accelerating sweep of technology. And then at the next level of analysis, attention needs to be given to the social implications of these individual statistics on the family and community structures resulting in far broader dynamics that can threaten the stability of the entire society.

Clearly a requirement for creative, if not massive, intervention is called for, if the disproportionate effects of such structural employment adjustments are not to wholly unravel the social structure of the black community as we have known it. Indeed, it may just be possible to see a partially causal relationship from such underlying employment shifts and the increased reliance on crime as a tool for economic survival, female headed households, and violent teenage rebellion. This is not to say that other factors are not involved. But such a recognition of economics as an important ingredient should serve as an added caution in any anticrime and welfare reform policies that ignore the need for secure job creation through high-tech preparation and small business development as part of any structural solutions.

These implications are interactively aggravated when entrepreneurship is added to employment trends. Just the broad outlines of the economic implications flowing from the paradigm shifts inherent in the coming Information Age, reflect both the opening and closing of employment and entrepreneurial opportunities that cannot be ignored. Between those two extremes of original and terminal economic activity, fall countless modifications and trend lines with direct implications for the African American labor markets and business communities never witnessed before.

The *entrepreneurial* mix that results from post-industrial readjustment leading to an information and service-based economy, are equally far reaching. With the Internet Shopping Malls and Home Shopping by television as the new points of purchase, department stores and other retail outlets can become obsolete. With home and workplace becoming a blur, the mass transit industries as we have known them, may become dinosaurs. From such developments and others, one can predict the ripple effects that will endlessly affect the ancillary vendors, concessionaires, and distributors required along the economic chain, as well as transportation routes, financial vehicles, construction industries, and other business entities. Hence, the brave new world of constant change or alternatively "world of instability" is born.

New ancillary business forms are likely to grow up alongside each major innovation, *e.g.* lap top computers require carrying cases, World Wide Web home pages generate new outlets for graphic artists, and other such innovative developments. But unlike the evolutionary pace of the industrial era, the lightening swift pace of the Information Age can leave whole trades, communities, or even cities behind overnight, when their single or primary economic contribution or product becomes obsolete. The effect is not only making individual employees insecure, but their entire economic environment will experience the resulting changes in buying habits, real estate patterns, tax policies, and a serious impact on investment decisions.

Indeed, the speed and reach of these changes promise to accelerate themselves further by virtue of the instant broadcasting of their arrival to the farthest reaches of intelligent listeners. The result of these developments will be simultaneous speculation and anticipation each time a change is introduced, thus adding to insecurities and caution, whether well founded or not.

Hence, it becomes a very demanding matter for long term public and private planning to come up with the means to facilitate the entrepreneurial migration of minority-owned businesses along with the others required to stay in sync with such constant and inconsistent macroeconomic adjustments. For if such problems are a general business population hardship, they will be particularly so in a minority community of entrepreneurs likely to be more thinly capitalized, less effectively networked into the economy and not consistently informed on developing high-tech options and trends before they unfold as common knowledge.

All of this will very certainly require a revisiting of the traditional patterns of entrepreneurship in technology for those geographical areas in which the black population is concentrated. At present, no local, state or federal cluster of policies or programs exist equal to addressing these far reaching portents. Nor have black communities themselves developed any general plans or operational theories of how they might harness the powers of high-tech entrepreneurship for the development of their communities. No one can say that there are not numerous small scale initiatives at work, such as community development corporations and neighborhood revitalization efforts engaged in small scale high-tech activity. But not one of these efforts has the hope or the scope of the type of multibillion dollar investments required to have palpable effects beyond block-by-block scattered site renewals. And even those rays of light which do exist are overshadowed by the encroaching economic *desertification* that has continuously dried up uptown, inner city, and sometimes even downtown economic districts in the urban areas in which black people are concentrated.

In a different sense, the required adjustments may be a combination of intellect, aesthetics, and self-assertion that can only spring from the bottoming out of such desperation. Faced with the impossibility of rationalized results, it becomes reasonable to step outside of purely efficiently reasoned strategies to pursue less measurable values. A deteriorating city may consider public space beautification or environmental improvements as new priorities, even though they may not be necessities. A community may be willing to accept slower construction schedules dictated by the economic necessity for more labor intensive employment demands from its own residents. But these will be the economic exceptions rather than the rule, more akin to the Luddites who tried to beat back the tides of the industrial process brought on by the mechanization in yesteryear England.

Entrepreneurial Innovations

Like the classic contrast of the pessimist and the optimist, based on whether they are preoccupied with the filled or empty half of the same glass, black entrepreneurs should take heart in the underserved high-tech communications demand, for it may alternatively represent a unique market opportunity.

From all of the historical discussion of electronics and communications in America, *it is clear that inventions only become economically important after their applications are made known to the masses of potential consumers.* When telephones were simply viewed as a novel means for officials to contact other agencies, their growth rate was marginal. When electricity was relegated to public street lights, the demand was limited. When cable television served only to supplement line of sight television broadcast reception, it was scarcely viable. Only when the average consumer became impressed with the commercial, life quality and entertainment possibilities, were new applications offered and large new markets born.

Accordingly, a lag exists in the black community's demand for computer assisted telecommunications, because no convincing case has been made regarding their unique and highly advantageous use. Indeed, given the way in which the industry has focused its priority applications on high speed data transfer, banking, industrial networks and Eurocentric cultural interests, it is scarcely surprising that the black community has yet to be awakened to the potential of computer and telecommunication power. And when coupled with marketing imagery that for the most part ignores them, their ho-hum reaction is fully predictable. Alternatively, the appeal of arcade games, low cost beepers, cellular phones and VCRs have met with widespread acceptance in the black marketplace.

The challenge for black entrepreneurs, then, is the tailoring of high-tech telecommunication applications and marketing to the special needs of the black community. By way of example, consider the following. Many teenage mothers would like to complete their high school education, but public schools won't allow their return with their infants. If distance learning could be provided through facilities that would not exclude toddlers and infants, the demand for GED courseware and the delivery would be considerable. For many with poor transportation systems, the need for public information goes unsatisfied because it is too time-consuming and difficult to collect. Were similar information provided by readily accessible networks at kiosks in public places in the same manner as a pay phone, the use could be enormous. Black organizations spend billions of dollars traveling to conferences and conventions. If the option was made known for teleconferencing at far less cost and loss of time, many organizations would use it along with low cost electronic mail and bulletin boards. If providers of Afrocentric products were available on World Wide Web home pages, their customer base could be international rather than a single neighborhood. If black doctors and lawyers could electronically and securely access neighborhood client centers by interactive video from a central location, they might very well increase their clientele exponentially. If a service existed for families to make virtual reality visits to prisons and hospitals, the demand could be phenomenal. If cultural repositories of Afrocentric collections were digitized for distance access as well as the distribution of products via CD-ROM formats, the interest in computers would be stimulated among those best able to afford ownership.

Consider also the potential of telecommunications as a vehicle through which the religious leadership of the black community could communicate with its membership. Through the use of such vehicles, local ministers could confer with each other, hold denominational meetings with distant church leaders, or speak directly with parishioners in their homes. These contacts could be for spiritual guidance or consultation, professional training and development, or for the mobilization of public opinion around a particular issue. Through such means the neighborhood cohesion, weakened by geographic dispersion, could be united again. The challenge is for black entrepreneurs, on their own or in collaboration with majority suppliers, to develop and promote an imaginative world of high-tech applications to motivate and activate black consumers.

Such market opportunities go beyond a purely domestic market. Throughout the Caribbean Islands and Africa, telecommunications are in their infancy. As a legacy of colonialism, most of the telephone delivery systems are dependent on overseas suppliers, obsolete in their capacities and dependent upon costly technological systems. There are major opportunities to assist in the development of state-of-the-art facilities throughout the Black Diaspora, using domestic satellite systems, cellular relays, smart cards for wireless messaging, and other innovative technologies. Indeed, networks linking the Third World institutions of higher education with HBCUs in America, represent major entrepreneurial possibilities as well.

One of the most vibrant opportunities exists in linking the entertainment industries of Africa with those of African Americans. The technology exists to deliver full length motion pictures by satellite in digital formats to theaters throughout the continent of Africa. The same technology will allow live concerts and conference delivery on a pay-for-view basis. Inadequate distribution channels plague both Africa and African Americans for their artistic works, in spite of the fact that they both have a ready audience which they simply cannot reach. Through satellite delivery systems the barrier of time and distance could for the first time be overcome. The commercial synergy that could result from such a transcontinental linkage could have a major impact in the economies of both communities.

The future may well need a new hybrid paradigm in black entrepreneurial, community and worker alliances that simultaneously tackles the access to capital, jobs and market share as a unified package. Under such a scenario, economic coalitions could be contrived which pool the political and economic clout of the whole black community to demand participation in both the high-tech business and employment opportunities it generates. Examples of these have sprung up around the country where boycotts have been organized to get jobs or contract opportunities. Where these have had success it has been because of the unique combination of activists able to garner broad popular support, combined with workers and labor unions. But very sophisticated models will be required to meet today's legal and business requirements and scrutiny. And while such self help strategies are clearly not without their own inherent racial dangers, they may nevertheless offer the last best alternative to despair.

Giving careful consideration for the *black future,* why isn't it completely feasible for the billion dollar black religious community to decide to become educational providers at the primary and secondary levels with the cooperation of entrepreneurs and HBCUs? With an extended base of more than a hundred thousand parcels of church real estate with a geographic and membership reach almost coterminous with the black population itself, it would be ideally situated to assume such work. The Congress of National Black Churches (CNBC), which includes the eight largest national denominations solely controlled by and for African Americans, claims an indirect membership of nineteen million persons and 85,000 church facilities. At least another twenty thousand churches and several million black worshippers belong to the integrated denominations but have the same needs. With the relentless political trend towards the privatization of education in America, black churches could become instrumental in providing heritage-based high-tech educational alternatives. As a precursor to such an initiative, these institutions could create their own online, cable and satellite operated community networks. They could use the same infrastructure to deliver pay-for-view entertainment, teleconferencing and cultural software of their own choosing. They could thus become proactive in the preservation of themselves economically and culturally. And later they can wade into the delivery of accredited public curricular education on a fee basis.

Given the competitive dynamics of computer driven telecommunications, it is highly probable that once such a course of action is articulated, more than one major industry player will come forward to trade its expertise and financial strength for the collaborative advantage of partnering to reach such a demonstrably lucrative, as well as underserved population section. After all, as we noted earlier, the collective earning capacity of *Black America* is better than $450 billion and equivalent to the twelfth largest GNP in the world if considered a separate nation. Hence, what began as a dooms day scenario of the black community losing out to technology in the 21st Century, can be reworked to give birth to an economic resurgence never before witnessed within the black community, based on the principles of self-help, collaboration and the need to reverse impending economic isolation.

What is suggested in high-tech educational renewal could also be explored in health care. Again the service deficiencies are glaring and worsening, alongside exploding health care technologies. At the same time, professional black health care providers are losing out on servicing the health maintenance organizations (HMOs) and the participation among other medical distributors, including pharmacies, nursing homes, and hospitals. Through the use of tele-medicine, Internet buying and specialized professional services, as well as distance learning, social service delivery can be decentralized to the point of being a new economic engine in black communities.

How Labor Fits the Picture

Not only is there a role for creative futuristic collaboration between black communities and entrepreneurs with majority businesses, but with organized labor as well. In point of fact, the very conditions of change altering the economics of the black community also apply to labor unions. Increasingly, the percentage of unionized labor is falling to the point that the labor movement constituency is approaching little more than 15 million members. Not only are workers demurring on union membership, but employers and legislatures express ever growing union hostility. And the labor movement is groping to find new strategies to revitalize itself. As a result, big labor has resolved to use its vast internal pension fund and financial resources to underwrite investments that can generate jobs and membership expansion in programs like the "J for Jobs" initiative.

Of considerable importance then, is the fact that the 1995 incoming leadership of the American Federation of Labor and the Congress of Industrial Organizations (AFL & CIO) publicly targeted greater attention on the plight of minority workers as one of its cardinal organizing objectives. But this will only be of significance if it carries with it new approaches that take technology into account. It will also require organized labor to increasingly use its economic resources to serve as engines of change. It will call for a creative use of the huge financial reserves of labor pension funds as vehicles for creating high-tech jobs for their union members and the high-tech training and preparation of the children of their current members. For the fact of the matter is that employment is becoming increasingly interactive with technology.

Therefore, another futuristic experiment could be for union pension funds to invest in the development of high-tech facilities in and for black communities. Coupled with public funds where possible, such collaborations might be applied to implement work requirements that modify or replace welfare systems as they currently exist and be extended into prison populations so they can earn their keep as well as acquire relevant skills while incarcerated.

The special economic applications of computer assisted telecommunications to deliver such training, could include new ownership patterns, such as employee stock ownership plans, as well as conventional business arrangements to increase the stake holding participation in the newly created industries.

At the outset of this chapter, it was noted that technological innovation has several stages: first, the theoretical, then the demonstrative, followed by major applications and finally widespread diffusion throughout the economy. Attention is needed at each of these stages within the black community, so that the blessings of the Information Age do not become *redlined* and limit their upward pull on the whole American population. A very special role suggests itself for the Historically Black College and University community, as well as those Blacks in key high-tech companies. As things currently stand, they uniquely represent the potential for liaisons between the complicated world of a computer driven economy and the potentials for black economic development. Just as the black church community is learning how their special resources can apply to the socially threatening separation between those "who know" and "those who do not" along racial lines, the black educational community can resist its demise with shrinking public funds and relentless pressure to merge with majority institutions or be content to wither away on their own.

It would be increasingly useful, as well as in their own self interest, for the HBCUs and corporate Blacks to find new ways to benefit their community with their talents, both as volunteers and through corporate staff lending programs, involving highly trained personnel. Where feasible, their physical facilities need to be made accessible in novel ways to the community. University and private sector small business incubators, internships, the generation of on-line training and distance learning programs call to mind experimental applications that can later lead to widespread applications throughout the black community. There is a need to complement the outreach of public education with business and community collaboration.

An important role also exists for the mainstream philanthropic community in connection with the information based needs of the black community. For many years such institutions spawned from the high social conscience of successful industrial moguls at the turn of the 20th Century. They have made large donations to ameliorate the conditions in which Blacks find themselves. Historically, such foundations have done much for Black America in a charitable mode, which needs to be creatively redirected to a high-tech economic development strategy on a profit-making capitalistic basis. Instead of giving the black community a fish, it can instead be enabled to fish for itself. Charity must not become a sedative, but a ladder.

Clearly, the lack of talent is not the determining factor in causing the absence of entrepreneurial Blacks traveling the Information Superhighway, rather the issue is capital. Whereas white entrepreneurs with advanced ideas in technology are either welcomed by allied industries or traditional venture capitalists, the same is not the experience of black pioneers and innovators. Crack cocaine dealers must not be the only source of venture capital in "the hood." The major foundations with a historic commitment to the problems of race could create a special high-tech venture capital fund to which African American entrepreneurs could apply. A special emphasis should be given to software developers and innovative applications and dissemination enterprises. Such an emphasis on software is justified because typically hardware innovations are already more readily received in the marketplace. Software on the other hand, especially if it happens to have any ethnic content, has been very difficult to market to venture capitalists. Hence only "mom and pop" or woefully under-funded black software developers exist to date, without a critical mass within the industry. This is particularly ironic, given the fact that the world of software represents the highest growth potential on all fronts in the high-tech arena.

In part, the reluctance to make capital available for black software developers is born of arrested expectations of black technical talent, on the other, it represents a depreciation of black intellectual products unless arbitrarily limited to entertainment. Based on what has already been accomplished by black software developers with little or no resources, there is every reason to expect big - if not revolutionary - things in the entrepreneurship of educational software, artistic expression, and scholarly information, once adequately given strong financial support.

The Multimedia Lab associated with the Massachusetts Institute of Technology comes to mind as a prototype for stimulating black software. As a facility launched to be a nonprofit vehicle, it soon moved from being dependent on governmental and philanthropic grants to negotiate major contracts from commercially driven corporate support groups. Now every major electronics, computer and software provider looks upon its financial relationship with MIT's Multimedia Lab as a cost effective vehicle for advanced research. While such a facility is missing in a fully free standing way in Black America, the beginnings of such a network exists among fourteen members of the "HBCU Network." Each of the participating institutions offers advanced degrees in engineering or computer science with a capacity to provide research and applications in high technical work. Those institutions like the Computational Science and Engineering Departments at Howard University as well as Clark-Atlanta University's Research Network Institute, represent the aggressive start of a new breed of black entrepreneurial academicians. Both centers are heavily supported by external contract awards, rather than by university resources. With the creatively pooled support of the philanthropic community, their efforts could lift the entire community of which they are a part. Equally important, (and of even greater significance) is the presence of black entrepreneurs participating in the discussion and exploration of the *road ahead* for applied technology, an important strategy that represents the only way to assure that our community's special needs, perspectives and interests stay in mainstream focus. What's needed here is a *Black Economic and Information Development Fund* (which could ultimately be an open-ended mutual fund), specifically focused and dedicated to investing millions or even billions of dollars in a

Black information Age Revolution.

As a capitalist country, America reserves special influence for businesspersons to impact public policy. The reality of this special role has been very strongly seen in the debate leading up to the passage of the historic new omnibus telecommunications legislation. Not only were influential companies pushing for their particular proprietary technologies and market niches, they were universally opposed to public interventions. For them the final arbiter was to be the omniscient marketplace. No black entrepreneur could feel safe with such a policy, given the historic marketplace behaviors on matters of race. But for the most part, black businesspersons were not in the debate, due to their absence in the marketplace.

Similarly, the paramount determination on whose behalf and at what prices the relevant technologies will be marketed, may well be private sector decisions of far greater importance than public statutes. Accordingly, the role of black entrepreneurs in the equitable making of public policy is critical. For an analogy one need only look at the predecessor policy development process that led to the Federal Communications Act of the 1930s and the line of legal cases and parallel administrative ruling from the Federal Communications Commission (FCC). In most instances, the underlying issues were the clash between commercial interests seeking to define the public interest. And it took some time for the growth and development of advocacy groups to come forward without commercially driven motives. Similarly, if one looks at the landscape of policy-shaping forces in molding the new telecommunications legislation, there are scarcely more than half a dozen voices raised on behalf of blacks and other minorities versus the thousands representing the industry. Because such patterns are not likely to change, it becomes particularly important that black business persons become part of the trade and industry machinery whose voice is predominant in shaping the course of public policy.

A case in point is the matter of legally determined differences in the common carrier rate structure that classes of customers must pay. Although a race neutral question on its face, it represents a philosophically fundamental issue of how the public property of the airways are to be allocated and paid for. Likewise, consider the issue of FCC-determined telephony and cable user rate structures shaped to consider the ability to pay. If minority businesspersons look to the economic conditions of their likely customer base, they will have to support special consideration on behalf of their minority constituents as predominantly low income consumers.

Furthermore, the economic trickle down of business interests into elective politics also speaks to the need for a strong black entrepreneurial presence in the computer and telecommunications industries that sit at the heart of the Information Age. History shows that the solidarity among current and would-be black radio station owners and black office holders was crucial in the development of procedures that greatly facilitated black ownership penetration. The same could be true in the lengthy and highly arcane regulatory process that will result over time under the new Telecommunications Act of 1996.

It is important to note the special importance of black professional participation in the legal community for their specialized but rippling effect on the industry. Black legal practitioners tend to play important roles, albeit hidden, as interpreters and defenders of their community's interests. It is therefore of great importance that efforts be made to assure the racial integration of the administrative bar that practices before the FCC. In most, but not all cases, it more than likely translates to black membership in the majority firms that represent major corporate players. The occasional black firm that emerges from break-away governmental lawyers, and law professors with telecommunications expertise, is not ruled out, but these will be few and far between. Again it will be important that major corporate and union players as well as the philanthropic community, affirmatively use their leverage in the legal marketplace to assure black partners and associates in any and all of the telecommunications firms they use.

Finally, if there is one universal reality in the economic picture for the foreseeable future in the economics of the information industry, it will be the requirement for constant and rapid change. Not only will merger mania continue, with the interlocking joint ventures described in our earlier chapter, but the potential for new player exclusions will become ever greater once the industry titans have fully developed their master plans (in most cases, by the year 2000). The sheer size and commercial diversification of the players will assure the exclusivity of the club. The same logic suggests that the only external participation allowed will be for the outsourcing to small highly competitive suppliers who are made or broken by their big brother tie-ins. This major industry development will assure the minority status of black business in America for the 21st Century. Hence, this makes for a very fragile life line for minority businesses in the game, unless they are sufficiently linked in the black consuming public to assure their existence and continuous growth cycles. Let us conspire to make the sellers beware for a change!

CHAPTER SIX

THE NEW INDUSTRIAL ERA and STRATEGIC PLANNING

Khafra K Om-Ra-Seti

On the morning of January 15, 2019, Ptah-Hotep sat motion less in deep meditation in the virtual reality environment called *Askia*, an adjoining room to his office at Universal-Kemet, headquartered in Atlanta, Georgia. A dynamic high-technology African American global corporate complex, Universal-Kemet was the brainchild of Ptah-Hotep and a group of black scientists and engineers, who for 25 years built a sci-tech complex and model for technological advances in the African American world. They pioneered the development of a major scientific renaissance of profound meaning and purpose, capturing the imaginations of millions of African Americans and people of African descent from around the world. By the start of the *Great Millennium,* they had set the stage for a new beginning in a revolutionary document entitled *The Age of Light: The African American Renaissance.* It was a call for unity and survival to save a devastated and demoralized African world, ravaged by AIDS, drugs, destructive images, educational decline, political and industrial ineptitude, and rampant and mindless violence. *The Age of Light* stressed the significance of an *Age of Enlightenment* which would remove the shadows and demons of over 500 years of destructive mental darkness. African Americans were clearly at the crossroads. Not everyone understood the mission, but for those who did, it marked an incredible turning point in their historical consciousness.

Ptah-Hotep was scheduled to deliver a speech before the international forum of black scientists, engineers, mathematicians, technologists, historians, economists and many other black professionals throughout the world. The African network of 49 hyper-netic satellites encircling the globe in geosynchronous orbit above the equator, would transmit the historic speech to over 400 locations around the world. Over 50,000 delegates had gathered in Atlanta to hear Ptah-Hotep's speech at the beautiful high-tech oasis of *Imhotep-GIZA*, a magnificent technological and scientific research complex composed of Universal-Kemet and nine other interconnected futuristic structures built in patterns of pyramids, globes and paragons. In the center of the complex stands a massive 250-foot black cellular obelisk, a web-like structure that absorbs sunlight by a peculiar method of photovoltaic technology, which powers the entire techno-complex. The scientists at Imhotep-GIZA named the structural design *The Solarium,* in acknowledgment of the central ability of the obelisk to provide power to the strategic orbits of the various structures. Ptah-Hotep's pioneering research in the science of solar energy and photonics provided the incredibly inexpensive source of energy that gives life to the miniature solar system. This scientific triumph earned him the title of *The Nommo* and the Nobel Peace prize for Physics in the year 2012.

Ptah-Hotep's current virtual reality environment is an ancient temple setting overlooking the Mediterranean Sea in the ancient city of Carthage. Askia is capable of 19 different historic settings, complete with an astounding array of special effects and real-life environments.

A short beeping sound awakens Ptah-Hotep from his meditations.
Depressing a small button on his platinum-based picture-phone watch,
he begins a visual conversation with Naja, the *adept technologist*. She
has called to remind him of his impending speech before the forum.

"It is time Ptah."

Ptah-Hotep smiles and nods in approval,

"Thank you Naja, I'll be right there."

Ptah-Hotep rises slowly and takes a long look at the Mediterranean
Sea below him, he then issues a loud voice command to Askia.

"Aton-so-relak."

The virtual reality environment returns to its normal appearance
of an empty, spacious gold-colored room. He leaves the setting and
joins Naja in the main reception area. From there they walk to a board-
ing station to catch a *levi-car transport,* an internal high-speed su-
perconductor powered transportation system. As they traveled to the
galactic space (the main open-air ancient temple coliseum), Ptah-Hotep's
thoughts were centered on what he must say and do next; his message
must convey a new mission for the organization.

> "The extraordinary scientific advances since the start of the
> Great Millennium have given mankind the power to revise
> reality and expand our reach into the mysteries of the uni-
> verse. We are now actively exploring Mars and the Moon for
> mineral and technological resources; our deep-sea hydrogen-
> powered underwater sea vessels are penetrating earth's last
> frontier; the science of superconductivity and levitation has
> evolved to the point of moving large objects with the assis-
> tance of *e-beam* laser technology; and mankind is now in the
> initial stages of producing the first prototype android. Progress
> has been rapid and at times uncontrollable. But the earth is
> dying and mankind has destroyed thousands of species of
> plant, insect and animal life in its quest for the control of
> nature. The planet's ozone layer is clearly being destroyed.

Our organization must accelerate our mission to build a universal society based on peace and harmony with nature and the universe, before we reach a critical impasse. The deep study of the ancients have taught us that there is a point that we must not go beyond in our scientific endeavors. I pray that my message will be understood, for I fear that we may not have much time. If we break the harmonious rhythm of the ageless flow of eternal life, it will mean utter chaos and a return to mental darkness."

The levi-car stopped at a special entrance to the coliseum and Ptah-Hotep and Naja are greeted by the special securities staff of Imhotep-GIZA. As they are escorted to the center stage area, a mysterious soothing futuristic jazz melody is heard in the background. On stage are seated the 24 elders (the governing body) of the international organization, who are all brilliant men and women chosen from the basic fields that collectively represent universal knowledge: twelve women and twelve men, the organic principle of the universal harmony of male and female. As Ptah-Hotep and Naja come into view on stage, all of the elders stand and begin an enthusiastic applause for this great man. They are joined by the entire audience, which leads to a nearly five minute joyous welcome for the creative multi-genius spirit of Ptah-Hotep, *The Nommo*.

A poet and philosopher, architect, scientist, economist and bold visionary, Ptah-Hotep had been instrumental in helping to construct a massive mental awakening in the African world, which had a profound impact on many societies. As he stood before the podium, all communication systems were fully activated, beaming the event to over 200 million people worldwide. When the applause ended, Ptah-Hotep looked patiently at the wide expanse of beautiful people that had come to hear his message; his voice would be a poetic melody for the next evolutionary phase in scientific knowledge.

IMPACT OF TECHNOLOGY

The brief story of Ptah-Hotep's technological dilemma is not meant to be some scientific fantasy that has no basis in the realm of techno-logical possibilities. Most of the scientific advances envisioned in our story are currently poised to achieve those high-tech levels of maturity. In Chapter Two we outlined many advances and provided a systematic vision of how these dynamic technologies will evolve and re-shape our future world. The message is clear and the handwriting is on the wall: we are on the threshold of the *fantastic*, and a scientific future that will alter our sense and perception of reality.

The Information Age revolution of the 1990s is the dawn of a *New Age* which is destined to have an enormous impact on the social, po-litical, economic, financial and cultural arenas of societies worldwide. What's happening in the 1990s, is not simply an American revolution or a Western Civilization phenomena; it's global in origin, and will evoke a vast, penetrating manifestation. This is tantamount to the spread of a new worldwide religion, except the subject of this proselytizing is sci-ence and technology on an unprecedented level. The entire world is at the crossroads and *now* is the time to completely understand that, and not after the smoke clears in the year 2000; for the future will defi-nitely belong to those who prepare for it!

By the year 2000 the impact of technology will present some of the following developments:

♦   Machines making machines in ever greater complexity and precision. Extreme worldwide competition will place the ro-botic worker in the center of all major manufacturing produc-tion and heavy industrial development.

♦   Expert computerized systems and other variations of artifi-cial intelligence (AI) involving higher-order thinking, will increasingly allow complex problems to be resolved very quickly. A problem or task that may have taken a few days or a week to resolve, will be solved in ten minutes. These computerized software systems will allow man the free time to explore and devise problems of greater complexity.

♦ A dramatic increase in the globalization of economic and financial activities will bring about the emergence of a world economy never before seen or developed in all of world history. Vast networks of tightly-linked computerized stock, currency, and bond markets will greatly simplify the process of global investing and economic transactions.

♦ Supercomputers with gigabyte memories (one billion bytes) will be available for home use for reasonable cost, placing an incredible amount of computing power in the hands of the individual.

♦ Supersonic air travel and high-speed levitated trains and ships will begin to move towards center stage as major modes of transportation systems for the majority of advanced societies. Enormous infrastructural projects will be implemented to overhaul obsolete systems.

♦ The science of biotechnology will bring about incredible creations, which no doubt, will generate huge worldwide religious debates over the issue of mankind's involvement in the creation of complete organisms in the laboratory. With the production of the first *Frankenstein* and the drive to create some version of a *Superman,* the world will need to come to practical terms with this new technology.

Such broad-sweeping developments are on-line to proliferate in a few short years. The information and communications revolution of the 1990s is the central force behind this massive move towards the internationalization and globalization of the world's economy. Rapid adoption of new technologies and innovations by the majority of the nations of the world will continue to speed up this entire snowballing process.

We are in the midst of a period of *radical innovation* in several related fields, which is spearheading the move to drastically change products and processes. Economists tell us that when there is a *clustering* of these radical innovations, new industries emerge which bring major paradigm shifts in societies. These large-scale revolutionary changes have occurred in periodic cycles throughout history. Author Peter Dicken cites the descriptive term "changes in the techno-economic paradigm" to describe this phenomenon.[1] This historic shift in techno-economic behavior forms a major part of *Long Wave Cycle* theory, that provides a system of thinking for our understanding of what is occurring in the 1990s.

KONDRATIEFF AND THE LONG CYCLE

The long wave cycle theory was popularized by the Russian agricultural economist Nikolai Dimitriyerick Kondratieff, who began publishing his theories in economic journals during the 1920s. He published *Long Economic Cycles* in 1928, which brought together the central hypothesis and critical ideas of his belief in super-long economic cycles. He based his statistical data on the capitalistic free market system, which eventually created some problems for him with the ruling communist elite of the Soviet Union. Kondratieff's book was published one year prior to the October 1929 stock market crash, and his theories indicated that a downward wave was in motion prior to the Great Depression of the 1930s. The beginning of the Roaring 20s carried the inflationary spiral to its last peak, and the 1930s produced the last phase (of deflation and depression) of the downward wave.[2]

According to Kondratieff 's theory, a long wave cycle will last from 45 to 60 years, with the average being 54 years. The statistical data he compiled covered a period of 140 years, which represented two and one-half cycles. Each completed cycle was broken into two phases: a rising wave and a downward wave. Each phase averaged roughly 25 to 27 years and would be characterized by certain economic, political, technological and social events. During the period of a complete cycle, one major depression would occur, and at least thirty years of technical innovations would be possible. Kondratieff based his original theories on data compiled from the United States, Germany, France, and England. The data consisted of a 19th Century price series that included interest rates, cash deposits, foreign trade figures, the average level of commodities, and the production of pig iron, lead and coal.

The foundation of the long wave cycle consists of massive investments in long-term capital goods, large plants, railways, bridges, canals, other types of infrastructural developments, and the rise of a skilled labor force to work in the new industries created by emerging technologies. Historical evidence indicates that great scientific breakthroughs and discoveries occur during the downward cycle, whereas the application of new technological inventions and innovations find their greatest support during the upswing cycles. As the world moves further into the 1990s, we are witnessing one of the most astounding periods of scientific discovery in the history of mankind. Breakthroughs in the areas of digital technology, solar energy, laser technology, superconductivity, hydrogen fusion, semiconductors, robotics, fiber optics, bioengineering, innovative communication systems, satellite systems, and many others are destined to replace entire industries and restructure the world of the 21st Century. Based on Kondratieff's theory, these developments indicate that the end of a long wave cycle is in progress during the 1990s.

The actual periods covered by Kondratieff's first two and one-half cycles consisted of the following:

First Cycle: the end of the 1780s to 1844-1851, reaching an inflationary peak between 1810 to 1817.

Second Cycle: from 1844-1851 to 1890-1896, reaching an inflationary peak between 1870-1875.

Third Cycle: began in 1890-1896 and peaked in 1914-1920, and was in its last phase when Kondratieff concluded his analysis.[3]

Modern Kondratieff exponents may disagree on the actual years that ended the third cycle and began the fourth. Our analysis conclude that the third cycle ended in 1940-1948, which would also indicate that the fourth cycle began during this period. This *fourth wave* will be concluded in the 1990s, the key technological transition period leading to the 21st Century. Out of the chaos of the massive restructuring process of the Information Age, the *fifth wave* will be born, which will carry us to approximately the mid-21st Century.

Significant historical evidence supports the thesis that major technological changes are associated with long wave cycles. What we will ultimately witness is a powerful "techno-economic paradigm shift" from one mode of operation to another. As mentioned in earlier sections, the 21st Century will be totally transformed by Information Age technologies. The end result will be what Peter Dicken describes as the "crystallization of a new paradigm, generating a new global economic reality." New modes of production, distribution, marketing and organization will form the core of many of the new revolutionary systems that will drive the global economy of the future.

Combining some of Dicken's analysis with our own, several key technological revolutions emerge as the central developments of each K-wave cycle. The following summaries of each period list the key techno-events and the primary countries associated with these developments:

First Cycle: the end of the 1780s to 1844-1851; technological forces (steam power, cotton textiles and iron), leading nations (Britain, France, and Belgium).

Second Cycle: from 1844-1851 to 1890-1896; technological forces (railways, iron, and steel); leading nations (Britain, France, Belgium, Germany and the United States).

Third Cycle: from 1890-1896 to 1940-1948; technological forces (electricity, chemicals, automobiles, airplanes, and cinematic film); leading nations (the United States, Germany, Britain, France, Belgium, Switzerland and the Netherlands).

Fourth Cycle: from 1940-1948 to the 1990s; technological forces (electronics, synthetic materials, pharmaceuticals, petrochemicals, integrated circuits, atomic power) leading nations (the United States, Japan, Sweden, Germany, Britain, France, Belgium, the Netherlands and Switzerland).

Fifth Cycle: the 1990s to approximately the mid-21st Century (based on the theoretical logic) technological forces (digital computers, laser technology, robotics, semiconductors, superconductivity, biotechnology, entire realm of Information Age technologies) leading nations (the United States, Japan, Germany, Britain, France, Belgium, the Netherlands, Switzerland, India, the four Tigers of Hong Kong, Singapore, Taiwan, and South Korea).[4]

There are certain important implications embedded in the above analysis. If Kondratieff's theory holds true, then by the mid-1990s the U.S. and world economy had entered the last phase of a downward wave, which will bottom out and end sometime before the year 2000.[5] A fifth wave will be born, and a new upward trend in economic and technological progress will become a manifestation throughout the world.

THE EMERGENCE OF NEW INDUSTRIES

New industry developments and formations are significant characteristics of the 1990s Information Age revolution. For mature industries, the state of competition by participants depends on five basic competitive forces: (1) rivalry; (2) substitution; (3) bargaining power of suppliers; (4) bargaining power of buyers; and (5) entry. Profit potential of an industry is ultimately determined by the collective strength of these forces. On the other hand, the essential characteristics of an emerging industry present a different set of parameters, wherein the rules of the game are not clearly specified. During this nascent stage, an industry is in a state of disequilibrium and firms generally have poor information about competitors, characteristics of customers, and industry conditions. Market share is basically unknown, as well as an assessment of the players in this new field. Many companies, both large and small, are attempting to lay foundations, consolidate market positions, test market products or services, secure suppliers and customers, and focus on many other related strategic initiatives. It is essentially a period of confusion, excitement, expectation, disappointment, and general uncertainty. There is very little attempt on any company's part to retaliate or block the entry of a new firm into the industry. The absence of rules and a clear direction is both a risk and a source of opportunity for all of the participants in this new game. This is precisely what we are witnessing in the 1990s; a period of *industry chaos,* as the players struggle to forge the new *COMMUNICATIONS' INDUSTRIAL EMPIRES* for the 21st Century.

Since the traditional barriers to enter this new industrial development are not fully in place, there is no serious threat to a new entrant. For an industry in a state of equilibrium, some of the familiar barriers to entry are as follows:

(1) Economies of Scale
(2) Product Differentiation
(3) Capital Requirements
(4) Access to Distribution Channels
(5) Government Policy.

In many respects, the circumstances of an emerging industry works to the advantage of the small firm attempting to develop into a larger entity. Thus, newly established firms determined to enter an Information Age industry in the 1990s, should consider carefully the targeted industry and selection of a strategic market niche, make a careful assessment of the internal strengths and weaknesses of the firm's resources and talents, and then move forward as destiny would have it. The early years of a firm are rough enough without having to fight strong competition, retaliatory actions, and government policies. The actual costs of these actions could be greater than the actual *risks* assumed in the proposed venture. Therefore, the conditions of an emerging industry are really favorable to the small player. With a good game plan, some strong alliances, and a little luck, the new enterprise could become the next IBM!

In John Naisbitt's book, *Global Paradox,* his thesis suggests that the more global the world's economy becomes, its smallest business and industry players correspondingly have a greater influence and success in the marketplace. This could lead to some very interesting developments, particularly in the emerging communications revolution of the 1990s. Naisbitt declares that, "riding on the wave of the telecommunication revolution, the opportunities for individual freedom and enterprise are totally unprecedented." For the African American, this thesis and scenario represents an important era of economic opportunities and global networking that should be totally explored.

The *paradox* that Naisbitt is describing points to a much greater role of the entrepreneur in the Information Age. At first glance it appears that his thesis is "pie-in-the-sky" and too rosy for entrepreneurs and small companies, however one has only to observe the downsizing, reengineering, and the active promotion of the *virtual* corporation during the early 1990s to understand what he is really identifying. This phenomenon is part of the paradigm shift (the reorganization of the world economy process) that we must comprehend as a major wave of the future. Much of the analysis we have presented here indicates that new business formations for the Information Age should begin in the 1990s in order to take full advantage of the expected upsurge in economic activity shortly after the year 2000: K-wave theory points to an upward wave in the early years of the 21st Century.

THE SILICON VALLEY AFFAIR

With the start of 1992, a nonprofit organization was started in Silicon Valley called Joint Venture: Silicon Valley or JVSV. The primary goal of this organization is the economic revival and rebirth of the world famous Silicon Valley infrastructural complex. After the first six months in operation, the organization issued its Phase I report entitled, *An Economy at Risk,* which examined some critical long-term problems facing the economic growth of the region. In June of 1993, JVSV issued its Phase II report entitled *Blueprint For A 21st Century Community,* which outlined a number of dynamic solutions that could resolve the challenges facing the local economy.

As the birthplace of the world's most advanced high-tech companies, Silicon Valley has been an extremely important geographic engine of growth for California regionally, and the United States globally. For decades Silicon Valley lead the way as the high-tech capital of the world. With its unique combination of leading-edge companies, its strong dynamic entrepreneurial culture and a diverse pool of knowledgeable workers, Silicon Valley residents perfected the art of *systematic innovation* to a point where the art of revolution became a way of life. In this one geographic location can be found the broadest and deepest range of scientific and technological expertise, coupled with an entrepreneurial flair for adventure. From the semiconductor to communication technologies, to major advances in business services, the regional base of Silicon Valley pioneered movements that ultimately changed the way people are educated, work, play, and enjoy the pleasures of modern civilization.

The major industry clusters that drove the dramatic growth periods are Semiconductors, Computers/Communication, Defense/Space, and Business Service. During the early 1990s, these areas were in a transformation stage while the emerging industry clusters of Software, Bioscience and Environment were positioned as additional growth clusters of the 21st Century. Thus, according to the Blueprint report, these seven export-oriented industry clusters represent the major lifeblood of the region's economy,

THE CLUSTER FACTOR

The presence of industry clusters is an important phenomenon for a regional economy. An industry cluster consists of geographic concentrations of interdependent and globally competitive companies in related industries. A combination of resources, talents, expertise, and production capacity provided by both domestic and foreign, large and small firms, fuel the growth and development of a dynamic cluster. This interaction and cross-fertilization of ideas, products, and services fosters a unique industrial self-generating environment that promotes dynamic growth throughout the local economy. With the support of a solid infrastructure consisting of state-of-the-art communication/information systems, modern transportation facilities, university/research environments, finance and marketing services, favorable governmental regulations, and strong export markets, industry cluster developments can become the main engines of economic growth and prosperity for a region. As this growth translates into domestic and international success, the region begins to attract and recruit brilliant minds from around the world. As the African general Hannibal said over 2000 years ago, "nothing succeeds like success," and this is what happens where there is a clustering of related firms and industries operating in the same geographic region.

An economic *multiplier effect* happens on many fronts. Local firms supply products and services for other firms located throughout the industrial region. Employees pump up the local economy by spending their paychecks at local stores and restaurants, and purchasing homes and automobiles. For the high-tech Silicon Valley, this economic phenomenon contributed greatly to a high standard of living throughout the four county network of Alameda, San Mateo, Santa Clara and Santa Cruz. The Blueprint report tells us that, "For every $100 in sales, cluster firms can induce as much as $300 of sales throughout the local economy by purchasing local goods and services with income *new* to the region."[6] Thus, the major seven key clusters of Silicon Valley are vital to the continued international strength of the region, and this is the main focus of the JVSV initiative. Many individual firms continue to prosper on a global basis, but expansion designs that consist of *outsourcing* and building new facilities in other regions, meant the gradual chipping away of the harmonious cluster-effect that made Silicon Valley a world class region in past periods.

With a changing economic picture in world affairs, intense international competition, particularly from Asian countries, and the rise of other high-tech regional industrial complexes in various parts of the world functioning with lower operating costs (wages, taxes, etc.), the Valley slowly drifted into a period of significant economic decline. Since 1984, 40,000 jobs were lost in manufacturing industries. From 1989 to 1993, job growth for the Valley was virtually stagnant. By the 1990s, worldwide competitive forces had restructured the high-tech world, compelling some leading-edge Valley companies to expand outside of the region. The emergence of Japan, the Four Tigers and India (with its large base of two to three million software programmers and developers) had a dramatic impact on Silicon Valley's worldwide prospects.

In a reality where few things remain the same, it seems that even the most powerful of entities cannot escape the inevitable cycles of birth, growth, maturity, death and in some cases, rebirth. The formation of the JVSV initiative had a mission to revive and restore the Silicon Valley's world class life-style and to put it firmly on track for the expected growth periods of the 21st Century. And according to our analysis, the timing for their *rebirth strategy* was on target, given the period of industry chaos during the opening stages of the Information Age.

REGIONAL COOPERATION

In the *Blueprint For A 21st Century Community,* JVSV promoted a strong regional collaboration of business, government, community and educational leaders to fundamentally reshape the future of Silicon Valley: the so-called *collaborative advantage.* More than 1000 government, business and community leaders in the Silicon Valley came together to work on this fundamental problem effecting their collective overall future. In response to the rapidly changing world economy and the extraordinary prospects of the 21st Century, the Phase II report recommended the following:

♦   The need to restructure the infrastructure of Silicon Valley to embrace the dynamics of *change* at a much faster rate. This includes being more responsive to the individual needs of the companies and industries that make up the Valley. The report made the observation that smaller, less complex regions like Austin, Texas or Singapore were often able to meet the rapidly changing needs of companies faster than Silicon Valley.

♦   Silicon Valley would go beyond its reputation as the *Valley of Entrepreneurs* to become the *Entrepreneurial Valley.* While the independent entrepreneur was the primary engine of the

Valley's initial growth, a new growth engine of the 21st Century will be the networked corporation having dynamic relationships with other companies and with many communities. The Valley will enjoy the fruits of individual entrepreneurs, but will also be able to capitalize on new ideas through strong networks of companies, institutions, and individuals.

♦   In the future, Silicon Valley will become the world's first truly *networked* region, nurturing the right environment to attract, retain, and grow the virtual corporations that are linked extensively to the global economy of the 21st Century. Instead of doing everything in-house in a single location, companies began locating activities globally to take advantage of each region's unique offerings. In the process, a new type of business has emerged, the networked or virtual corporation which has unprecedented responsiveness and productivity.

♦   Flexible networks that link contractors, subcontractors, and customers in an elaborate web of relationships have become the dominant organizational pattern. These networks are both local and global.[7]

♦   In June of 1994, JVSV announced the formation of the first *environmental incubator* program in America. Eight entrepreneurial start-up companies moved into a 20,600 square-foot building in San Jose, California and began their two year nesting periods, which will provide them with inexpensive space, free office furniture and management help for the emergence and hatching of their technologies commercially. Other incubator programs such as defense conversion, multimedia, and software development are prime examples of the Valley's commitment towards assisting the systematic development of new technologies.

The overall success of the JVSV plan depended on a number of factors, but central to this issue is the ultimate impact of the Information Age of the 1990s and the rapid growth of the global economy in the 21st Century. Silicon Valley is a prime example of a major industrial development region transforming itself to compete in a rapidly changing world environment.

The Blueprint report brings to light an important lesson and something that will be the cornerstone for success of all industry developments in the 21st Century; the issue of cooperation and the collaborative advantage. This represents a critical factor for African Americans attempting to develop vital and enriching organizations in the Information Age. Cooperation, trust and respect will represent the moral fiber of strong and dynamic organizations. Commitment to a common vision and unity in organizational focus, can inspire a movement of cross-fertilization of ideas, concepts, resources, productive capacities, and expertise on a level conducive toward industrial strength. These types of institutional principals must guide our actions or there will be no significant presence of African Americans in the Information Age. Industrial cooperation is essential if maximum efficiency, with corresponding reduction in waste and energy, is to become a model for 21st Century African American, techno-economic development: *KyberGenesis!*

As we entered 1996, the revitalization of Silicon Valley was clearly on track. The cooperative spirit and the dynamics and sense of urgency initiated a *rebirth* and a clear example of what can be done when people are united behind a common goal. Driven by a red hot stock market, the dynamics of new technologies for the Internet (Netscape), and Information Age euphoria, Silicon Valley came back to position itself as a much stronger region in the global economy. This type of industrial policy will ultimately maximize efficiency and energy, and reduce waste. This is a TECHNOLOGICAL MODEL African Americans need to study very closely. African Americans need to develop an industrial model for the 21st Century.

OBSOLESCENCE AND TRENDS

Our analysis in previous sections reveal that the emergence of new generic technologies creates new system designs that in turn parent the development of new industries. Current trends in scientific progress are scheduled to bring into existence large arrays of new products and services that will either replace or enhance existing products and processes: various products in today's markets will become obsolete. Witness the demise of the turntable and vinyl records; similar events will take place in many other fields. By the year 2020, the automobile of the day will probably be electric, solar or hydrogen-fueled. Resource limitations, in the petrochemical field, technological advances, a population explosion (100 million people were added to the world's population in 1995), and environmental factors will converge to drive this massive conversion process. Our shipping industry will be revolutionized by ships powered by large superconducting magnets, allowing for high-speed ocean travel and rapid transport of international commerce. These types of massive changes bring into existence new support industries that supply the necessary parts and services required by the new technological realities. The techno-formation of these and other major breakthroughs will happen in the last decade of the 20th Century and the first decade of the 21st Century. We will witness the rise and fall of industries on a scale not seen in the annals of industrial and economic history.

Product Life Cycle, IBM and the "Dinosaur Syndrome"

The early 1990s witnessed the obsolescent stage of the product life cycle of mainframe computers. As the most successful company to emerge out of the computer revolution of the late 1940s, IBM needs no introduction; for over three decades the computer giant dominated the global mainframe business. However, by 1990 it was painfully clear that a new era in computing power and system designs would be the new standards for the 21st Century and beyond. Traditional mainframe systems were being de-emphasized for multivendor, client/server environments that offered greater flexibility and cheaper operating expenses.

From 1989 to 1994, the mainframe market maintained a steady course of declines. In 1993 the market declined 21%, which was in part due to industry-wide price slashes of 35% per year since the beginning of the 1990s. For the years 1992 and 1993, IBM racked up enormous losses of $13 billion, which forced the company to reengineer its entire corporate operations and to layoff 40,000 employees in 1992. IBM's mainframe revenues for 1993 were $6.6 billion (not to shabby for a dinosaur), which was about half that of 1990.

Other mainframe producers were brutally beaten as well by the technological revolution. Amdahl Corp., Unisys Corp., and Hitachi Data Systems all initiated drastic price cuts, reworked the insides of their machines, and struggled to reposition themselves in a fundamentally changed technological environment. Unisys began calling its newly revised mainframe *enterprise servers*, to reflect its quantum shift into a new arena.[8] In 1993, Amdahl's corporate sales nearly dried up, a clear indication of the new direction in the computing environment.[9]

Despite these painful economic and technological blows, the obsolescent period and shift out of the mainframe arena will not be an overnight affair. With billions of dollars invested in hardware, software applications, programmers and various types of system analysts, the conversion and replacement process will be a slow but steady progression over the next decade. Nearly 90 percent of Fortune 500 companies still perform most of their data operations in the mainframe computer environment. Thus, the proposition for reengineering is an enormous multi-billion dollar investment, given the fifty to sixty thousand mainframe population that are potential candidates for conversion. This industry dilemma is analogous to telecom companies faced with the enormous proposition of replacing millions of miles of copper wire with fiber optics: in both cases, a hybrid solution is readily adopted in order to avoid a painful operation!

Thus, while the traditional mainframe computer will be *Gone With The Wind* within a decade, a new evolutionary, mini-style version will emerge as a practical reality for the 21st Century. IBM and Amdahl are rapidly reshaping their corporate missions in response to the onslaught of the communications revolution of the 1990s. Like the telecommunications industry and vinyl records and turntables, mainframe computers became a target in the path of the most broad-sweeping technological revolution in history.

Nevertheless, for IBM this story is far from over. Like the "Silicon Valley Affair," by late 1996 IBM had recovered from the previous periods of declines. The company's new mainframes, PCs, and minicomputers received respectable acceptance in the marketplace. In addition, IBM's new strategy gave an even stronger emphasis on customer needs and requirements. Strategic alliances and acquisitions that focus on new technologies and software (Sun Microsystems' Java programming and other related software and hardware revisions) enabled IBM to successfully incorporate the digital wave of the future in its new global strategy. For 1996, customers spent roughly $59 billion with IBM, representing a 8% increase over revenues of $54 billion in 1995. The cover story for *Business Week* (December 9, 1996) spoke to IBM's dramatic resurgence: "How IBM Became A Growth Company Again".[10] The company's continued success in the future will depend on how well it can manage *change*.

SYSTEMATIC INNOVATION

Peter F. Drucker's book entitled *Innovation and Entrepreneurship,* offers some very important lessons regarding the basic nature of innovation. His central thesis informs us that:

> There must be a systematic search for innovation and opportunities, a systematic examination of the areas of change that typically offer entrepreneurial development ... One needs to

pick an area of interest and personal expertise and study systematically the emergence of the innovative opportunity.[11]

Drucker's analysis points to a critical technological movement that began during the 20th Century: the attitude and technological mission of systematically searching for the breakthrough product, concept or service. The entire process of innovation shifted in its focus and organization in the 20th Century: it became an organized effort supported by research laboratories and procedures which produced many of the inventions of this era.

Drucker tells us that since the 1940s the process of innovation has been a highly organized venture conducted by educated professionals. The process of searching for and developing breakthrough products has become a profession in which "the inventor has become an engineer, the craftsman a professional." In short, the innovative process was institutionalized and financed by deep corporate pockets. This became a significant part of the paradigm shift in the workplace and a major contributor to the rapid advancement of new technologies in our era.

Drucker identifies seven key sources of innovative opportunities that give rise to new industry developments. Entrepreneurial behavior and attitude exploits the advantages presented by these new opportunities. The seven areas identified in his thesis are:

(1) Unexpected events (whether success or failure) and outside developments can produce an innovative opportunity. An unintentional and unplanned development can be the source of a major breakthrough. What may appear to be a failure on the surface, could in fact hold the key to a golden opportunity.

(2) Dramatic changes in industry structure or market structure can bring about windows of innovative opportunities, while

condemning obsolete designs and systems to extinction. This part of his analysis is especially critical, particularly as it relates to the enormous structural upheavals taking place throughout the world in the 1990s. Accordingly, this represents a period of *innovative opportunity.*

(3) Drucker identifies something called *the incongruity* in the innovation process. Here the thinker/researcher needs to pay close attention to that gray area "between reality as it actually is and reality as it is assumed to be." Major innovative opportunities that are the results of incongruities will emerge out of the political, social, cultural and economic revelations of the Information Age revolution. Industry-wide macro changes may go unnoticed by the majority of industry participants, however, small and highly-focused enterprises can seize the opportune moment and begin new movements. African Americans need to be glued to these emerging new trends and be prepared to flow with a new and dynamic shift in industry developments. The world is going to change in ways many people never in their fondest dreams imagined.

(4) Innovative enhancements based on perfecting existing processes will be developed by new knowledge. As new discoveries take place, the opportunity for new applications and redesigns will present themselves throughout the revolution. Essentially, old product designs with weak links or outdated techniques, will be improved with new product knowledge.

(5) Massive changes in demographics will present opportunities for innovative ideas. The worldwide communications revolution in the 21st Century will be a significant factor in the changes of populations, their size, structure, migration patterns, age, composition, employment, education, income and other statistically important elements. New population trends will present extraordinary innovative opportunities.

(6) New knowledge in many areas (not just technological or scientific) will help to uncover the search for new developments. What we are presently witnessing in the 1990s is a revolutionary movement in the *convergence* of diverse areas of knowledge. Unlike the other areas of innovative opportunities, Drucker tells us that innovations based on new knowledge have a specific *window* period in which an entrepreneur can seize a position in an emerging industry. Since the 1950s, this window period has averaged about five to six years, and after it closes a period of *shakeout* begins. According to Drucker, "The 'shakeout' sets in as soon as the majority of ventures started during the 'window' period do not survive the shakeout..." In the Information Age revolution of the 1990s the contest is global and the number of participants will ultimately include tens of thousands. When the shakeout comes (and it always does) the casualty rate will be heavy and economically punishing to many companies from around the world. The survivors may not necessarily include all of the major powerhouses of the latter 20th Century, but is very likely to witness the emergence of some new superstars. A number of factors will determine the outcome, but chief among them is a superior awareness of the evolutionary spirit of our times.

(7) Changes in perception, mood and the meaning of life, are the beginning stages of new innovative periods. Few people can deny that our perceptions of life and reality will be profoundly shaken in coming periods. The individual will be empowered as never before, and this will bring about major cultural and historical changes.

The above analysis is important, and a careful study of these sources (of innovative opportunities) will yield some very fruitful results. Strategic planning in this area should consider the cross-fertilization of ideas, 21st Century multidimensional business formations, and the collaborative advantage in reaching predetermined goals. For African Americans, target areas of significant penetration should be those that are not broadly considered by the major industry(s) participants. According to Drucker, this is "Hitting them where they ain't," and that's precisely what will be the winning strategy in the majority of cases. The focus should be on particular market segments and demographic categories. A clear design and strategy in this area will yield some very profitable results in future periods. It's important for African Americans to realize that we are in the initial stages of a new era, which will generate major changes in many areas. A major requirement will be the need to take off the old hat and mindset of 19th and 20th Century thinking, and start developing new visions for the 21st Century. Establish a bold *vision* for the new century and consider the *KyberGenesis* factor as a key revolutionary technological force in world development.

PRODUCT LIFE CYCLE AND THE INNOVATIVE THRUST

The introduction of new technologies in the world happens in stages and difficult periods of trial and error. The actual adoption of new technologies is often slow at first, then the market growth rate begins to increase rapidly as consumer acceptance accelerates. The basic technological stages of the innovative process are summed up in Figure 1. In general, stages 1 through 3 take many years to complete. The current trend of innovative advances indicates that this will no longer be the case. Moving from stages 6 to 7 traditionally took up to five years. It took eighteen years for Xerography to move from stage 1 to stage 7, and another five years to achieve the goal of producing an effective office copier. Widespread adoption of television came about a decade after the introduction of the first television set. Integrated circuits took twelve years to move from stage 1 through 7, and the laser reached stage 6 in about five years. Thus, the innovative process for different innovative technologies varies in length and is influenced by economic considerations, the social environment, and governmental policies in operation during the initial stages. And again, the late 1990s climate is favorable in all of these critical areas.

In the 1990s, international competition, governmental deregulation, and societal expectation of 21st Century technologies, are prime incentives for innovation, particularly in the United States or North America. There is a rapid pace of innovative advancements, with synergy movements in full swing. Laser technology reaching stage 6 in roughly five years indicates four very important realities: (1) the presence of intense worldwide competition; (2) the rapid recognition of the superior performance of laser and digital technologies; (3) quick acceptance by the movers and shakers of worldwide industrial development to embrace the wave of the future; and (4) consumer/buyer acceptance of the new laser technologies (which has been phenomenal). Laser technology has multiple uses and its proliferation will continue at a strong pace.

TIMING

We would like to leave you with one last thought in regards to strategic planning and innovation; the paramount issue of timing. For this message we turn to an unlikely source; the famous sixteenth century Japanese swordsman, Miyamoto Musashi. During the closing years of his illustrious sword fighting career, Musashi wrote a book entitled, *The Book of Five Rings (Go Rin No Sho),* which during the 1980s became source reading material in business graduate schools at various universities in America. This book provides an excellent treatment of strategy, and presents some very interesting insights on the nature of *timing.* On this subject Musashi tells us:

CREATIVE STAGES IN TECHNOLOGICAL INNOVATION

PRIMARY   RESEARCH

(1) A new idea or opportunity is presented.
(2) A platform is established to carefully examine the theoretical premises of the idea and concept.

APPLIED   RESEARCH

(3) A design and model of the idea is taken into the laboratory for
verification and refinement.
(4) The application is taken through a demonstration process.

MARKET   INTRODUCTION

(5 The prototype stage and field testing.
(6) Initiation of commercial use of the new product or service.

MASS   PRODUCTION   AND   MARKETING

(7) Widespread adoption in the marketplace:
general public acceptance for the new product.
(8) Proliferation: the technology is used in other fields,
which promotes widespread usage of the original concept.

FIGURE 1: Adopted from data provided by *The Changing Environment of Business.*

There is timing in everything. Timing in strategy cannot be mastered without a great deal of practice...In all skills and abilities there is timing...there is timing in the way of the merchant, in the rise and fall of capital...It is especially important to know the background timing...If you do not look at things on a large scale it will be difficult for you to master strategy...[12]

THE MULTIDIMENSIONAL CORPORATION OF THE 21st CENTURY

In the wake of the digital revolution and the *dinosaur syndrome* of the 1990s, the standard organizational/business system that dominates the 20th Century, particularly the highly successful American model, has reached a point where it must either evolve or perish. Throughout America and other industrialized nations, corporate entities in various industries submitted to radical restructuring programs under a new system labeled *reengineering*. New concepts such as the virtual corporation have taken root in the 1990s, indicating a paradigm shift in the actual organizational structure and way a company processes information and produces a product or service. The digital and information revolution has brought into existence a significant movement in the very nature of how and in what way successful businesses will operate in the future. This new reengineered, virtual corporation is taking on the characteristics of a multidimensional entity functioning throughout several industries simultaneously. In the communications arena, this has become the de-facto norm and goal of many global corporations. Multidimensional is nothing new in the world of science and physics, but in the dawn of this new era, it has taken on an expanded reality in the everyday world of the common man. This represents a historical shift in business and organizational development, similar to the enormous restructuring developments of the Industrial Revolution.

REENGINEERING

With the collapse of communism in the early 1990s and the enormous triumph of the worldwide free enterprise movement, trade barriers and restrictions began to fall in nation after nation throughout the world, opening a doorway for the 21st Century global age. As we approach the 21st Century, the broadest use of the term reengineering can be applied to governmental management of infrastructural developments within their borders. Much like the global technological hurricane of the Industrial Revolution, the nations that did not participate in the new technologies and organizational shifts in business developments, were systematically left behind and ultimately subjugated by their more sophisticated and powerful competitors. We have entered a similar period wherein many small and economically depressed nations will be forced to make some very tough decisions. In order for *any* nation to be commercially successful in the 21st Century, state-of-the-art multi-billion dollar infrastructural communication networks will need to be an established reality. Investments in roads, transportation systems, schools and universities, hospitals and medicine, and implementation of policies allowing for full competition and interaction with the global community, will be mandatory. In short, reengineering societies, corporations and institutions for the next century has become a matter of survival and a blueprint for success in the future. Those leaders intent on ignoring the enormous implications of the revolution of our era, will ultimately witness the demise of their governments, institutions, and companies in the wake of our historic global paradigm shift towards the new age. Strategic actions taken in the 1990s will greatly improve their chances for survival and success in the coming period.

Authors Michael Hammer and James Champy, the acknowledged gurus of the reengineering movement of the 1990s, have been very instrumental in convincing many American (and non-American) corporations to restructure their entire business operations. In their international bestseller, *Reengineering The Corporation: A Manifesto For Business*

Revolution, the authors inform corporate leaders that we have arrived at a point in history when it is imperative that the American corporate model undergo a systematic revision. In their thesis we learn that, "the classical American corporation is sadly obsolete," and so we are faced with a corporate revolution as we make the transition towards the 21st Century. American corporations led the world for more than 100 years with superior corporate organization, but that heyday is over. Much of this organizational transformation can be attributed to the explosive power of advanced technologies.

In the global era of the 21st Century, corporations will have to compete with the world's best movers and shakers in markets throughout the world. We have seen the destructive and creative powers of the dinosaur syndrome; the massive revolution in the telecommunication industry and AT&T; the astounding progress in the computer industry that resulted in the demise of IBM's dominance; the rise and imminence of the multimedia juggernaut of the 1990s; and the massive restructure of several media industries; all of which brought fundamental shifts and ripple effects throughout many techno-industries. The reengineering proposition is a poignant statement and testimony of our times: large corporate organizations are forced to restructure themselves in ways that are radically different from how they operated in the past. This is technological revolution at its best, tearing down old systems and erecting new ones to take their place.

THE VIRTUAL CORPORATION

The new corporate species arising out of the ashes of the reengineering movement is the virtual corporation. Driven by the technological revolution and other global economic, political, social, and cultural forces, the virtual corporation is designed to be more flexible, innovative, responsive and less bureaucratic than its predecessor. The transformation is traumatic in many cases, as companies move to streamline their operations, replacing certain functions and processes with computers and robots, and eliminating middle management in re-structured departments. The virtual corporation must adapt to the needs of the end-user, and the emphasis is increasingly focused on the empowered individual of the global community. The winds of change are responding to this new reality.

This movement is far-reaching in many ways. Technological advances in telecommunications and computing in the 1990s, has started to eliminate permanent office environments for many employees for certain types of organizations. The strategy here is the reduction of office costs and leased space requirements, which next to salaries, are the largest drain on a company's financial performance. *Hoteling* or the *virtual office* is one of the business strategies emerging out of the new virtual environment. Instead of an employee having a full-time permanent office space exclusively, that space is shared by others, and in turn, all are required to make reservations for the time slots needed for in-house periods. This system works well for employees that routinely spend 50 to 90 percent of their time in the field, such as sales people, auditors, management consultants, and various occupations that require a great deal of travel. The virtual office phenomenon will have a significant impact on the availability of office space in many major cities.

It appears that the advent of the *virtual product* (customized products with heavy customer participation and information content, such as the personalized/customized automobile) is one of the driving forces necessitating the need for the virtual corporation. Global alliances and partnerships consisting of manufacturers, suppliers, distributors and increasingly customers, are the building blocks of the new types of global arrangements. Increasingly, mutually beneficial relationships based on mutual trust and a shared destiny by corporations and their global partners, employees, and customers will make the difference between success or failure in the marketplace. Loyalty and affiliations in the future will be based on a different set of global parameters.

The coming global struggle between the *blue-collar worker* and the *robot* will create some new alliances among people who were previously indifferent to each other's political and economic problems. Broad-sweeping changes in government and corporate environments will bring about confrontations between old allies, and establish new playing fields. New industries will arise to take the place of those that fall: the watch word will be constant *change.*

THE MULTIMEDIA AND MULTIDIMENSIONAL FACTOR

Given the estimated $3 trillion pot of gold awaiting the victors at the end of the rainbow (the competitive global struggles), many large corporate conglomerates in the United States are restructuring themselves for the multimedia 21st Century. As one of the major dynamic forces driving the Information Age, the emergence of multimedia has brought about massive industry realignments and cross-industrial developments. As one publication stated "America is the heartland of multimedia," and as we entered 1994 it became apparent that this nation was also leading a multimedia global revolution. The United States was establishing the global model, and this model will be duplicated all over the world by the year 2000.

The metamorphosis of the conservative and FCC controlled $193 billion telecommunication industry, dramatically illustrates the significance of the multimedia techno-factor. As we have seen in previous sections, industry barriers are falling and outdated policies and legislated laws on the books have become obsolete. Digital technology has essentially torn down the walls between telephone companies, broadcast TV, cable TV, the film industry, and computer hardware and software companies. They are all in the same business; the *communications business*! Federal regulators, particularly the FCC, are racing to catch up to the full implications of this major paradigm shift. As the traditional barriers are removed one by one, what is slowly emerging from the creative cauldron is the *multidimensional corporation,* the new corporate species for the communications arena. Either as a result of mergers and acquisitions, or strategic alliances and partnerships, this new species is coming into existence in the 1990s.

In observing this situation in the second half of the 1990s, it is difficult to say what will emerge by the year 2000; whether there will be a multidimensional global corporation and an industry established in the same name. It is also difficult to anticipate the arrival of other participating industries in the struggle for the global communication dominance. However, in the early stages of this techno-revolution, the key industries that have taken the lead toward convergence in forming the nascent multimedia alliances are:

(1) Telecommunications: both the wireless and wireline
   industries
(2) Network/Broadcast TV
(3) Cable TV
(4) The Film Industry
(5) Computer Hardware
(6) Computer Software
(7) Direct Broadcast Satellite (DBS)

THE PIPELINE CONNECTION

The first phase in the development of the multimedia future has been a mad rush to control the *pipeline* - the cable systems, broadcast TV, the telephone systems, the fiber optic networks, and the wireless cellular and satellite networks. These arenas represent the basic foundation of the new *information superhighway,* which has become the rallying chorus for the restructuring of the communications systems in America and ultimately throughout the world. The cost of this mammoth overhaul is estimated to be between $100 to $150 billion. When the new foundation has been put in place, it will be the industry standard of the 21st Century and beyond. All other media systems and new developments will evolve out of the basic pipelines of the future.

All of the major players have agreed on one central point: the cost to build the information superhighway is too high for any one company. This is one of the primary factors that is driving the merger mania of the 1990s. According to the Securities Data Co., the announced American merger volume reached $275.2 billion in 1993. During the first nine months of 1995, merger deals totaled nearly $249 billion. Much of this activity was driven by the feeding frenzy in the emerging multimedia arena. These companies are being brought together by economies of scale, innovative technologies, synergy needs, financial and economic necessity, and federal and local regulations. The new techno-media complex they are forming will offer a vast array of services to homes and businesses. Within the next few years major developments will clearly define who and what will be the industry leaders. A significant shakeout in these key industries will witness the demise of many corporate entities. By the year 2000, the new species should be alive and well.

THE NETWORK TV CONNECTION

In 1993, many analysts were wondering whether network television was heading for extinction, another casualty of the dinosaur syndrome. From 1950 to the early 1990s, network TV traveled through the life cycle of birth, growth, maturity, decline and rebirth. The Big Three: CBS, Cap Cities/ABC, and NBC are rapidly being propelled towards a new role in the multimedia world of tomorrow. By late 1994, it was clear that network monopoly in the home entertainment business was over. Like IBM and AT&T, Network TV was compelled to pursue a strategy that would shift its industrial position to a place in a much larger universe of media offerings.

The significant period of decline that began in the 1970s with the advent of home video, direct broadcast satellite, and cable TV, has been relentless. The Information Age revolution in the 1990s will ultimately accelerate the pace towards a media form of obsolescence or revision, with a dramatic reconfiguration of the system's base of power. Network TV will not die a violent death or be left to wither away like vinyl records and the turntable, but instead will play a significant role in the multimedia universe of the 21st Century. However, the major point to be made here is that the basic system of networking, distributive media stations and other types of information delivery technologies is not on the decline; what has declined and will diminish in importance is the *Big Three* dominance over the airwaves. It's a new day and the movers and shakers are developing a new *game.*

Some of the key issues and factors that have defined the dinosaur syndrome for network TV are as follows:

- ■ In the late 1970s, network TV commanded a 90% market share of homes watching television; by 1994 the Big Three held a 61% share. In its heyday, with an omnipresent network distributive system, the Big Three reached 98 % of U.S. homes.

- ■ The relentless onslaught of cable, home video, and Direct Broadcast Satellite (DBS) during the 1980s and early 1990s, had a significant impact on the Big Three's audience shares. In 1980, 23% of U.S. homes were subscribers of basic cable TV; by 1994 that number had swelled to 63%! Total revenues for the home video market in 1993 were nearly $14 billion, and by 1994 the world was in the midst of a major revolution in satellite systems.

- ■ The 1990s marketplace is crowded with many competitors and competitive forces: Pay-per-view, HBO, BET, Independent TV, video classrooms and conferencing, direct broadcast satellite channels, the shift to a 500 channel universe and movies-on-demand, interactive games and other forms of interactivity, and the Internet. In this brave new media world the consumer is king/queen, with a cornucopia of viewer choices.

■ Since the beginning of television back in the late 1940s and early 1950s, its primary objective for many decades has been the selling of advertising and using programs as fillers. Giant corporations with mass advertising needs, have been heavily dependent on network TV to lure millions of passive viewers to their TV screens on a daily basis. By the early 1990s, they were spending roughly $30 billion annually on TV advertising, with approximately $9 billion earmarked for the Big Three. However, by the year 2000, the advertising budgets of such giant corporations as Procter & Gamble will be divided among a much larger array of media offerings, and the entire notion of advertising will go through a period of intense revolution.

■ Deregulation of the network TV industry will open up a new chapter in the competitive struggle for the control of the air waves. In 1993, the FCC set the stage by discontinuing most of the restrictions set forth by the "financial interest and syndication" rules which banned the networks from the production of more than a fraction of their TV programs and disallowed them to participate in the lucrative syndication business. By 1994, the networks could enter into full-time production of TV shows, and by the end of 1995, the domestic syndication rules were removed. Federal Communication

Commission (FCC) deregulations cleared the way for the megamerger deal of Walt Disney Co.'s acquisition of Capital Cities/ABC, valued at nearly $19 billion! As other possible merger announcements hit the airwaves (i.e. CBS and Westinghouse Electric Corporation), FCC Commissioner Andrew Barrett pondered a future of fewer competitors. As he observed the merger mania of 1995, he stated that, "By the year 2000 we'll probably see 10 to 12 companies controlling everything we see, hear and convey in entertainment, voice and data." Across the board deregulation is clearly the road that America is taking in the 1990s.

- In the late 1980s, New Corp's Fox Inc. was established as a nascent fourth TV network in America. In December of 1993, Fox Incorporated acquired the broadcast rights to the NFL's National Conference games (a $1.56 billion deal over a four year period), outbidding CBS by $400 million, who had held the contract for 38 years. With this major deal in its war chest, Fox's strategic plan was to solidify a stronger network position in America. In May 1994, Fox engineered a masterful deflection of 12 major stations from the Big Three, with CBS losing key station affiliates in such lucrative markets as Detroit, Cleveland, Atlanta, Tampa, and Milwaukee

- In the wake of the FCC decision to deregulate network TV and the historic corporate brilliance of the "Fox maneuver," Time Warner's Warner Bro's (WB) studio and Viacom's Inc.'s Paramount studio, announced plans to start their own mini-TV networks during the 1994-95 season. The WB Network and United Paramount Network (UPN) increased the total to six network stations in America.

Thus, given these and other historic changes in the entire communications arena, it is clear that major evolutionary and economic forces are redefining the entire spectrum of communication systems. For African Americans it is a time of opportunity and a period where major advances can be made.

PART THREE

CHALLENGES OF THE NEW ERA

CHAPTER SEVEN

Telecommunication and the Wireless Revolution

Khafra K Om-Ra-Seti

T raditional frontiers and industry barriers in the telecommunications industry collapsed in the 1990s under the enormous weight and pressure of digital technology and the advent of the Information Age. This spectacular set of circumstances is yet another sign of the winds of change. The communications revolution sweeping across America in the 1990s, is like a gale-force wind that is destined to establish the standard model for the globalization of communications in the 21st Century. Starting in 1993, America took center stage as the global leader in setting the standards for building the new organizational structures in telecommunication for the future. The entire world will be reshaped by the dynamics of a new *communications paradigm.*

MA BELL: THE MOTHER OF AMERICAN TELECOMMUNICATIONS

Alexander Graham Bell is generally credited as the inventor of the telephone. Historians tell us that the patent awarded to Bell on February 17, 1876 (one hour before Elisha Gray's telephone patent) would ultimately be challenged in court by 600 law suits over a period of eleven years. Supporters of many inventors fought long and protracted legal battles to prove that their telephone inventions preceded Bell's patent design.

Nevertheless, as history would have it, Bell (a voice teacher), won the honor and proceeded to organize the effort to build a telephone system in America. An interesting observation of the latter years of the 1870s reveal that the public's perception of a new medium that would be able to transmit the human voice, was very dim; it was considered science fiction, and in some circles, unbelievable. This represented the beginning of a paradigm shift and a techno-economic event destined to change the course of human societies. History offers us many lessons, however the periods of great paradigm shifts are of extreme importance in the long history of mankind.

American Bell and Western Electric Company (the manufacturing arm of the Bell system) were incorporated by the early 1880s. On February 28, 1885, American Telephone and Telegraph Company (AT&T) was born, and originally established as a long-distance subsidiary of American Bell. In deep competitive struggles with Western Union (at the time, the nation's largest telecommunications company) and many other independent phone companies, American Bell concentrated on expansion and protecting its patents (in hundreds of law suits) up to the early 1890s.

In 1893, when Bell's patents expired, there were only a total of 291,253 telephones in the United States. By the turn of the century, Bell's strategic plans were revised in order to prepare for a major campaign to capture a huge share of the rapidly growing telecommunications industry. After remaining a subsidiary of American Bell for 15 years, AT&T absorbed American Bell in 1900 and began a new era of consolidation for the emerging 20th Century. The years 1907-1908 marked a major turning point in the development of the modern commercial communications system that became the AT&T/ Bell monopoly. Some of the key events that initiated this dramatic shift are as follows:

♦   In 1907, an aggressive Theodore Vail (newly elected President of AT&T) and the Morgan banking interests, spearheaded the leadership that led to the modern, vertically integrated AT&T, with a firm vision and goal of building a regulated monopoly with universal coverage. Offers of consolidations were presented to many independent phone companies to join *Ma Bell's* communications family.

♦   By 1907, over six million telephones were in operation in America, with nearly three million supplied by the 15,527 independent exchanges. Vail's public appeal in 1908 of "One policy, one system, universal service," began to create a new image of AT&T.

The financial panic and stock market crash of 1907-08, dealt a fatal blow to Western Union (AT&T's arch competitor) and other independent phone companies. This presented an opportunity for AT&T to take control over the majority of communication markets in America. By 1910, AT&T had 5,882,719 telephone lines in operation. Through consolidations and acquisitions, AT&T was well on its way to becoming a deeply entrenched telecommunications monopoly in America.

In the decades that followed, AT&T continued to consolidate its hold on the telecommunications industry in both the local and long-distance arenas. Western Electric Company manufactured all of the equipment that customers used exclusively throughout the Bell system, and Bell Laboratories (the research arm) moved to the forefront as an important source of innovative ideas, products and services. As an organization, AT&T and the Bell system now consisted of 21 operating companies, with a parent/headquarters operation providing research, financing, patents, the interconnecting long distance lines, and critical development for the rapidly growing enterprises extending their services in the continental United States.

With the collapse of the stock market in 1929 and the onset of the decade of the Great Depression, Roosevelt's New Deal policies gave birth to the Communications Act of 1934 that fully established telecommunications as a regulated industry. The Federal Communications Commission (FCC) was created with the prime objectives to stabilize prices, insure universal access, and make available affordable telephone service throughout America. At that time public policy favored a regulated, protected monopoly that could provide universal service under governmental control. In 1934, nearly three quarters of the American population did not have phones, and even in the midst of a depression, the stage was set for a growth period when the economy started to move again. AT&T's cozy relationship with the government went beyond the issue of universal coverage; during World War II the company supplied radar equipment and other communication devices to the military.

Starting in the late 1950s, the insulated world of AT&T began to unravel. Some of the key decisions and events that began that process are as follows:

♦   A court ruling in 1957 allowed AT&T customers (first time) to attach non-AT&T equipment to their telephones, provided that the devices did not interfere with the public network.

♦   The *Carterfone* decision in 1968 took the equipment issue a step further; non-telephone company equipment could now be connected to telephone lines. This landmark decision opened the door to competition to Western Electric's manufacturing private domain.

♦   In 1969, MCI Communications Corporation was granted a license to begin private line services between Chicago and St. Louis. Continued growth and expansion, along with FCC approvals to allow switched long-distance services, moved MCI into a strong competitive position with AT&T for long-distance customers. At the time, AT&T was providing end-to-end service to about 80 percent of the U.S. telephone market, and controlled 90 percent of all long-distance connections.

♦   In 1974, MCI filed an antitrust suit against AT&T, which eventually led to the U.S. Justice Department taking legal action to prevent what was then considered illegal activities by AT&T in restricting competition in the telecommunications market. That began eight years of legal battles, with AT&T spending hundreds of millions of dollars on its small army (hundreds) of the best telecom lawyers in the country, producing some 12 million pages of legal documents to preserve its protective monopoly status and massive empire. But, the world was changing; new technologies were reshaping the communications and electronic landscape, and the old established model was no longer considered the ideal system for America.

MA BELL AND THE BIRTH OF THE BABY BELLS

In January 1982, the United States Department of Justice announced (in the case US vs. AT&T) the Consent Decree for the divestiture of the local operating companies from AT&T. This represented the effective breakup of AT&T and began the process to end its monopoly in America. The impact of dismantling the largest corporation in the world was similar in scope to the breakup of the Soviet Union in the political arena: a large powerful entity would be divided into its component parts. AT&T was a superpower regulated monopoly, with extensive networks and enormous influence.

The Consent Decree ruling in January 1982 gave AT&T a two year period to prepare for the actual separation of its total operations. D-Day occurred on January 1, 1984, establishing the new era of the seven Baby Bells. Brooke Tunstall, a veteran of the divestiture proceedings, described the process as, "the dismantling of AT&T's integrated nationwide local and long-distance network and of the company's financial and management structure into eight discrete corporate entities."

The 22 Bell operating companies were reorganized into seven new regional holding companies or RHCs (the Baby Bells: US West, Ameritech, Nynex, SouthWestern Bell, Bell Atlantic, BellSouth, and the Pacific Telesis Group). These restructured holding companies were prohibited from entering the long-distance market, manufacture phone equipment, and participating in the development of information services. Under its newly revised organizational structure, AT&T was allowed to keep its long-distance network, Western Electric (its manufacturing facilities and arrangements), and Bell Laboratories, one of the largest private research centers in the world. It would also be allowed to enter the high growth arena of computer information markets and the manufacture of computers.

However, one of the technological ironies of this century is the fact that Bell Labs was responsible for many of the innovations that eventually brought about the transformation of the communications industry, hence the breakup of AT&T. Bell Labs pioneered in integrated circuitry, laser technology, satellite systems, and many other innovative products and services. When we step back and observe the tremendous amount of technological progress that has occurred throughout the 20th century, it seems inevitable that the mammoth telecommunications paradigm would be forced to evolve to another level: AT&T simply became a dinosaur in its monopolistic structure. America's strategic shift in the 1990s to the next technological level, will force the rest of the world to adopt the new emerging communications paradigm.

TELECOM'S EVOLUTIONARY SHIFT TO THE 21ST CENTURY

In the aftermath of the breakup of AT&T, some observers started predicting that the complete transformation of the entire system would take approximately 20 years. The historic breakup represented the first phase (*Phase I Edict*) of this enormous transformation process. The second phase (*Phase II Edict*) began in the early 1990s and is witnessing a near-complete deregulation of the telecommunications industry, the unleashing of multifaceted competitive forces, and the rapid advance of technological forces on a national and international level.

In the initial stages of the Phase II Edict, there is a great deal of risk and confusion in designing and building the future networks. The major players are struggling to position themselves for the new opportunities imagined for the 21st Century world. It is a multi-billion dollar high-tech gamble to gain a significant foothold in a global marketplace estimated to swell to over $3 trillion by the year 2000. The technological possibilities and complexities, organizational structures and designs, and the impact of the global competitive struggles by many of the world's largest corporations, will result in many new opportunities and a total revision of global business practices. We have truly entered what can be described as the *Global Era.*

The Phase II Edict is also revealing signs of what may likely emerge as new business trends in the new era. Communication decentralization and networking, alliances and integration of technological forces, are emerging as significant business and system developments. Continued deregulation has caused major tremors in the territory-based world of telecommunications. Traditional system designs and barriers are being uprooted, bringing about territorial invasion. The 1990s is a time when the global players and trend setters will openly try to outwit, outmaneuver and wage business wars to capture territories. Intense competition between the local "Bells", long-distance carriers, cable companies and others, will eventually generate new types of business arrangements. The end goal will be to produce a low-cost communication system for the 21st Century. To clarify some of these issues, it's important to examine the industrial developments that took shape in the early 1990s.

AT&T and the LONG-DISTANCE MARKET

AT&T is at the forefront of the development of the global communication networks of the 21st Century. The emergence of a global infrastructure in business services has been the main driving force behind this movement. By 1994, the world's 2500 multinational corporations were stressing the need for seamless telecommunication services linking their enormous international networks. Vast networks of banking and financial services, currency, bond and stock markets, airline reservation, hotel and travel services, advertising and marketing services, and many other communication requirements of business and governmental organizations are actively promoting the global communications revolution. The market value of the corporate global juggernaut is estimated to be over $10 billion. However, as we move closer to the globalization of economic activity, the value of global communication services will be immeasurable.

In the U.S., the long-distance market is dominated by AT&T, MCI, and Sprint. In 1993, the Big Three accounted for nearly 87% of long-distance market activity. AT&T held a commanding lead of 60% of the market; MCI, 18%; Sprint, with a little over 9%, and LDDS, WilTel, Metromedia Communications, Litel Telecommunications, Allnet and 475 smaller carriers together held a roughly 13.5% market share. Total revenues were $62 billion, which represented a 6% rise over 1992. Access costs (payments to access customer lines in local phone territories) as a monopolistic practice, will experience dramatic changes as federal deregulations level the playing fields. Some of the major changes that will eventually restructure the long-distance arena are:

(1) Deregulation of the telecommunication industry in America, which will allow the powerful Baby Bells to enter the long-distance arena, manufacture equipment, and offer a variety of information services. Industry analysts expect revenues for the Big Three to decline or be sluggish in the domestic markets due to the Baby Bells' competitive challenge. The intense competitive struggle is expected to lower costs for all categories of consumer telephone services.

(2) The dramatic rise and rapid growth of the *wireless* revolution, which many of the long-distance players regard as a vital part of the future development of long-distance networks. To reduce access expenses, long-distance carriers have moved towards a strategy of merger and acquisition in both the cable and wireless markets.

(3) Technological innovations in digital and fiber-optic networks and other areas of communication transmissions, will continue to redefine the total nature and system of communication. The synergy of voice, data, and video is an area of intense technological revision. During the early 1990s, data transmission (fax, computer downloads, etc.) grew 20% annually, while voice transmissions have grown only 6% to 7% by comparison. The

synergistic combination of computer, telephone, fiber-optic, and video will open a new chapter in revenue generation across multi-industry frontiers.

These and other trends will continue to bring about a massive restructuring of the telecommunications industry. In 1993, communication companies eliminated 50,000 jobs in efforts to reengineer, downsize, and streamline their operations for greater network flexibility in future markets. Industry analysts reported that for the single month of January 1994, 44,314 jobs were eliminated, indicating a trend of continued job cuts as communication companies consolidate and streamline their operations. AT&T announced in February 1994, that it would be eliminating 14,000 to 15,000 jobs in future periods in an effort to save $900 million a year in operating costs. The technological shift is merciless in many job categories; white-collar management jobs also experienced major hits in their ranks.

In the merger and acquisition game, nearly 50% of the deals consummated in 1993 were in the communications field. By late 1994, AT&T had picked up McCaw Cellular for $12.6 billion, setting the stage for a major national cellular communications network. The McCaw strategic purchase was in part undertaken to allow AT&T to bypass the local Baby Bell monopoly on access costs for completing long-distance calls. Sprint acquired Centel Corporation in March 1993, which gave it an important presence in many types of communication markets. Centel owns local telephone systems in seven states and 44 cellular communication markets that have 392,000 subscribers. Sprint also became a member of the Motorola-led consortium investing in Iridium, the global satellite-based communications network.

REGULATORY LIBERATION FOR THE BABY BELLS

With the advent of deregulation, the Baby Bells will become full-service universal companies, able to participate in the long-distance arena, manufacture equipment, offer cable television and a broad range of information services, and compete fully in the domestic and international markets. In the early 1990s, local operating exchange territories were exposed to intense competition by the forces of the digital age, new technologies, and regulatory actions in competing industry environments, allowing them to chip away monopoly barriers that had been in place for decades. In June 1993, the FCC unleashed a wave of new competitive pressures in the local markets. The protective monopolistic territorial frontiers of the Baby Bells, preserved by the FCC and the local PUCs (Public Utility Commissions that regulate communication within their jurisdictions) had essentially entered a period similar to the 1982 breakup of the AT&T U.S. monopoly. The telecommunication paradigm shift was clearly entering the next evolutionary phase.

Before the year 2000, local telephone and/or specialized communication services will be offered by cable television providers, radio-based cellular carriers, electric utilities, long-distance carriers extending their distribution designs, fiber-based metropolitan independent area networks (such as competitive access providers (CAPS) that offer private-line traffic by linking business customers to the long-distance market), and other local exchange companies seeking to operate outside of their own particular areas. Hence, the need to provide a level playing field for the Baby Bells so that they may take full advantage of the new-age opportunities and expand into global communication networks. The *dinosaur syndrome* simultaneously brings about extinction and creation within the broad framework of evolution. Also, by unleashing the power of the Baby Bells, America will have a stronger lineup of telecommunication giants competing for the leadership of the global age.

The ultimate impact of the new regulatory environment will be to make both the long distance and local exchanges look alike organizationally, establish lower prices for services throughout the industry, and motivate a major movement towards consolidation and strategic alliances between various players from diverse industries. Technological advances are supplying alternative service providers with the capability to offer a wide range of services and to serve virtually all telecommunication users. Thus, the Phase II Edict completes the mission of accelerating the growth and innovative capacities of all the central players in this new evolving global environment. By February 1994, the FCC had opened the interstate access market to major competitive forces. The revenue earned in this area by the Baby Bells is roughly $25 billion annually and represents 25% to 28% of their total earnings. This was another clear indication that the local monopolistic frontiers were collapsing as steadily as the Berlin Wall fell in 1989; symbolic and technological signs of the times.

Local wireless carriers offer essentially the same service as the local wireline exchanges, with the major difference of price. Wireless carriers charge a substantial premium (due to mobility of the service) for their service calls. However, industry analysts are predicting that the price for both wireless and wireline services will be roughly the same by the year 2000 or shortly thereafter. In such a scenario, some observers feel that many customers will switch to the wireless system, which will cause a radical restructure of the communication world. The years 1995 through 2000 will witness the extreme revolutionary changes of the Phase II Edict. However, the Baby Bells were not sitting still and waiting for the dinosaur syndrome to bring about their demise; they invested in the cellular market in both the domestic and international arenas, started wireline data services, and formed alliances, mergers and consolidation partnerships in the cablevision industry and satellite markets. Some of the events and industry developments shaping their future are as follows:

■   The Pacific Telesis Group announced in January 1994 that it would be eliminating 10,000 jobs by year-end 1997. On April 1, 1994, the company divided its overall operations, setting up a separate corporate entity for its wireless venture. Pac Bell would remain the traditional phone company, with plans to invest billions of dollars in a broadband network to provide voice, data and video communications for its local customers. AirTouch Communications, the cellular operation, announced its company vision to, "become a global leader in wireless communications." A stock offering on Wall Street raised $1.3 billion to help finance this stated mission. In July 1994, AirTouch began merger discussions with US West (a Baby Bell) to link their domestic operations, which would give both parties an opportunity to develop a nationwide telecommunication system. This merger arrangement will cover 21 states with the potential to reach 53 million subscribers in 16 of the top 30 markets. In addition, the participants plan to form a joint venture to tap into the emerging PCS (Personal Communications Services) market. If this trend in mergers and alliances continues, the wireless telecommunications industry will eventually be dominated by several major players.

■   US West Incorporated formed a strategic alliance with Time Warner (the second largest cable system operator in America) in 1993 to successfully compete in the rapidly evolving global communication environment. In August 1994, Time Warner, in a deal worth hundreds of millions of dollars, purchased phone switches and high-end digital network equipment from AT&T. The company purchased switching equipment for voice calls and for advanced data and video usage transmissions. The stated goal was to offer phone connections in the markets where Time Warner runs cable systems.

■   The dizzying speed of developments in the technological field rendered much of the telecommunications legislation obsolete. Deregulation of the industry became not only politically expedient, but also economically necessary. The first major overhaul of the 1934 Communications Act that created the FCC, was hotly debated in Congress throughout 1994, exactly 60 years after the passage of the historic depression-era legislation. However, the actual struggle to make legislative changes had been on the table since the late 1980s. The House of Representatives voted in June 1994, overwhelmingly in favor of two bills that sponsored the removal of barriers and greater competition in the telecommunication industry. One of the principal bills, *The Antitrust and Communications Reform Act of 1994 (HR3626),* coauthored by Judiciary Committee Chairman Jack Brooks (D-Texas) and House Energy and Commerce Committee Chairman John Dingell (D-Mch.), would essentially legislate the conditions and timetables under which the Baby Bells would be allowed to enter the long-distance phone market, manufacture telecommunications equipment, offer cable television, alarm services and electronic publishing, and deliver other various types of information services to homes and businesses. The other bill, *The National Communications Competition and Information Infrastructure Act of 1993 (HR3636),* sponsored by Massachusetts Democrat Ed Markey, Chairman of the House telecommunications subcommittee, and Republican Jack Fields of Texas, sought to open local telephone monopolies to competition and to tear down the barriers prohibiting telephone companies from competing with cable-TV operators to service customers with video programming. The ultimate Telecommunication Competition and Deregulation Act will essentially be a rewrite of the 1934 Communication Act.

As we entered 1996, legislation was still pending in Congress for deregulation, however, by February the way was cleared. Congress, in a near unanimous vote, took the giant step to deregulate communication systems in America. The bill cleared the House 444 to 16 and the Senate 91 to 5, with the Clinton Administration standing in the wings promising to sign the bill within a weeks' time. It marked the end of an era when, on February 8, 1996, President Clinton signed into law new legislation that would revamp the 1934 Communications Act. The monumental significance of this new deregulatory beginning is yet another indication of the *winds of change.* Some analysts began to predict that by the start of the 21st Century, perhaps fewer than a dozen mega-corporations will dominate the communication arena, offering everything from basic phone service to global banking, investing and entertainment. Proponents cited job growth and lower rates and fees for phone and cable services; critics pointed to structural changes that would promote job losses (reengineering, mergers and acquisitions, and new technologies) with rates for cable and telephone increasing. One thing for certain, in 1996 America made the decision to take the communications revolution to the next level: its a *bold* new agenda and clearly establishes this nation as the leader of the Information Age Revolution of the 1990s.

■ In a stunning announcement in September 1995, AT&T unveiled a plan to divide itself into three independent publicly traded companies. The breakup was scheduled to be completed by late 1996, and created the following three companies:

(1) AT&T: A slimmer version of the $50 billion a year telecommunication giant which consists of long distance operations, cellular phone and wireless systems, credit card and consulting businesses.

(2) Global Information Solutions: An $8 billion a year computer-making operation.

(3) Lucent Technologies: This company will consist of the world famous Bell Laboratories, the telephone manufacturing operation, and the Network Systems switch-making unit. These combined units generate approximately $20 billion in annual revenue.

During a period when most corporations were feverishly pushing for mergers and acquisitions, AT&T chose an opposite strategy to effectively compete in the new deregulated era. Analysts predict that one part of the AT&T strategic plan will be to acquire a Baby Bell in the new deregulated environment. The telecommunication giant was clearly preparing itself for the intense competition from the Baby Bells and others in the new communications' reality.

■   AT&T and Africa One (Africa Optical Network): Unveiled in 1995, AT&T is aggressively pursuing a project to install a telecommunications network for the African continent. By employing the AT&T Submarine System's unit, the company plans to lay 21,000 miles of undersea fiber-optic cable, which will literally form a ring around the entire continent. During its initial phase, 41 coastal African countries and islands (with the inclusion of Saudi Arabia and Italy) will form a linkage with the huge network. Satellite, microwave and other fiber-optic connections will be used to provide telecommunication links for those countries that are landlocked on the African continent. One of the expressed goals of this project is to, "help the continent move from an aid-based to a trade-based economy."[1]

■   Throughout the remaining years of the 1990s, strategic alliances, mergers and acquisitions, network developments, global partnership arrangements, and other types of formal alliances will be aggressively pursued by major corporations hoping to form global operations earning nonstop revenues. Some of these ventures will fail miserably, losing billions in the process while others will become the new global *titans* of the 21st Century, with round the clock operations earning income every second of the day.

THE TECHNOLOGICAL ENGINE OF CHANGE

As we have seen, technological advances reshaped the regulatory environment in America and literally rendered many industry restrictions obsolete. In both the wireless and wired world, digital technology is lowering the cost of transmitting information and is rapidly making available new ways to construct local networks and provide a large array of services to those areas. Greater efficiencies are being offered along with a larger variety of exportable products that can be delivered to markets throughout the world.

In the wired world, fiber optic technology is clearly one of the waves of the future. Since its introduction in the 1970s, fiber optic technology has moved to the center stage to become the heart and arteries of communication transmission systems. It is the heart of the network and the primary determinant of system performance. Experience through the years has proven that the fiber option is more cost effective; the glass fibers have proven to be stronger, thinner, and more flexible than other materials, and the unlimited bandwidth offers an incredible capacity to transmit enormous amounts of information quickly. By 1987, seven million miles of fiber optic cable had been installed worldwide. During the early 1990s, the use of fiber-optic technology exploded. In 1990 alone, over seven million kilometers of optical fiber was installed worldwide.

Glass fibers are the best materials for high-speed networks. Undersea fiber-optic communication links represent a main source of forging the development of the global communications networks. By the end of 1993, there were a total of 289 undersea fiber optic international network system links. With prices decreasing, the trend indicates enormous growth in this area. Inherent weaknesses in other systems such as copper and satellites, makes a compelling case for a tremendous growth period. Since only light travels through the cable, transmissions are not disturbed by electrical or radio frequency interference. Also, unlike its copper counterpart, fiber-optic transmissions *don't leak* electrical information (the cable itself does not conduct electricity) and cannot be physically tapped without detection. Satellite transmissions often suffer from inherent delays and possible interruptions. Fiber is receiving rapid deployment in local area networks (LANS) and other types of system designs.

However, the problem with many well-established worldwide telecommunication systems is the presence of hundreds of millions of miles of copper wire, which in most cases will not be replaced. Ripping out the old copper wire cable and replacing it with fiber would cost billions of dollars. Thus, for many industry players, the option will be to construct hybrid systems that combine copper, fiber, satellite, cellular, and cable technologies. Of course, systems that will be 100% totally fiber will outperform wireline systems that are not. This represents yet another interesting aspect of the Information Age revolution.

The technological engine of change has led to the formation of new types of organizational group formations and network evolution. The emergence of an explosive period of innovations has led to intense competition and expansion, which creates breeding grounds for new types of coalition network relationships and linkages. The remaining years of the 1990s will be characterized by numerous organizational developments (and some deals will collapse like Bell Atlantic and Telecommunications Inc.) towards mergers and acquisitions, partnerships and global networking arrangements.

SYSTEMS INTEGRATOR

One of the organizational business operations that will likely prevail as a model in future periods is the *systems integrator.* Under this business development program, communication professionals and specialists will assemble packages consisting of various types of services, equipment, etc., in a one-stop shopping commercial environment, for both domestic and international markets. In this scenario, transmission of data will be viewed as a commodity, and the central task of the systems integrator will be to design and customize a package of informational requirements based on a customer's needs. Businesses and individuals will be able to purchase their communication products and services in a unique deregulated, decentralized global environment. Telecommunication systems will have unlimited capacity to serve the most voracious corporate appetites with a large array of fantastic/futuristic services.

THE WIRELESS REVOLUTION OF THE 1990S

Wireless technologies have moved onto the fastest growth curve in the communications arena in the 1990s. Indeed, the shift to wireless may eventually cut a deep path into the revenues of the dominant wireline markets. Here again, advances in semiconductor technology and microprocessors, sophisticated software systems, and digital wireless networks have moved the wireless juggernaut onto center stage. Such areas as cellular phones, specialized mobile radio (SMR), pagers, personal digital assistants, and satellite technology experienced phenomenal growth in the early 1990s. Consumers are fascinated with the convenience and mobility provided by the wireless systems.

The growth rates of cellular and paging devices has been 40% annually, with 14,000 new subscribers joining the revolution daily. In 1990, there were 5.3 million cellular users in the U.S.; by 1993 that number had grown to 14 to 15 million. At some point prior to the year 2000, it may be more cost-efficient for many more customers to switch over to the wireless mode of communications. With each significant decrease in price, more consumers are adopting the wireless way of life. Analysts have observed that with price reductions of a factor of ten, the market growth rates are greater than a factor of ten. The years 1995-96 witnessed a tremendous amount of foundation building and infrastructure developments in new and existing wireless systems. After this phase, an explosive period of growth is expected to occur prior to the year 2000. With approximately 30 million cellular users worldwide in 1994, future projections indicate 100 million by the year 2002; and this is really a conservative estimate.

Worldwide, the wireless movement is snowballing, with demand in China, Eastern Europe and Latin America experiencing extraordinary growth. By August 1994, the top ten cellular carriers in the U.S. included several of the Baby Bell subsidiaries or newly established separate companies. Table 4 illustrates the approximate number of cellular subscribers for each of the leading companies of 1994.

TOP TEN CELLULAR COMPANIES: AUGUST 1994

COMPANY	SUBSCRIBERS
	(millions)
SouthWestern Bell	2.1
BellSouth Cellular	1.9
McCaw Cellular	1.6
LIN Broadcasting	1.4
AirTouch Cellular	1.2
GTE Mobilenet	1.1
Bell Atlantic Mobile	1.03
Ameritech Cellular	0.9
Sprint Cellular	0.6
US West Cellular	0.6

Table 4

Adapted from data provided by Datastream International, SF RCR Publications.

Technological breakthroughs have had enormous impact on the growth and wide adoption of the wireless juggernaut. Billions of dollars invested in outmoded equipment by both cellular and telephone companies had reached the point of critical obsolescence in 1994. Most of the cellular and telecommunication companies (particularly the Baby Bells, which in 1994, served about half of the 14 to 15 million cellular customers) have to upgrade from analog systems (which converts speech to sound waves) to digital systems capable of converting text, speech, graphics, and video into rivers of ones and zeros. Thus, cellular systems that do not upgrade to the most advanced digital system of computers and signal processors, will not be able to offer the multiplicity of services envisioned for the industry. Also, by the mid-1990s, the wireless industry had not adopted an industry-wide *standardized system* for the propagation of the wireless revolution. Unlike the leadership of the compact disc arena (discussed in Chapter Two), industry leaders were still in disagreement on the issue of technological standards in products and services.

PERSONAL COMMUNICATION SERVICES (PCS)

In 1994 the next generation of wireless technology became the focus of attention by many movers and shakers both inside and outside the communications arena. The FCC began conducting auctions to sell PCS licenses to the highest bidders for frequency allotments on the electromagnetic spectrum. The new levels of wireless spectrum were envisioned to offer greater power and technical range than the existing wireless frequencies for cellular phone services. The FCC made available a wider and higher range of frequencies for PCS, spectrum that would not be as crowded as cellular. PCS would be 100% digital and capable of offering a wide range of services, which includes multimedia, video, and faxes. During an auction held in July and October of 1994, the FCC raised over $1 billion in the sale of PCS licenses for paging and interactive video. The enormous broadband PCS auction held from December 1994 to March 1995, was billed as the start of a new dynamic industry development in America; a broad expansion of wireless digital communication. The stakes are high, however, the next level of wireless services are expected to be very dynamic and powerful. Table 5 illustrates the various levels of the radio frequency (RF bands) of spectrum allocation.

For those of us raised on the continuing saga of the *Star Trek*

RADIO FREQUENCY SPECTRUM

(Low Frequencies to Extremely high Frequencies)

SPECTRUM RANGE	BAND IDENTIFIER	COMM. USER
30-300 kHz	Low Frequency (LF)	Maritime and aeronautical navigational services.
300-3 mHz	Medium Frequency (NT)	Ham radio, AM radio, long-distance aeronautical services.
3 mHz-30 mHz	High Frequency (BF)	Shortwave radio, citizens'band radio (CB), Ham radio.
30 mHz-300 mHz	Very High Frequency (VHF)	FM radio, VHF Television broadcasting, public safety radio such as police and fire dispatch
300 mHz-3 gHz	Ultra High Frequency (UHF)	Cellular phones, PCS, UHF TV, pagers, Mobile radio, wireless data.
3 gHz-30 gHz	Super High Frequency (SHF)	Commercial satellite radar, microwave trans missions, cellular vision (wireless video).
30 gHz-300 gHz	Extreme High Frequency (EHF)	Military and satellite users, research.

Table 5

NOTE: The RF Spectrum presented here represents only a small portion of the possible spectrum that is actually available. For instance, laser-optical systems operate outside of the Spectrum and in prac-tice would use visible light as its source.

series, the PCS revolution incorporates wireless communication devices used in the future time periods popularized by the show. Small, lightweight, battery-powered and very portable devices in the PCS realm will enable people to place and receive calls virtually anyplace and anytime: a phone number will be associated with a person and not a physical location. Personal digital assistants (PDAs) will eventually expand the service range of PCS: this one device will ultimately incorporate a pager, cellular phone, a wireless fax machine, electronic mail service, calculator, and a pen-based note pad. This will be a truly futuristic device, setting the technological pace for the 21st Century: the forerunner of *Star Trek's* multipurpose/intelligent hand-held communication system.

Personal Communication Networks (PCNs) will keep track of a person's location and manage the technical problems of routing incoming and outgoing communication data. Unlike cellular systems, the PCS system will employ a micro-cellular digital network that will consist of low powered devices, based on high frequency radio waves in the 1.8 gHZ range. First generation cellular phone transmissions move from cell to cell within defined sections of a geographical region (a range of one to 20 miles), wherein each cell facilitates transmissions with high-powered transmitters. Under the expanded PCS system, the transmitters will be the size of bricks and can be mounted on utility poles, with the distance between cells (in many cases) less than a few hundred feet. The reductions in size, distance, power, and costs of the devices and overall system, along with the multi-service factor, will move the PCS technological system to the forefront of the wireless revolution by the year 2000. Overall, the wireless revolution of the 1990s is one of the major forces reshaping the entire communications arena for the 21st Century.

CHAPTER EIGHT

THE POLITICS and ETHICS of TELECOM

Timothy L. Jenkins

Thus far in our writing we have examined the subject of high-tech telecommunication as though it were discrete technical, economic, and social phenomena affecting the black community. However, when all three of these factors are considered together the matter becomes a political and ethical phenomenon that is greater than the sum of its parts. The ethical side of telecommunications has many dimensions. The *distributive* dimension answers who will be allowed to own various property rights in telecommunications. The *regulatory* dimension determines how such ownership rights can be exercised as a balance between public and private interests when disputes arise and new rules are proposed affecting telecommunication uses. Finally, the *democratic* or *nondemocratic* impact of telecommunication policy, controls and access may well become the controlling dimension of the 21st Century, creating the underserved both in the United States and throughout the world. And whenever that occurs, race and ethnicity must be considered shadowy elements with profound significance.

A public policy subculture has grown up in which new buzz words have been given a virtual reality. Terms like info-privacy and crypto-security, public-interest access, universal service requirements, pay-for-view, open architecture, open platform, and other new age lingo have, by frequent repetition, become the emergent lexicon for policy discussion in telecommunication. As a result, the language obscures the message. For many, the Information Age threatens to become an electronic nightmare with serious dangers for individual liberty. As the amount of personal data accumulates in electronic files, the invasion of individual privacy becomes an easier proposition. The security of personal information will be a challenge, not only technologically, but legislatively. Both the civil and criminal codes will need major revisions to accommodate these new realities.

The issues of equity, universal service, and public interest access are concepts that run to the very core of democracy, and will become all the more critical as the population continues to shift to electronics for news, information, and advocacy. Buried in the movement to *reinvent government* is the assumption that high-tech alternatives can be found to bypass traditional government bureaucracy to streamline traditional services such as motor vehicle, health and welfare programs. All of this presupposes the access and knowledge to use these new technologies, as well as, the ability to pay for their ongoing availability. How effective these tools will be, is dependent upon systems designs that are coordinated as networks. Certain designs are better than others for facilitating political and civic dialogue, but it will be important to assure that users can travel *upstream* and speak to decision-makers as well as being *downstream* constituents.

Transmission capacity will determine how interactive a system can be. A broadband network with fiber-optics or coaxial cable provides all options. Because these have limited availability, some restrictions may be required by more readily available technologies such as compression enhanced telephone lines. The issue of *open architecture* is important because this has been defined to assure two-way exchanges that allow the position of listener and speaker to be interchangeable.

The matter of an *open platform* is important because this speaks to the mutual technical capabilities built into the hardware and software designs to accommodate the widest possible compatibility with varied equipment specifications, characteristics, and proprietary products. Both hardware and software adaptations will be essential for optimal use because both are essential keys to solving the puzzle of user-friendliness. As the VHS and Beta competition illustrated in the world of VCRs, the survivor need not always be the logically designated *fittest*: it may simply be the one that manages to become the most popular or the most widely available. Properly introduced, the emerging information infrastructure can affect society as profoundly as the Gutenberg printing press; therefore, it is of no small importance that democratic scrutiny be given to each and every aspect of the design, ownership, regulation, and use of these new tools.

The framework for considering the distribution of telecommunication property rights, has its roots in the legal and regulatory history of the telegraph, telephone, radio, and television industries. While certain analogous elements of these frameworks continue into the multimedia era, important aspects of change render traditional political approaches to such single source communications obsolete. Since the first comprehensive federal legislation was adopted in 1934, the Congress, the courts, and the Federal Communications Commission (FCC) have been treating the airways (through which messages and information are passed) as a public domain. As a result, state criteria for ownership followed because the amount of airway space (differentiated as channel frequencies) was considered to be both finite as well as scarce.

Implicit in these ownership allocation decisions are the constitutional questions of First Amendment free speech. For years the debate has raged between free speech protections belonging to owners and the public's access rights to electronic means of expression. Among the early concepts were the *equal time rule* and the *fairness doctrine,* fashioned by the FCC in 1949 to foster evenhanded treatment of political candidates and controversial viewpoints. These same rules were repealed in 1987, with the argument that the proliferation of media no longer required such protectionist rules.

A more recent example of competition management is the court ordered breakup of AT&T into the nation's Regional Bell Operating Companies (RBOCs), colloquially referred to as the Baby Bells. Without getting drawn into the RBOC discussion too deeply, it is important to fully understand the impact of Federal communications legislation that will greatly alter the playing field of regional telephony with the introduction of a host of both new ancillary and alternative telecommunications usages beyond voice transmission. Phone companies have struggled long and hard against the cable and satellite lobbies seeking to alter regulatory schemes to accommodate one or the other's competitive advantage. While it is not always easy to discern how the black community or other minorities will fare with varied scenarios, all will agree that no communication interests will be exempt from experiencing some impact.

While discussing the political and ethical aspects, it is also necessary to remember that the economic considerations of size, resources, reach, and concentration of ownership are necessarily tied-in with all political discussion. According to the traditions of diversity, public policy has favored guarantees for widely parceling out media ownership, so as to avoid any single source becoming overly powerful or monopolistic. Hence, prohibitions have been made on how many radio or TV stations could be commonly held. Predominant ownership in print media has also been made a relevant consideration in granting licenses or ordering divestitures of electronic media. Others argue that such notions of antitrust have become less relevant with the remarkable breakthroughs in technology that expand signal reach worldwide (as opposed to overlapping plus or minus fifty-mile circles). Since new supply-side competitive forces have come into play, the plot continues to thicken. Similarly, with the prospect of delivering as many as 500 separate channels of information simultaneously, and through digitization's quadrupling of cable capacity, traditional concepts of competition take on an altered meaning, due to radical changes in the competitive arena.

For years the black community waged telecommunications battles to assure increased license ownership and public access. In some instances this has been through rule making proceedings before the FCC; in others it has meant congressional action. Now these traditional battles will need to take new forms. For instance, the paramount interest of Blacks has long been to have free public announcements and public access to free time on cable networks. In many instances this right has been won at the local level when individual franchises were awarded. But just how much value is there in free cable access *per se,* without supportive professional means for set design, script writing, camera and lighting technicians, and other related professions that are required for *effective* use of such access? Accordingly, while a certain number of radio and TV channels may be dedicated to public nonprofit broadcasting, how meaningful will this be if public taxpayer support is simultaneously withdrawn, making the exercise of such ownership economically impractical?

In a report issued by the FCC in 1995, it was shown that the black ownership of radio licenses throughout the country actually suffered a slight decrease, while Hispanic radio ownership increased. It should also be noted that the FCC and courts in 1995 withdrew earlier rules to provide a statistical advantage to minority bidders on licenses for wireless personal communications services and cellular phone territories. The latter actions can be directly attributed to the change in political as well as the judicial climate away from affirmative action techniques created to account for past exclusion or the promotion of future diversity. From the black community's perspective, two simultaneous strategies need development:

(1) How do we articulate meaningful standards for ownership participation and access in the face of the exploding delivery capacity of multimedia?

(2) How might we be able to leverage private resources to assure a presence for ourselves and our points of view in the newly complicated media mix, especially in the face of declining support for regulations as well as affirmative action remedies?

Clearly, with the shift in public thinking away from financial resource redistributions on behalf of the disadvantaged, greater attention on nonfinancial resource allocations are needed. Consider the doctrine of *easements* in real property rights. While the common law generally protected the exclusive ownership and control of land, it also came to recognize the rival rights to access or trespass over privately held land to serve broader community interests called easements. Similarly, while private property ownership is universally respected in the United States, the state has also been granted the rights of *eminent domain,* which is capable of overriding private ownership for compelling public reasons, carefully justified and established through due process of law with provisions for adequate compensation for any property publicly taken.

While it might not be politically or economically feasible to grant outright public ownership rights or minority ownership rights to communication channels and networks in the future, it may be possible to allocate periodic access "easements" for programming, along with required multimedia protections and backstops that guarantee a wide diversity of opinions. Furthermore, applying *"Moore's Law,"* that every eighteen months the capacities of computer-driven technology doubles and costs are drastically reduced, the future may provide even more creative ways to accommodate minority opinions and players without being inconsistent with mainstream market trends. A form of "eminent domain" might come into play to reserve some of the additional communication space for public use when the channels of existing ownership increase through digitization. This is the type of thinking needed from black scholars and theoreticians in the law as well as in the business of communications.

REGULATORY   REORDERING

Part of the issue of redesign is updating the 18th Century concept of the First Amendment to 21st Century realities. In the beginning, the commonly held notion was that the relatively minor economic barriers to enter the print market avoided the need for public regulation. On the other hand, the business of broadcasting presents a broader level of concerns, in part because of the heavy financial resources required to enter the industry. Hence, regulators have posed various limitations of size, geography, duplicative media outlets, and other types of restrictions to assure a level playing field. For years, courts have worried over the differences between print and broadcasts in sanctioning electronic ownership regulations and protecting free speech. The issues now go beyond the ability to speak, to also include the ability to both hear and be heard in the media forums of our society.

With the ongoing patterns of merger mania occurring throughout the communications sector, it is altogether possible that the future will see but a handful of powerfully integrated multimedia corporate giants capable of controlling information previously known to only governmental entities. This concentration carries with it the power to suppress, as well as the power to promote, particular ideas at the expense of others. A free market approach that continues to assume equality between the individual consumer and the tools of the corporation, may be something of an anachronism. While this trend has been at work for some time, the crescendo it has now reached alters quality as well as quantity in the debate. There is no easy resolution of the competing interests, except through experimentation with a variety of models. In one model, the audience will only be able to hear what the owner wishes to offer; in another, the audience will tune into only those sources it wishes to hear. Additional models will offer interactive exchanges and allow access providers the option to demand an equity interest in content providers as part of the access toll. For example, certain shopping networks insist on only carrying materials they themselves buy at low wholesale prices before offering them through the high-priced retail home shopping outlets they control. Certain other networks give priority time and place preferences to those shows they produce. Through both of these devices the access provider is using leverage to assure its interests over the common carrier users and their audiences.

Public regulation needs to catch up with such practices, because the implications of such practices could become quite ominous, particularly for black merchandisers and producers historically kept from the marketplace. Other ways in which the thumb of the access provider can influence the scales for those seeking an outlet for their products or ideas, will be price differences, dial placement, marketing support, billing arrangements, and other marketing and distribution services. These amount to private forms of regulation largely ignored, up until now, by the public sector debates on censorship and access. Even at the more basic level of regulation, it must be remembered that the only reasons most minor or geographically remote markets enjoy telephone service in the United States at all, is due to a public policy to subsidize the weaker markets with revenues from the stronger markets. Therefore, the continuing role of regulation looms large on the agenda, if Blacks and other minorities who make up the core of many inner cities are to enjoy the technology promise that the private sector is currently restricting to its preferred major commercial markets and consumers.

When communications deregulation is proposed across the board, it is never annotated in racial terms. Yet issues of protecting diversity, unpopular opinions and speech considered by some to be offensive *per se,* are frequently the racial flip-side of a large portion of communications policy. These have not surfaced in bold formats in cyberspace, because of the relative novelty of the subject matter. It will not take long, however, for the novelty to wear off and reveal the underlying basics. Consider the way in which pornography on the Internet quickly became a hot legislative target as soon as it was noticed and generally publicized on ideological and political grounds. To some it makes sense to deregulate certain electronic media, while maintaining it in others. The main problem to emerge, is when one form of media changes seamlessly into another by virtue of common ownership. Again, the formation of public policies that cope with such nuances have yet to be developed.

Constitutional and Democratic Implications

The black community must be especially vigilant in defining its democratic and constitutional interests in new forms of media. Under varied definitions, electronic media has been held to be public, quasi-public, or private but open to the public. Broadcasting and cable television are frequently considered quasi-public because they allow privately imposed preconditions to determine public access. On the other hand, switched telephone networks are generally considered public, because they operate as regulated common carriers open to everyone without user discrimination. In part, the niceties of these distinctions ignore the fact that all of them make use of governmentally owned rights of way, public streets, and publicly-owned airways, such that each is infected with public investments. The complexity of distinguishing public from private property rights in communications becomes greater with the ownership differences in media, where telephone wires, specially laid cables, and satellite signals have been distinguished without real differences.

Lest it be forgotten in this discussion of the public investments in creating the present value of telecommunication property, those contributions are not limited to rights of way. Indeed, the basic research and development that led to the birth and diffusion of the computer industry as a whole, came from expenditures made in national defense. From the logistical requirements for the *Battle of the Bulge* to the need to decode Nazi messages during World War II, the U.S. military has been at the core of creating the intellectual property and prototype hardware that now represents all of these multi-billion dollar information industries. The Internet itself was grandfathered into existence by the Defense Department's need to facilitate the collaboration between the far-flung university research centers and scientists at work on its myriad of projects. In light of this governmental ancestry, it is all the more startling to hear the disingenuous umbrage taken by the industry today whenever the question of public interest controls and constraints are suggested.

The importance of this public/private distinction to the African American community is great, because it has been our slow and arduous struggle to assure equal *public* access for the past hundred years through the Fourteenth Amendment to the Constitution. Now if this newly emerging electronic space becomes mostly *privatized*, once again Blacks may find themselves without a legally guaranteed right of access through constitutional protections. In considering the converse of this argument, after we gain access through private means, we may find ourselves at the mercy of owner censorship whenever it happens not to share black political and economic perspectives. This will grow as a subject of importance as the Information Superhighway assumes the position as an indispensable means of exchange.

The double threats of public and private censorship requires special black vigilance *now*, because the ground rules are still being made. While it is easy to expect that the traditional interest of our community lies on the side of unfettered use of these new wired systems and airways, the rapid expansion of extremist use of such media for hateful mobilizations give reason for pause. It may be the case that the carriers of such socially, if not physically, destructive information have to be required to control the extreme elements among their users, so as not to grant safe haven for the actual undermining of our society. Indeed, the Constitution anticipates such balance (as the courts have interpreted it) so as not to require social suicide in the name of being fair in the allowance of free speech.

Beyond the abstract level of constitutional discussion, there comes the practical stuff of every day politics. Already, candidates for President consider it indispensable to have world wide web sites that enable them to spread their message. Predictably, the same mechanism of private networks will continue to be organized along political party lines, both for and against candidates in the future: the major parties have already reached this point! With the attendant sophistication and cost required to engage in high capacity network management, it will become increasingly important that the black presence be as widely tuned into the large scale networks of others as possible.

As a portent of things to come, The American Bar Association has created a special committee on the political adaptations of on-line communications. The charter of this Special Committee is the consideration of a host of proposals for political uses of on-line networks, from casting absentee ballots for soldiers in far away bases, to kiosk type terminals in common polling places across the land. For those of us who can still remember the insidious machinations of Southern literacy tests and poll taxes to purge black voters, state controlled on-line voting systems are fraught with danger. Even without invidious intent, as long as technophobia and basic computer unfamiliarity is widespread among Blacks and other minorities, a new on-line voting system may have a direct impact on minority ballot participation.

Advocacy Access

Telecommunications technology can be effective in increasing both awareness and knowledge about policy issues. It can even facilitate substantive dialogue between citizens and public officials, with candidates and campaigns for open evaluation through tele-technology. From the widespread use of these devices, new public mandates can surface as public agenda topics. How effective these tools will be, depends largely on how they are designed, for what purposes, and by whom. At the same time, black-owned electronic networks will be increasingly important to assure uncensored communications on political subjects, including candidate choices, legislative initiatives, and current controversies.

In addition to the use of such systems to exchange ideas, there is also the economic dimension of political mobilization to be considered. To date, the political fund-raising capacity of network systems is just beginning to mature. As such, it may well come to represent the people's equivalent to the highly touted political action committees. With widespread outreach and hourly updated information, political propaganda will become a tactical science capable of generating fast opinion shifts right up to when the last ballots are cast. As a result, little known candidates and controversial causes will be capable of visibility previously reserved for super stars. This can be as destabilizing as it may be promising in free speech. Information and misinformation may be indistinguishable, if they are allowed to be spread too late to be answered, causing new forms of sabotage.

But information alone will never be an empowering solution unless better ways to order and present it are developed, that enable the would-be recipient to know where to look and how it can be made accessible according to highly filtered personal interests. The only way in which that type of Afrocentric sorting will occur, is for black political scientists and politicians to become active users and publishers through on-line multimedia. To date that has not happened and there is no sign that it soon will.

International Democratic Implications

Not only will the political impact of multimedia delivery be felt in the United States, but interactively throughout the world. The 1995 insurgency of indigenous people in southern Mexico leveraged its influence by involving activist sympathizers in other countries. Through Internet linkages, daily bulletins were able to coordinate demonstrations in the capitals of the world, collect contributions with the speed of light, and most importantly, provide instant rebuttals to dis-information of their government. Historically, these human rights campaigns have only been possible with enormous organizing effort, speaking tours, fund-raising, and pamphleteering. Now they can be mounted from a laptop computer at a remote mountain phone line and relayed through multi-points beyond the reach of any single government. However, since the technology itself is neutral, it also predicts similarly widespread uses by counter-democratic forces.

As illustrated daily, abundant mischief can flow from anonymous hackers seeking to mis-characterize themselves to discredit movements they oppose or wish to destroy. Consider the invasion of the Nation of Islam's World Wide Web site, as it was infiltrated and trashed by a group of antagonists on the eve of the *Million Man March* in 1995. These same sources, using computer chains, form letters, and phony messages aimed at deluging political decision makers at state and federal levels of government (before critical actions or votes), are capable of simulating false ground swell phenomena with little or no virtual reality. Still, we can consider it a mile post in the march of civilization for antagonists to be able to carry on their wars with words rather than guns through these new media. Conceivably, the outlet of *pro* and *con* radical speech might provide some of the therapy needed as an alternative to violence, to allow political ventilation to occur between genders, classes, generations, and political groups not easily facilitated through mainstream media and publication channels. This happy result can only occur on an inclusive basis, to the extent that those segments of our community with something to say will take the time to learn the technicalities required to say it electronically as well as exercise continuing vigilance to protect it from corruption from break-in hackers.

Just as intelligence gathering has worked against us in countless ways, we can make it work for us by browsing through Internet discussion groups, bulletin boards, and public forums organized by those opposed to our best interests. Hopefully, it will be possible to engage in such conversations without resorting to the *flaming* tactics of derogatory rhetoric so common among on-line antagonists of the day. Properly organized as teleconferencing events, people of vastly different perspectives might even find a common platform from which to explain their differences. If this cannot be achieved on uncontrolled public space, perhaps it could become a vehicle for private network or Intranet exchange.

Thus, in the black community of the United States, it will be absolutely critical to have widespread access to the political messaging capabilities of multimedia. Especially important is its capacity to bypass established information gatekeepers and an exclusive reliance on written text, as well as the higher cost for composing and distributing hard copy propaganda. The community of black colleges and universities will be performing an additional service by preparing the next generation to use these powerful tools. When the doctrines of racial inferiority were advanced in defense of segregation, it was largely the HBCU community that took on the mission of setting the record straight. They published learned documents, they organized symposiums, and in some instances, formed delegations to call on public officials in need of better factual understandings. In this respect, they played an intellectually activist role that went well beyond their campus responsibilities. Likewise, class uplift, political awareness and social responsibility were made an integral part of the curriculum. While these added roles for black academia continue, they can now be made more far reaching when leveraged through technology.

The Political Economy of Race and Communications

Many well intended writers have hailed a declining significance of race in all aspects of American life. Some of these commentators rely on the degree and extent of the upward mobility that has produced the upper income statistics among African Americans. Increasingly, others with the same conclusions make the point that race relations must be considered in the context of the political economy and therefore cannot be isolated from nonracial social problems. This latter group finds it easy to overlook race embodied in structural inequalities. Robert Newby who shares such views argues, "by placing race relations in the context of the political economy, we can easily discern that race is rooted more in society's productive structures than in people's psyches." Such analysis has led to conclusions that in different periods, the changing forces of production gives rise to different social relations based solely on productive processes, with racial conflict more often than not, a passive ingredient. Henry Lee Moon writing in *Crisis* Magazine as early as 1968, said that what had started the century of Negro protests, by the last third of the century had become a problem of education and economics. Somewhat later, the late Vivian Henderson considered that "any efforts to treat Blacks separately from the rest of the nation are likely to lead to frustration, heighten racial animosities, and waste the country's resources as well as the precious resources of black people." These men were not racists.

The truth of these observations poses particularly difficult challenges for black public policy-makers in the field of telecommunications. Because of the novelty of the situation, it will take considerable effort to come up with promising fusion strategies. But major shifts in strategy are not new to the black community. Beginning with the 1950s, the movement was for *Civil Rights*. By the mid sixties, there came the *black liberation* movement. Then in the seventies the push was on for greater *black electoral politics*. At each shift, there were frictions with the leadership and tactics of the preceding movement directions.

The term, movement, has been variously defined as "a more or less continuous conscious interaction toward a goal," or "an activist phenomena directed toward social change." Whatever the precise definition, a movement is felt by its ability to mobilize its participants in coordinated ways toward shared objectives. In the politics of telecommunications, a fusion movement is called for that enables all current and would-be participants to appreciate their collective need for each other. Industry executives in the telecommunication arena need to consider the need for new minority customers for their products, at the same time they seek to maximize profits by labor force reductions and overseas relocation. Labor leaders in high technology areas need to appreciate the need for more minority outreach as well as the disincentives of strong arm negotiations that lead to reduced American price competitiveness with overseas suppliers.

Governmental officials groping for new telecommunications policies must come to grips with the essential need for balance between totally market-driven directions and long-term socially inclusive strategies. And black leaders ought to appreciate the economic necessity of their constituency's serious engagement in every way possible in using, learning, earning from, and owning the expanding tools of computer-assisted telecommunications, both independently as well as in coordination with other groups.

Ironically, a promising new way in which Blacks can benefit from the politics of telecommunications, is by the strategic subordination of their racial identities to emphasize the common characteristics with the larger population. The apparent contradiction of this approach and what we have said elsewhere needs clarification. The way the majority of black people suffer and may continue to suffer in the Information Age is similar to, if not the same, as all of those who are poor, less educated, vocationally untrained, geographically isolated and politically ignored, regardless of color. Based on these criteria, Blacks have a promising pool of allies among Hispanics, Native Americans, and the unemployed and low-income whites. The challenge is (and will remain) finding parallel ways to communicate and emphasize these elements of solidarity to form the critical mass required to influence national telecommunications policy, while at the same time pursuing independent actions.

To date, there are only fragmented efforts in this direction because, absent a foundation funded conference, the parties do not assemble to talk to one another. This points up the need for policy-shaping coalitions which bring the missing perspectives to the table for those outside and looking in on the telecommunications arena. The very technology itself offers a potential communications vehicle which must not be lost or misunderstood in the quest for economic liberation. Such constituencies need help in becoming tele-literate in relevant policies, as well as the techniques needed to allow on-line discussion and mobilization.

For the sake of example, the telecommunications needs of public education, serving each of the above constituency groups, can provide a priority area for such coalition attention. The foundation and public interest sectors should reconsider their program priorities and find ways to support such coordination and coalescence. Such an alliance represents the most promising means by which universal access, affordability, and social relevance can be advanced in the formulation of the Information Superhighway through educational policy. By observing the need for greater efforts in this regard, we are not ignoring the fact that certain foundations and others have done yeoman's work in making known to policy makers how important it is for them to listen to "The Other America." The problem is that many grassroots organizations that would be able to benefit from and contribute to such discussions, are not yet included.

The Politics of Appropriate Technology

Billions of dollars are spent on technology research for telecommunications, but practically nothing goes towards solving the communications problems of the disadvantaged. In part, this is true because the *appropriate technology* for the communications needs of the disadvantaged is not easy to describe, partly because it means different things to different people; partly because it is a changing, growing concept; partly because by definition, it involves the heresy that a technology appropriate to one place, time, purpose, and people, may not be right for another. So the specific technologies to which the term *appropriate* might apply will vary according to circumstances.

For purposes of example, the concept can be narrowed to that which is consistent with the resources and needs of low income communities. This coincides with the notion of technology compatible with survival in a world of limited resources. Another aspect of appropriate technology is that it involves process as well as hardware. We need to consider the what, why and specific use of a technology; there is clearly a need for revolutionary approaches and bold insights.

The following attributes are essential elements of appropriateness:

- Simplicity: easy to do, make, or repair.
- Economy: involving low capital requirements.
- Energy efficiency: requiring little nonrenewable energy to operate,

- Humane: compatible with health and environmental interests.

Each of the characteristics is prescribed to overcome the limiting conditions of income, fragmented communities, and deteriorated physical environments in which the disadvantaged are confined. Making telecommunications technology appropriate for various niche communities may be the frontier for its social diffusion. Accordingly, as a matter of growing public policy importance, the political discussion of telecommunications must include the special needs of the economic *have nots*. Rather than an initiative required by the state, this discussion should emerge as a logical assessment of future national needs from the communications industry itself.

However, it would not be wise for the black or low income communities to leave the matter wholly to industry initiative. Efforts need to be made to coordinate collective political and economic influence to raise the issue of appropriate technology, alongside the engineering efficiencies and priorities which normally hold center stage during political discussions of technology. At the heart of these questions are the most fundamental political considerations of all: on whose behalf are these new technologies to be introduced, with what specified applications, in what order of priority, and with what price/subsidy considerations?

A concrete example of the political economics of appropriate technology is offered in the discussion of the technology which allows a standard television set to access the Internet without the expensive necessity of a personal computer. This represents an example of needed quasi-political collective bargaining on behalf of low income consumers once they become aware of the interests at stake.

The politics and ethics of telecommunications come in many forms. It involves the judgments that affect technology ownership, as well as use and access regulation. It addresses the matter of free speech along with the private versus public interventions. But the matters of politics also reach broad discussions of the political economy within which various segments of the society exercise political and economic influence. The issues of politics in telecommunications are also international, determining not only the electronic signals allowed to be sent out, but also those allowed to come in. Here, issues of democracy may clash with issues of state sovereignty and dominant morality. In any case, the political and ethical dimensions of telecommunications remain both deep and wide areas for exploration.

Conflicts of Interest

It was Frederick Douglass who reminded us that those who wish to achieve progress without conflict would like to enjoy a summer's rain without the discomforts of thunder and lightning. In much of our discussion of tele-politics, we have spoken as though the only necessity is that we adequately inform ourselves and agree to speak out in order to exercise influence on the industry. Such wishful thinking would be a tad shallow. Instead we must recognize that with multi-billions of dollars at stake, any and every political initiative aimed at influencing the relevant industries, is not only likely to be at someone's theoretical expense, it also is likely to be hotly contested. Hence, if spokespersons for the black or disadvantaged communities make known their price concerns, their geographical opposition on applications or voicing opinions on any proprietary aspect of telecommunications, they may find themselves pariahs throughout the industry.

Let's face it, the computer and telecommunications industries represent a very powerful confluence of media, money, and mindsets. They came into being historically as an outgrowth of the defense industries, made up of very large corporations. With the exception of certain software newcomers, most of those involved represent old-monied power well adapted to the rough and tumble of government influenced competition. It may be a bit difficult then to expect to blend one's legislative and regulatory independence with being able to enjoy the philanthropic largesse, research collaboration or subcontract opportunities without being a member in good standing of the industry's club. Just as Ralph Nader and other consumer advocates learned, it can get a bit rough to find oneself up against such Fortune 500 opposition on matters of principle. This is true for would-be crusaders and scholars as well as elected officials. This makes it all the more important that the communities of those currently excluded from telecommunications sector influence, develop strong alliances among themselves before they go public.

As we have come to understand the facts of life, there are very few public interest players in the world of computers, multimedia, and telecommunications, who stand totally without some form of industry support, if not sponsorship. Either through recycled equipment, donated software, and shared facilities, the industry generously encircles those whom it knows to have relevant inputs. This poses a problem not unlike that of officials who regularly deal with public utilities, you want to be close but not overly close, lest you lose your perspective or your independence. One might consider such a concern a bit premature, since no Blacks to date have come seductively close to such conflicting invitations or temptations. But as software and hardware companies become the functional successors to textbook publishers for large state educational markets, they will likely exhibit some of the same wily characteristics toward anyone seeking to change the way they've grown used to doing business.

It was also Fred Douglass who instructed, "Power concedes nothing without a demand. It never has and it never will." Let a word to the wise be sufficient. If we are to express political opinions in the arena of computers, multimedia and telecommunications, we have to be prepared to take the likely heat that comes with such spokesmenship.

Prescribing The Future

Herman Kahn, a futurist most of us can appreciate for both his factual and philosophical grasp, asked, "Do we have free will or is everything determined?" He went on to say, "I don't have an answer I'm sure of, but I am convinced that people behave better when they think they have free will. They take responsibility more and they think about their choices more." In the discussion of politics in telecommunications, it has been our objective to both concentrate on public policy choices as well as assume greater responsibility for their side effects along with their intentional results. The tendency in the discussion of technology is to speak mostly in the third person as though its development were wholly external or maybe even abstract. But to do so represents a fatal danger. It allows us to disown the small individual parts we play in making vast tidal waves of change. Our part is played nevertheless, even if we opt not to choose one, because by that option we have cast an absentee ballot for the majority. It is important that we *wake up* to the implications of continued silence and inaction on the politics of telecommunications. The economic and technological implications of the 21st Century are far too important for black people to not be full and totally committed participants.

Among the many reasons for resignation in dealing with this aspect of technology, is the awareness of how small and how brief the part is for anyone. A sense of distance from its practical results comes from knowing how complex the interactions are that combine to influence each outcome. But these are the same reasons for self assertion. By becoming party to the political dynamics of vast change, we make it possible to influence unforeseen elements of its direction in ways that defy prediction.

Nowhere is the case stronger for political involvement in telecommunications politics than for African Americans. Theirs is the population trailing farthest behind. They will have the most to gain, if they push themselves to the vanguard of this age of change. Furthermore, for the first time, all of the facts are lined up to provide a clear forecast of the promising potential of this new age, contrasted with the devastation awaiting the failure to exercise the option for greater initiative. The most intimidating aspect of all of this, is the sense of helplessness that makes modest efforts appear insignificant when statistically contrasted against the size of the social needs and obstacles. René Dubos comes to the rescue to those overwhelmed by such odds with his dictum, "Think globally, act locally." It is a mistake to study the macropolitical trends with frustration, without giving thought to the requirements of one's neighborhood. For too long have the basic policies of telecommunication run from the top down instead of the other way around.

Increasingly, local leaders will need to approach their politicians and corporate moguls with proposals and demands instead of passively reading about change in the newspapers. This set of circumstances is the reason for much of the waste in national reformist initiatives in telecommunications; it results from poor local understanding and even poorer local program absorption. When solutions are proposed, based on small scale realities, it is less likely that they will become corrupted when applied more broadly than *vice versa*. Toward this end, greater emphasis is needed on leadership training among local leaders in the politics of telecommunications policy, so they can develop intelligent insights into how their communities can and should benefit.

It is no accident that along with the upheaval in technology has come an upheaval in perspective, that sometimes *less is more*. This is a message not to be lost in the black community. The degree to which local people know politically what they can and should be able to get from their local telephone company, cable and TV operators, will determine the reality of better service delivery. Toward this end, greater attention needs to be afforded to these scattered *local guerrilla* technology projects and their mostly volunteer leadership, because these may be the best sources from which improved national telecommunications policy can be derived. By *local guerrilla* projects, we mean those numerous homegrown efforts that have sprouted around the country in which techies have assumed the leadership for mobilizing communities to do what public education has largely ignored; prepare the next generation of black people for living in the Information Age. With no common name or leadership structure, these hundreds of seedlings, that need to be nurtured to bear fruit, illustrate the collective power of individual responsibility and the importance of intelligent choices. Let us all roll up our sleeves and get *busy* building and preparing for the 21st Century!

CHAPTER NINE

A Work In Progress

Timothy L. Jenkins

The peculiar fascination with the subject matter of this book is the unpredictable dynamics of its underlying subject matter driven by ever unfolding technological breakthroughs. In the few months that intervened between our writing the first chapter and this final one, new commercial applications are challenging many of the fundamental understandings and market predictions then in vogue. Accordingly, these changes have not only altered the nature of the marketplace (its underlying legal framework for regulation, and the nature of the business entities), but they have also shifted in unpredictable ways the possibilities for collaborative arrangements as well as new forms of competition.

Principal among these technological factors have been the explosive appearance of the Internet and World Wide Web. Within this context has emerged alternative hardware, new network systems, and a formidable challenge to the PC as the indispensable and dominant communications device. These new developments have each contributed to the accelerating roller coaster ride which lends such excitement to the cyberspace phenomenon. Their combined effect has been the geometric leveraging of information use as a socioeconomic tool in society.

In keeping with the primary motive of this book, we will resist the temptation of devoting this final chapter to an in-depth treatment of any one of these many unfolding technical developments, in favor of a summary listing of the most dramatic recent occurrences coupled with some speculations about their importance and possible consequences. While some may criticize this approach as fragmentary, any effort to do more is likely to reach detailed conclusions that will only have to be abandoned when the inevitable actually occurs. Recent history suggests that the best mental attitude throughout this process is for all of us to expect to be surprised no matter how carefully we study the available tea leaves.

A COUNTRY OF LAWS NOT OF MEN

Equally important, these recent scientific occurrences and technology diffusions are taking place in a rapidly changing national regulatory environment struggling to keep a pace with laboratory and marketplace developments. With the historic passage of the Telecommunications Act of 1996, the nation for the first time since the 1930s, has completely overhauled the statutory framework of public policy in telecommunications. In many ways this Act may be said to be the by-product of the intensifying lovers' quarrel among broadcast, computer, cable TV, and telephone company interests. It is not surprising, therefore, that the Act contains considerable ambiguity and inconsistency. Under its provisions, both the commercial and noncommercial implications of information distribution are entering a new state of flux, if not turmoil. Some have likened these public policy challenges to the impossible task of trying to rationally manage chaos. The burden of protecting the public interest is all the more troublesome with the democratic masses so uniformed on the economic and technological nuances that affect regulatory choices. Indeed, it can be said that the Congress itself played only a *pro forma* role to that of industry in this grand enactment; a potentially dangerous precedent. Along with this is the fact that when the chairman of the Federal Communications Commission (FCC) issued his first call for an advisory conference on the implementation of the Act, the very day after its enactment, there is no record that a single black participant was solicited, irrespective of stature or celebrity.

In order to address the many sweeping implications of this legislation, it was our thought that they could be summarized best by listing the highlights of key provisions. What follows then, is our subjective judgment on the most important elements. Previously, the FCC had issued rules which narrowly limited any one radio or TV owner from holding more than token media combinations in the same market. The 1996 Act changed that rule to allow an unlimited number of stations to be commonly owned, as long as no one operator exceeds 35 percent of the national listening audience or more than eight licenses in the same local markets. Simultaneously, the Act repealed the bar to joint ownership of radio, TV broadcast networks and cable systems in the same market. Furthermore, the *liberal waiver policy* for joint TV and radio combinations has been extended to the entire top 50 markets, which comprise the majority of the U.S. population, making it far easier for media ownership concentrations to develop. Similarly, the national ownership of AM and FM radio stations has been freed from most antitrust restraints (regardless of concentration or saturation), with uniform eight year renewal reviews replacing the previously shorter licensing terms of seven years for radio and five years for television. This is now coupled with a streamlined review process that assumes routine renewal, absent a *pattern of abuse* or a *serious* violation of FCC rules. This makes it reasonable to assume that few, if any, involuntary transfers of media ownership will occur for the foreseeable future. This new process has also eliminated the long standing *ascertainment* rules calling for affirmative proof of diversity in broadcast programming as a prerequisite test for licensing renewals. Heretofore, these have been the sole method by which public grievances against broadcasters could be officially aired with the threat of major sanctions that could not be ignored. With the stroke of a pen, *ascertainment* has become history.

Within the six months that followed the adoption of the Act, it has been dramatically observed that more than $11 billion worth of mergers and acquisitions occurred. For example, until February 1996, CBS only had 12 stations, it now boasts 80 or more. This has allowed CBS to dominate the radio advertising in 8 out of 10 major markets.

Such powerful owners can only expect to grow stronger as advertisers emphasize national reach over local markets. The expansion has allowed CBS radio to command nearly one billion dollars in advertising, added to another billion from its 14 owned and operated television stations. And CBS is not the only media mogul to have experienced such unprecedented growth.

It is highly unlikely that any black consortium of entrepreneurs will ever be able to match or compete successfully against this type of purchasing power, and in the financial marketplace they are likely to pay triple the cost of money for commercial loans to make new acquisitions. This may even mean that many of the 200 or so black station owners out of more than ten thousand, will in short order be obliged to sell to national syndicates, leading to an unprecedented consolidation of ownership in all of the top 50 radio markets throughout the nation and the virtual disappearance of the African American presence in mass telecommunications.

The implications of this rearrangement are far more than economic when you consider the role black stations played in the recent local and national elections, the airing of such controversial matters as the CIA involvement in big city drug dealing, and any number of other important counterculture crusades both locally and nationally, likely to be frowned upon by national advertisers.

Elsewhere, the broadcast standards established to promote equal employment opportunity, although never vigorously enforced, have also been summarily eliminated. In fact, it was in the very same week of the Act's passage that the FCC met to roll back virtually all of its explicit equal employment guidelines and requirements. This represents a public policy shift that is likely to freeze the upward employment movement for black employees and other minorities. This in an industry notorious for its elaborate buddy systems as the primary method of workforce entry and promotion, as well as its proclivity for on-the-air stereotyping, based on an established lack of diversity among programmers and top executives. Equally important is the fact that relevant executive experience is often the indispensable antecedent for media entrepreneurship, making it all the less likely that such managerial training for the next generation of black and other minority media owners will continue to occur.

We take the time to examine these elements of the Act regarding traditional radio and TV broadcasting, because we believe their linkage with new higher communications technology is inseparable. Not only is it likely that those who own the old technologies will also own and control the new, but it is also likely that the public policy approaches will be similar as well. In a larger sense, the allocation of ownership along the airways spectrum is an even more critical area of public policy. It is not only limited in terms of supply, it is also the only means whereby those who may be economically left out of the new technologies can still become connected regardless of their geographic locations and demographics.

As for the thorny consumer issue of *universal service* in the evolving field of new telecommunications, this has been relegated by the Act to a Federal/State Board for follow-up recommendations based on a medley of euphemistic principles: 1) providing advanced services at just, reasonable and affordable rates; 2) nationwide access; 3) low income consumer access in rural and high cost areas in proportion to those in *non-redlined* urban areas; 4) equitable access by secondary schools, libraries and rural health care providers; 5) adequate federal and state regulation; and 6) such other principles as the Joint Board may deem appropriate. Hence, the hottest of all the current public policy hot potatoes - universal access - has been passed on to an *ad hoc* deliberative body instead of a standard public agency with long term accountability and *due process* self-correcting mechanisms that provide guarantees for curing its mistakes along the way.

In other areas the Act goes well beyond ownership, equity and access issues. Of major significance, the Act repeals the ban on telephone company entry into video programming and vice versa. Local telephone companies are now obliged to negotiate with would-be competitors on interconnections, number portability, dialing parity and access rights of way. This was Congress' way of facilitating the development of a seamless system of communications to avoid the Balkanization of various media and geographic locations throughout the United States, without explicit guidance on how it must be done. Given the litigious life style of the communications industry, it is likely to be years before the courts have finally settled on a common interpretation of these glowing mandates sufficient to allow predictable rules.

Furthermore, with a newly minimized U.S. Justice Department and FCC review process, local telephone companies are now authorized to offer long distance services. Telephone companies are also free to manufacture equipment and offer electronic publishing services (news, entertainment, education, and other media information) subject to case by case FCC approvals. All of which is likely to heighten the incest of news, entertainment and publishing with serious threats to free speech for all but the most powerful.

In the wake of these sweeping changes in the legislative landscape, numerous mega-billion dollar corporate reorganizations, acquisitions and alliances have already been spawned, and many are in the making. These developments promise to result in realignments of the marketplace to both increase and decrease competition, market shares and the potential number of corporate players both vertically and horizontally in the corporate environment. In the midst of this free-for-all, minority group interest will be increasingly difficult to define as well as protect. *All of which points to the necessity of black people getting involved as competitive suppliers (rather than merely consumers), in order to have any significant impact and presence in the marketplace.* As of this writing, there are no less than four of the seven regional Bell operating companies engaged in merger negotiations. In addition to these, the Bell Atlantic/NYNEX merger resulted in the second largest telecommunications presence in the nation, stretching along the Eastern seaboard from the Southern mid-Atlantic to the tip of New England. Whether or not these economies of scale will be shared with consumers rather than shareholders, is questionable and certainly not an encouraging prospect.

Now with the sanction of courts in steering the FCC away from auction set asides in the rapidly expanding cellular telephone spectrum, there is very little likelihood that affirmative action for telecommunications ownership will exist in any form. This points to the need for new ways of thinking among organized blocks of black consumers to become proactive in a manner never previously demonstrated. Given the magnitude and importance of African American consumers, it is entirely conceivable that they could move to the next level and combine their purchasing power to demand business opportunities as subcontractors and suppliers of strategic requirements from the dominant players. But to do this they must make a serious effort to study and learn about some of the long term implications of the emerging Information Age.

Here the issue goes far beyond the matter of entrepreneurship *per se*, it also affects the related job markets and community survival in inner cities as well as rural enclaves where African Americans live. As the telecommunications infrastructure undergoes changes of the type suggested throughout this book, the modernization is likely to be more offshore or suburban than urban. Hence the jobs being generated are more likely than not to also go to a foreign or suburban workforce. As a result, the cycle of deterioration could have an unstoppable domino effect as the Information Age unfolds, affecting public schools, real estate, tax bases, and many other governmental services in the areas abandoned or underserved.

As a seedling innovation, the Act does create a Telecommunications Development Fund; a new corporate body that can make loans and provide financial advice to small businesses (under $50 million in annual revenues) in the telecommunications industry. The objective of the Fund is to promote access to capital, new technology, research assistance, employment and training. The Fund will gain most of its resources from the modest financial pool created by spectrum auction deposits. While this will not represent much, this Fund can serve as a prototype for the mechanisms ultimately required to allow minority and women owned businesses to gain a better foothold in the high-tech range of the telecommunications industry. This activity, therefore, needs to be carefully monitored and nurtured from the outset. Meanwhile at the state level, jurisdictions like Tennessee have begun experiments with the finance pools derived from state imposed fees to create local funding to support small business entry in telecommunications.

Of Networks and Webs

Superimposed on these recent dynamics is the soaring popularity and surprisingly rapid ascendancy of the Internet World Wide Web, as the coming medium of choice for the telecommunication of large arrays of information. The emergence of this blockbusting phenomenon is likely to radically affect all aspects of telecommunications from now on.

As observed elsewhere in the book, although the availability of the Internet as a medium of information exchange dates back at least three decades, it has been in the last five years that its use has become more than exotic. In its earlier history it was the information vehicle of government-supported research at the academy. The Internet has now become vogue for commercial activities that were once frowned upon by its founding scholars. Indeed, it is hard to remember that not very long ago, the early denizens of what is now affectionately called, *the Net*, were universally committed to taking collective umbrage in no uncertain terms should anyone dare violate the code of strictly non-profit usage. This gave rise to the use of *flaming*, the colorful term used to describe derogatory E-mail intended to embarrass or chastise the recipient for the commercial breach of *Netiquette*. But today those precepts have been stood on their head.

Net commercialism is now the name of the game. Hence any business, whether or not worthy of the name, has launched its own Internet address. Web sites are doubling every 50 days and a new home page is said to be given birth every four seconds. Nicholas Negroponte of MIT's Multimedia Lab predicts that by the year 2000 there will be at least one billion people signed onto the Internet based on a current growth rate of 10% per month. Yet in spite of this feeding frenzy among commercial users (some would even say because of it), there is precious little evidence that anyone has found the silver bullet or "killer application," which assures commercial success through its use. To be sure, there are those limited number of retailers whose products have found a profitable new pathway to the market via the Internet, but these are the exceptions rather that the rule. Indeed as more and more commercial domains crowd onto the Internet, it threatens to become *increasingly* difficult for the consumer to be able to find the products and services he/she seeks; turning what used to be a pastoral environment into a virtual jungle. As a result, we have been witnessing something of a gold rush to the Internet, with little or no gold being unearthed.

To overcome this embarrassment of riches with more things to read than anyone ever wished to know, powerful *search engines* have emerged at the hands of inventive software creators to cull through almost endless reams of available data. Information about Internet information is now becoming king, just as *TV Guide* long ago outpaced the profits of all of the four television networks and as the *Yellow Pages* have earned more profits for regional telephone operating companies than any other segment of their other business services.

Significantly, Netscape has exploded on both the Wall Street and the technology scene, with a dozen look alike competitors to rescue the Net surfer from the deluge of raw data. As the dominant player, Netscape is found on 85% of all Internet PCs, prompting the software giant, Microsoft, to dive in not only as a potential rival but for its very survival. But the more powerful these browsers and search engines become as navigational tools, the more important it becomes to filter the subcategories of inquiry to limit and target their instantly discovered findings. The potential silver lining in all of this is that it offers a new way for inventive black-owned multimedia enterprises to add their voices to this growing chorus of *intelligent agents*. At least one of these, Unlimited Visions, Inc. (UVI), associated with the authors, has developed a program which orders the whole body of formal library holdings in ways that facilitate those interested in Afrocentric research. Through the UVI technology, one can type in a search phrase like "Ethiopian Christian Church," and collect all news articles of the last year, any Internet mention of the subject, any anthologies mentioning the subject as well as pay-for-view access to any published articles or books with on-line optional purchasing instructions.

Armed with such vehicles, the Information Superhighway can become the *Info-bahn* that ends the obscurity associated with the old world of researching Black Studies as a occult art, as well as the time consuming requirement for constantly reinventing the Afrocentric wheel. It can also be the way in which alternative scholarship, long excluded from mainstream distribution channels, can finally enjoy its place in the sun through worldwide electronic means of publishing as well as retrieval.

A Wave of New Internet Access Devices

A further breakthrough in potential Internet access has been the explosion of major companies offering cheaper alternatives than a complete PC system. These new devices are designed to allow the household TV to become an on-ramp to the Internet, facilitated by a mechanical adapter hookup to the standard telephone line.

Priced to be competitive with the current VCR, these new devices, variously known as *Internet Access Boxes*, *Set Top Boxes*, *Network Computers* or *Web TV's* will enable a new class of couch potato browsers to extend the reach of their common TV to the World Wide Web. Some commercial versions come with wireless keyboards and printers for E-mail as well as downloading from Web sites and remote databases. Others will essentially be read-only hardware at minimal cost. As the common man's surfing vehicles, these new appliances promise to move beyond the previous paradigm of 500 TV channels, to millions of sites, unless or until the traffic overload forces the Internet system to implode. Already many researchers in the university community (in apprehension of the enormous traffic) have formed a multi-million dollar investment fund to launch their own proprietary *Internet II.*

Most recently the Clinton Administration has also weighed in with the President pledging $100 million government dollars to assure public rights of way in the coming sequel to the Internet. These initiatives are fueled by threatened log jams that will surely result once the current *Internet I* has been overly subscribed.

Personal Computers vs Network Computers

As the Darwinian successor to the PC, the Network Computer (NC) championed by the industry leader, Oracle, is creating additional chaos in an extremely competitive arena. Oracle, along with others, believes that more often than not those who use computers are only interested in the basics of word processing, graphic presentation, E-mail, and Web browsing, free of the complicated applications used by information professionals. But heretofore, there have been no scaled down versions limited to such uses. In comes the NC to serve variously as a portable computer, screen equipped phone, set top box or a TV. It will not have a hard drive, instead it will hook up to the World Wide Web or a corporate computer network, and reach into the data and operating systems housed on massive database servers. As a result, the cost of such a device will only be a fraction of that required for a regular PC, and that is now estimated to fall below $500.

With its emphasis on the off-site memory of the network servers and switching mechanisms that are universally compatible with all hardware formats, the NC represents a virtual dagger aimed at the heart of gigantic Microsoft, which has been the dominant source of operating software. Heretofore, Microsoft products have all been sold over the counter in hard copy installments or delivered on a pay-for-use basis, with anticipated upgrades fueling a perpetual cash cow. Impressively, Oracle and Netscape have been joined in this new exploration by a veritable *who's who* in the computer and telecommunications industries, that includes almost every major player in any aspect of the trade.

Allied with this NC market innovation, yet separate and distinct from it, is Sun Microsystems' off-site operating software trade-named, *Java*. This has grown in the past year from a commonplace programming language among many similar varieties, into a major brand uniquely compatible with a horde of varied hardware and software technologies. As such, it is in the process of trying to become the *de facto* standard for providing operating instructions for networked computers (with limited memory storage) to enable them to perform a variety of functions, independent of the need to purchase any operating software or their subsequent upgrades. Such an off-site memory has the benefits of reduced maintenance and software development costs, greater interactive capabilities and security. This has led to it being licensed by every significant player in the computing and telecommunications industries, and has also been the impetus for a wave of start-up companies. Lucent Technologies has similarly launched its proprietary (it says superior) technology, called *Inferno,* designed to out perform Java in the areas of scale, compatibility and versatility. Let the market decide!

While this can all lead to a mother-load of opportunities, the emergence of a new low cost apparatus connected to large network management systems, can also suggest new forms of *broadcasting* and *narrowcasting* that make reaching out to new niche markets cost effective for the first time. For instance, now a mass based organization such as the African Methodist Episcopal (AME) Church (with its 3.5 million membership) can provide a quality format of after school programming that stretches across all four time zones to compete with the ubiquitous presence of Rap music and MTV delivered via cable and satellite. Low cost alternative Internet access devices can be the source of distance learning, either in the home or conveniently located public facilities.

With the new emphasis on preparing welfare recipients for the world of work, such low cost devices can well become the vehicles of choice for new forms of distance learning for those who otherwise might never see the inside of a college classroom or training at a state-of-art technical facility. Hence, this could lead to a university or training facility, not only without walls, but without faculty or prohibitive tuitions.

Bringing The Net Back Home

However, the wave of the future is not likely to only be driven by technological competition of material science and microelectronics, it will also be driven by the infinite variety of human needs which seeks to make use of telecommunications for quality of life improvements.

In this connection it is important to note that not all of these Internet and Intranet applications have to be global in their scope. It is equally urgent to apply the wealth of interactive telephone-delivered computer networks to neighborhood needs. Indeed, many have found the fad for emphasizing global and national connections at the expense of local ties, profoundly destabilizing. Attention is shifting away from local realities to national and global abstractions. This trend can be troubling because it holds the seeds for alienation among those left behind. Some have predicted the day when many will not feel like true citizens in their country because they are not connected to the information technology, which is the bloodstream of America. This may also threaten to generate perceptions of new technologies as dis-empowering vehicles for many disconnected rural and inner city communities. More often than not, discussions about information technology usually focus on networks and resources outside these communities. Still, many of the most devastating problems arise from local factors rather than national forces. It is often around local issues that people can affect the most change and thereby develop a sense of their own empowerment.

Whether it is television, radio, CD's or the Internet, media technologies are rarely conceived of as a means with which the average person can become more productive. Nevertheless, networking need not be limited to passive consumer models; and it would be a great misfortune if we do not break out of this mind-set.

In a recent doctoral thesis, Alan Shaw, a young black futurist at the Massachusetts Institute of Technology (MIT), demonstrates that low income neighborhoods can be uniquely empowered to self improvement by the use of interactive local area networks, called *Intranets*. These networks which he dubbed M.U.S.I.C. (Multi-User Sessions in Community), can allow participation at the local level around issues of local concern. Whether in discussions on community development, crime, city services, jobs or housing, through 24-hour neighbor exchanges of ideas, calendars, reference materials, pictures and voice conferencing at the neighborhood level, communities can truly interact on a real time basis. This reexamination of *small is better,* provides an alternative to the National Information Infrastructure (NII) in favor of a Local Information Infrastructure (LII). This could also lead to neighborhoods rediscovering a collective voice, as well as a means to benefit from an information infrastructure it owns and controls. This represents an innovation in the top down producer/consumer model (owned and controlled by others), and may well become the next wave of exciting developments among software designers.

The Technicalities of Delivery

With the coming improvements of compression techniques to expand available *bandwidths* to accommodate better audio and video transmission, the Internet can also become a competitive alternative to long distance telephone, radio and TV, each of which requires *broadband* delivery capacity. The importance of bandwidth, therefore, lurks behind all aspects of the discussion of telecommunications. In layman's words, bandwidth and broadband transmission simply refers to the speed at which electronic data can flow. This affects how long it takes for complicated electronic messages to be sent or received. Complex audio and visual information is necessarily broadband or requires very high electronic transmission capacity. As a result, these technical realities have traditionally been major problems for transmission over standard phone lines.

Simply stated, there are an ever expanding series of alphabetical labels given for enhanced modems and wire connections which can be applied to plain old copper telephone lines to enable more data transfers per second. These technologies are known as ISDN's (integrated services digital network), ATM's (asynchronous transfer mode), ADSL's (asymmetrical digital subscriber loop) and most recently SDSL's (symmetric digital subscriber line). Each of these transfer technologies tend to be more robust than the one before. In other words, the transfer capacity of plain old telephone services (POTS) lines can now be heightened to the point of a thousand times, provided the user's ability to afford the sending and receiving hardware required to compress and then reopen condensed electronic files. This means that instead of being limited to text and only black and white still pictures, new transfer systems can now deliver full motion color video with high quality digital sound, without abandoning the traditional telephone medium. This also suggests enhancements to allow a single telephone line to support simultaneous channels for PCs, TVs, and telephones without the necessity of extensive neighborhood rewiring. It also means the ability to simultaneously watch and receive on the Internet on the same line, provided they each require limited bandwidths.

In the current marketplace, *pipelines* which accommodate high speed transfers have demanded a price premium that has kept them out of the hands of noncommercial users. One would hope that this will change with the Telecommunications Act of 1996 giving emphasis to schools, rural health clinics and libraries as special access beneficiaries, among others.

In addition to these developments, new software alternatives have been introduced that will allow high volume traffic to be delivered via the Internet directly to the hard drive of a PC overnight, thereby avoiding the download waiting time and phone line congestion during regular business hours. Through the use of such software techniques, it will be possible to send customized packets of information to individuals on a daily basis (equivalent to a newly printed book per day), allowing the recipient to scan and select only what is needed, and await the receipt of the next night's installment.

It is hard to overstate the importance of these developments as potential alternatives to the mega-billions in investment to rewire America with either fiber optic cable and long distance wire lines known as T-1 up to T-3. Such options were previously only affordable by the high-end users for banking, stock trading and upscale governmental communications. We can only hope that with the new competitive reality introduced by the passage of the 1996 Telecommunications Act, the pricing of these enhanced pipelines will continue to fall so that they can become at least as ubiquitous as POTS has been. This is highly significant given the fact that there are some 750 million copper lines in operation today, representing over one trillion dollars worth of investment, which conceivably won't have to be duplicated or abandoned any time soon.

It also needs to be mentioned that similar extensions of bandwidth have been occurring in the world of cable TV. Using latent cable technologies has enabled many cable companies to deliver voice, data, entertainment, interactive and informational services through to a single device. Already beta testing is at work to establish the cost effectiveness of cable as a vehicle for multimedia delivery.

In combination, these developments have added considerable new meaning to the term multimedia and the dynamics of *conversion technology,* in which computer hardware and software overlap with distribution networks and various forms of content. The result, to be meaningful, requires an unending involvement of industry players, policy innovators and a growing consumer demand base. Thus, the challenge for Black America is for greater participation in all aspects of this new reality to protect its economic, political and cultural interests.

While such participation has always been a problem, it is difficult to know the many ways in which the Telecommunications Act, along with leading edge technology will ultimately exacerbate or relieve such trends. At the 5% present rate of replacement of copper wire infrastructure (as a function of routine maintenance), it will take some twenty years before a comprehensive system of fiber can be established as a universal successor medium. This means that in the intervening two decades, it will be critical for African Americans to position themselves to benefit from these incremental changes.

Meanwhile the *wireless* phenomenon, regulated and allocated by the FCC, may be the last best hope to enable those residential areas inhabited by minorities to become connected in record speed, thereby leap frog into technologies far more advanced than commonly available to the general population. Thus, we may have finally discovered a means whereby *the last can become first* for a change. It becomes critical that every effort be made to protect such publicly owned assets for the public's good.

Final Word

Because this is a "work in progress" in a highly dynamic field, there can be no truly concluding chapter. On the contrary, all of what has been written here is intended, in a larger sense, to be an *opening chapter* for a new paradigm in the way computer knowledge and telecommunications can become tools for invigorating our liberation strategies - *KyberGenesis.*

Hopefully, what has been written here will make it abundantly clear that these unfamiliar aspects of the future cannot be ignored or avoided, except at a terrible price.

Most importantly this is an assignment of too much importance to be left to technicians and the market place without vigilant moral, political and humanistic oversights. Far from an intimidation, this is a challenge we can welcome. Properly perceived and exploited, the technology of computer-assisted telecommunication provides a major component in our struggle to overcome recent accidents of history to become, in major respects, a brand new people.

The high cost of achieving these grand designs, is a realistic belief in creative promise of effort and imagination!

NOTES

Foreword

1. Andrew Young, *A Way Out Of No Way,* (Thomas Nelson Inc. Publishers, Nashville, Tennessee, 1994) p. xi.

2. IBID. p 2.

3. Andrew Young, *An Easy Burden,* (Harper Collins Publishers, 1996)

CHAPTER TWO

1. Khafra K Om-Ra-Seti, *World Economic Collapse: The Last Decade and the Global Depression* (KMT Publications, San Francisco, 1994) p. 49.

2. The invention of the transistor marked the birth of *microelectronics,* and it's considered the first electronic device with the ability to conduct electrons within solid materials. Development of the transistor took place at Bell Laboratory in Murray Hills, New Jersey.

3. Jose V. Pimienta-Bey, "Moorish Spain: Academic Source and foundation for the rise and success of Western European Universities in the Middle Ages", *Golden Age of the Moor,* Ivan Van Sertima (editor: Transaction Publications, New Brunswick, 1993) p. 205. **NOTE**: The Moors were largely responsible for the scientific Renaissance that took place in Europe during the medieval period of the 12th and 13th Centuries.

4. During the late 1980s, gallium arsenide surfaced as a semiconductor with greater potential than silicon for speed and flexibility. It was reported by scientists that the material allowed for a faster switching system and was 50 times faster than the best available silicon transistors. Some of the other interesting features of gallium arsenide are: (1) As an element, it is more resistant to radiation influences than silicon circuits (2) It emits photons and the circuitry is both electron and photon sensitive (3) the gallium arsenide circuit requires less power than its silicon counterpart (4) the element can operate at higher temperature conditions; it has a greater tolerance than silicon towards higher temperatures. However, the downside of this element is that it is a more expensive proposition, and unlike silicon, is only capable of producing low-density circuit wafers. The element is about 34th in terms of its abundance in the crust of our planet. It is considered a metallic element.

5. Otis Port, "The Keys to the Future," *Business Week/The Information Revolution 1994,* (May, 1994) p. 60.

6. The etching process takes place in microns, which are millionths of an inch. Since the early 1970s revolution in chip design, evolutionary developments in the art of chip-making enabled engineers to etch lines on silicon that were 6.5 to 0.5 microns in size. After seven technology generations, the fine art of chip design and computer advancements is shifting gears into *light speed.*

7. Associated Press, "Chipmakers Form Research Alliance", *San Francisco Chronicle,* July 28, 1994, p. B3.

8. The U.S. Patent Office made several material errors in not granting a patent to Mr. Gould in 1959. The new laser idea was developed by Gordon Gould while he was a graduate student working on his thesis on light at Columbia University. The type of laser he developed is the most commonly used laser on the market and can be found on laserdisc recording and playback equipment. In 1977, one of Gordon Gould's claims were recognized by the U.S. Patent Office court.

9. Charles Platt, "A Million Mhz CPU?", *WIRED,* January 1995, pp. 124-129.

10. Nec Corporation estimate that CD ROM capacity will more than quadruple within five years by the use of *blue lasers.* These lasers have shorter wavelengths that can focus on smaller dots on a disc.

11. Paul Nicholls, "Title Wave", *CD-ROM World,* July/August 1994, p. 38.

12. Chris Sherman, *The CD ROM Handbook,* (Mcgraw Hill Book Company, New York, 1988) p. 21. **NOTE:** Microsoft was founded in 1977 by Bill Gates and company. Gates stated in a 1985 interview that the *vision* of his company was "To put a microcomputer on every desk in every home with Microsoft making that a reality".

13. Reuters, "MultiMedia CD War Starting to Heat Up", *San Francisco Chronicle,* April 26, 1995, p. B3.

14. Dennis Normile, "Get Set for the Super Disc", *Popular Science,* (February 1996), pp. 55-58.

15. Microcomputers will continue to be loaded with many new features and advanced components. In addition to internal fax machines,

CD-ROM, voice mail, speakerphones and internal modems, new systems will feature cameras and other equipment for videoconferencing and digital components for *Videophones.*

16. Les Cowan, "trends in Roll-Your-Own ROMs," *Multimedia Producer,* October 1995, p. 16.

17. Frederick Rose, "Bringing It Home", *Wall Street Journal,* March 21, 1994, p. R12.

18. Charles Oppenheim (editor), *CD-ROM: Fundamentals To Applications,* (Butterworths & Co., London, 1988) p. 39.

19. Daniel J. Jefferson, "Tommy In Cyberspace", *Wall Street Journal,* March 21, 1994, p. R15.

20. Kathy Rebello and Paul Eng, "Digital Pioneers", *Business Week,* May 2, 1994, p. 98.

21. Ibid., Jefferson, *Wall Street Journal,* p. R15.

22. Ibid., Charles Oppenheim, pp. 40-42. **NOTE:** CD-ROM certainly had a more sophisticated beginning than *Home Video.* For the first five years of Home Video (roughly 1975 to 1980), pornographic films dominated the market. In the period 1981-83, the major studios began to release thousands of theatrical titles on video. As a result of that move, 14,000 video specialty stores came into existence during that period.

23. One of the main reasons that African Americans have not established a major industrial development movement in America, is a serious lack of an *unselfish vision* for business and technological unity. Also, many forces (racist, political, and economic; within and outside America) have worked against this unified policy.

24. Thomas R. King, "Lucasvision", *Wall Street Journal,* March 21, 1994, p. R20.

25. Ibid, King, *Wall Street Journal,* p. R20.

26. Ibid, King, p. R20.

27. A similar type of movement is needed to sound the alarm in the *Black World* regarding the significance of science and technology, and the 21st Century. The new *KyberGenesis* era is critical for survival in the next century.

28. Ibid., Om-Ra-Seti, p. 25.

29. Ibid., Om-Ra-Seti, p. 51.

30. Richard A. Jenkins, *Supercomputers of Today and Tomorrow: The Parallel Processing Revolution,* (Tab Books Inc., Blue Ridge Summit, PA., 1986) p.10.

31. Scientists are experimenting with networks of specially designed computer chips called silicon neurons, custom designed to perform similar to the data capabilities of brain cells. The *Frankenstein* and/ or *Superman* concept may evolve out of some enterprising *mad* scientist's laboratory, particularly if man continues to press on with the idea of creating androids made of entirely biological materials. In addition, the issue of *cloning* human beings came on stage in early 1997, which indicates the rapid speed and changes that are taking place in these scientific arenas prior to the new millennium. Science fiction is rapidly becoming reality.

32. Khafra K Om-Ra-Seti, *Analysis of the Optical Disk Industry & Business Plan for a Start-up Company - KMT, Inc.* (Masters Thesis,

San Francisco State University, San Francisco, May, 1987) pp. 19-
21.

33. SEE Chapter Three: "Black Scientific Legacy".

34. Robert K.G. Temple, *The Sirius Mystery,* (Destiny Books, Roch-
ester, Vermount, 1987) pp. 1-7.

35. John J. Keller and Don Clark, "McCaw-Gates Satellite Plan Draws
Skeptical Reviews," *Wall Street Journal,* March 22, 1994, p. B4.

CHAPTER   THREE

1. The transition from the Morse Code Telegraph system to the telephone was not a smooth historical event. Western Union, which dominated the Morse code telegraph business in America, went from a
$500,000 enterprise to a $41 million business empire within an eleven
year period, with telegraph wires stretching across the full extent of
America. With the introduction of telephone, the Western Union
monopoly was threatened. There was an intense industry struggle
between the two technologies: court battles, fierce competitive activities (which at times prevented Bell Telephone from erecting lines
in various locations), and predatory tactics to kill off the new technological challenge, were all part of this major business war. Western
Union failed to stop Bell Telephone primarily because the new service was far superior to the Morse code system. Bell went on to become the American Telephone & Telegraph Company (AT&T), one
of the largest monopolies in American and world history.

2. Robert C. Hayden, *EIGHT BLACK AMERICAN INVENTORS,*
(Addison-Wesley, Reading, Massachusetts, 1972) p. 126.

3. James G. Spady, "Elmer Samuel Imes: Pioneer Black Physicist", *Blacks in Science: ancient and modern,* (editor: Ivan Van Sertima, Transaction Books, Rutgers, New Brunswick, New Jersey, 1986) pp. 262-263.

4. James G. Spady, "The Changing Perceptions of C.A. Diop and his Work: The Preeminence of a Scientific Spirit", *Great African Thinkers: Cheikh Anta Diop,* (editor: Ivan Van Sertima, Transaction Books, Rutgers, New Brunswick, New Jersey, 1986) pp. 89-100. **NOTE:** During the early 1960s, Diop proposed the establishment of the following scientific institutions for the African continent: research institutes for electronics, physics, nuclear chemistry, aeronautics and astronautics, health, tropical agronomy and biochemistry, applied chemistry for industry and agriculture, and other specialized areas in science (p. 99). Diop was one of the most brilliant black scientists of the 20th Century.

5. Ivan Van Sertima (Editor), "African-American Scientists Played Major Role In Atomic Bomb Development", *Egypt: Child of Africa,* (Transaction Publishers, New Brunswick, 1994) pp. 270-272.

6. Dr. Henry T. Sampson and Dr. George H. Miley, United States Patent #3,591,860, *Gamma-Electric Cell,* patented July 6, 1971. Dr. Henry T. Sampson and Dr. G.H. Miley, "High Voltage Gamma-Electric Cell Operation," *Nuclear Applications Vol. 5,* September 1968.

7. James G. Spady, "BLACKSPACE," *Blacks in Science* (Ivan Van Sertima, Editor, Transaction Books, New Brunswick, 1986) p. 261.

8. Ibid, *Blacks in Science,* pp. 273-294.

CHAPTER SIX

1. Peter Dicken, *Global Shift: The Internationalization of Economic Activity,* (The Guilford Press, New York, 1992) p. 98.

2. Ibid., Om-Ra-Seti, pp. 127-129.

3. James B. Shuman and David Rosenau, *The Kondratieff Wave,* (World Publishing, New York, 1972) p. 29.

4. Ibid., Dicken, pp. 98-102. **NOTE:** Dicken's selected data identifies five key "generic" technologies that create new technology systems (some of which we mention): (1) information technology; (2) biotechnology; (3) materials technology; (4) energy technology; and (5) space technology. In the "fourth cycle" we included atomic power, which had an enormous economic, military and political impact on the world after World War II. The cessation of the second world war and the birth of the atomic age set the stage for the most extraordinary military buildups in the history of the world. Trillions of dollars were spent during the long 45 year period of the Cold War.

5. The date(s) for the ending of the "second cycle" in the 19th Century were 1890-1896. Shortly after the year 1900, the film, automobile and telecommunication industries began major growth periods.

6. Joint Venture: Silicon Valley, *Blueprint For A 21st Century Community: The Phase II Report June 1993,* (Wilson SanSini Goodrich & Rosati, Blueprint Underwriters).

7. Ibid., Blueprint, p. 26.

8. Bart Ziegler, "If Mainframe Computers Are Dinosaurs, Why Is IBM Creating A New Generation?", *Wall Street Journal,* April 4, 1994, p. B1.

9. Robert D. Hof, "Amdahl Escapes 'Death Valley,' But Now What?", *Business Week,* May 16, 1994, p. 88.

10. Ira Sager (Cover Story), "How IBM Became A Growth Company Again," *Business Week,* December 9, 1996, pp. 154-162.

11. Peter F. Drucker, *Innovation and Entrepreneurship,* (Harper & Row, New York, 1985).

12. Miyamoto Musashi, *A Book Of Five Rings,* Translated by Victor Harris, (The Overlook Press, New York, 1974) **NOTE:** During the 16th and 17th century samurai period of Japan, Miyamoto Musashi became one of the most revered swordsmen of his day. His single-minded devotion to the perfection of the *Way of the sword* led to his fighting and winning many duels, and becoming a legend in his time. Before he was 29, Musashi had fought and won more than 60 duels. During the last two years of his life, living in a mountain cave in deep contemplation of *the Way,* Musashi wrote *Go Rin No Sho,* his last will and testament.

CHAPTER SEVEN

1) UPDATE, *Africa Report,* May-June 1995, p.6.

GLOSSARY

ADSL: Asymmetrical Digital Subscriber Loop is a compression technology used to expand the available *bandwidths* of telephone systems to facilitate the transmission of digitized audio and video signals. For Internet users, ADSL will allow them to download Web pages as much as 50 times faster than the standard telephone lines with speeds between 1.5 to 6 million bits per second.

AGE OF LIGHT: Refers to the coming "speed of light" rate of data transmission and manipulation in computer assisted telecommunications. It will be a new age commencing sometime after the year 2000, in which we will witness an expanded intellectual universe. It will enable unpredictable scientific breakthroughs and elevated levels of consciousness.

ARTIFICIAL INTELLIGENCE (AI): Refers to the ability of a computer to perform *intelligent thinking* and make *intelligent decisions.* It involves the combination of complex and simple software elements to bring about a simulated form of applied logic. AI is the ability of a device to perform various functions similar to human intelligence, variously called reasoning, planning, learning, problem solving and pattern recognition.

ATM: Asynchronous transfer mode is essentially the segmented transfer of data in digitized packets to be reassembled in an orderly sequence at specified destinations. ATM refers to how digitized bits of information are transmitted in indifferent sequences to maximize or economize on available bandwidths. Packets of data are "queue upped" (in proper order for reception) in a system and transmitted as specified. An example would be the transmission of a two hour movie to one destination (a customer's home) in a few seconds.

BOOMING 80s: The 1980s was an "exhilarating" period of Reaganomics, a period of massive U.S. budget deficits, the rise of the Pacific Rim, and the emergence of a relatively large number of billionaires. It was also a period of rampant speculation, hyperinflation, merger mania, and the rise of billion dollar worldwide illegal narcotics. The *Booming 80s* like the *Roaring 20s,* was also a highly speculative period in the world of investment and finance.

CASHLESS SOCIETY: As the digital revolution in the 1990s continues to evolve, the use of paper currencies as a means of economic and financial exchange will possibly be replaced by more sophisticated credit/debit cards, and other forms of "digi-cash and cyber money." According to author Joel Kurtzman, we may be moved from a "gold to a megabyte standard," monetary systems based on microchips, computer memory and high speed transmission systems. Whether we use free-floating exchange rates or a gold standard, the underlining power of the system will be dependant on massive computer systems. Sometime in the 21st Century we will probably witness the conversion to a complete cashless society dominated by mega-global banking and financial systems.

COMPUTER GENERATED IMAGES (CGI): The revolution in digital technology has enabled computers to create "true-to-life" pictorial or picto-graphic images, such as the dinosaurs witnessed in the film *Jurassic Park.* CGI will continue to evolve as new hardware and software systems are created to build complete "realities" in computer environments. In short, what we witnessed in *Jurassic Park* is just the beginning of an enormous revolution in the film industry and other forms of multimedia development.

DEPRESSION: In an economic depression, such as the one that occurred in the 1930s, an economy simultaneously experiences sudden and severe business contraction, rising unemployment, deflation, reduction in consumer purchasing power, public insecurity and a buildup of inventories. For the majority of people, basic necessities dominate economic planning, which wipes out many consumer demands and services that cater to nonessential needs.

DINOSAUR SYNDROME: As used in this publication, this term refers to the imminent extinction of various systems, technologies, organizational designs and infrastructures during the evolutionary phase of the Information Age Revolution. As old system designs complete their historic cycles, new information age technologies will move in as replacements for the new era.

ECONOMIC MULTIPLIER EFFECT: This economic event occurs as success on one level ripples throughout an entire economic region or local economy. This allows successful businesses to generate huge profits, pay better salaries and bonuses, which allows employees to purchase more goods and services in the local economy. Local firms will supply products and services for other firms in the region, furthering the recycling of dollars and raising the standard of living for the entire region. The same effects can operate *vice versa.*

FLAMING: The use of aggressive or insulting e-mail to discourage, embarrass or chastise the addressee.

GLOBAL ECONOMY: Refers to the worldwide free movement of goods and services. The world is considered one big marketplace, with free enterprise systems and institutions operating on every shore. The *free enterprise system* has been instrumental in furthering the designs and commercial developments of the rapidly rising international economy of the 1990s.

INDUSTRIAL REVOLUTION: This period marks the turning point in the history of man that witnessed rapid advancements in the rate at which things could be done through the use of mechanical technologies. Centered in Europe (with Britain as the central driving force), it brought the 18th and 19th Centuries new developments and concepts like the assembly line system, steam engines, electronic communication systems, rapid firing guns and much more. Productivity increases in the newly industrialized nations generated the need for more raw materials, machines, factories and labor. As a by-product the colonization movement was sped up, as the more powerful nations scrambled for natural resources, land and wealth.

INFORMATION AGE: This period represents the *post-industrial period,* as the next evolutionary stage in worldwide technological development. It is the era of wealth creation based on the high-tech production and distribution of various forms of information. This new era is characterized by the development of the thinking machine, knowledge intensive industries and the synergistic use of information and electronic systems to generate new creations and designs.

INTRANET: Essentially a scale down version of the Internet that is mainly in use as a closed communication system, offering a new form of internal or limited access networking, complete with web sites, teleconferencing capabilities and many other Internet-like features. By 1996, between 70,000 to 140,000 companies had adopted Intranet platforms, which represents the first phase of a major new form of communications systems sometimes referred to as the "silent networks."

ISDN: Integrated Services Digital Network is an enhanced alternative to plain old telephone systems (POTS) used to transmit audio signals. It extends the bandwidth of telephones to accommodate up to 136,000 bits per second speeds.

KYBERGENESIS: Is an ideological and scientific revolution in *black thought and practice* to make use of the Information Age. It calls for collective black effort to seize the opportunities of this emerging era and build a new beginning for the 21st Century. The *KyberGenesis Connection* is a call to the black world to shift its priorities to a concentrated development of science and technology, economic and financial infrastructures, as well as local, national and global distribution systems.

MPEG: Is the Motion Pictures Expert Group agreed upon consensus for digitized compression standards for the transmission and storage of video signals. MPEG-1 through MPEG-4 are four ascending standards developed to facilitate slow to high transmission speeds for various forms of media, such as CD-ROMs, broadcast television and HDTV.

MYTH-INFORMATION: Is the reliance on folk tales rather than on sound scientific principles and facts. Prime examples would be to teach people that the world is flat or that the entire continent of Africa has never given birth to any great civilizations.

MULTIDIMENSIONAL CORPORATION: This term refers to the emergence of a new corporate entity that fully adapts itself to the multimedia wave of the Digital Age. These new corporate entities will ultimately operate simultaneously on many platforms and in many business environments, providing (in some instances) a complete line of products and services to a highly varied global consumer base.

PARADIGM SHIFT: Represents a period in history when broad inter-related changes are made in the way societies function, conduct transactions and organize the production and distribution of products and services. Its effects alter existing frameworks and require significant infrastructure developments to accommodate new system designs and technologies. Prime examples of paradigm shifts in global affairs are the Industrial Revolution and the emergence of the Information Age Revolution.

PHASE I EDICT: This term refers to the historic Federal Court Consent Decree in January 1982, that gave AT&T a two year period to prepare for the complete breakup of its operations. D-Day came on January 1, 1984, which established the era of the Regional Bell Operating Companies (sometimes called the seven Baby Bells) as well as AT&T reorganization in the long distance arena.

PHASE II EDICT: This term refers to the continued deregulation of the telecommunication industry in the 1990s (in the U.S.), which culminated in the implementation of the Telecommunication Competition and Deregulation Act of 1996. President Clinton signed the new legislation on February 8, 1996, marking the end of an era.

POTS: Plain Old Telephone Services refers to the basic information transfer system of the telephone industry that transmit through copper wire.

SDSL: Symmetric Digital Subscriber Line is a high-end compression transfer system used to compress and reopen condensed electronic signals.

TELE-LITERACY: This is knowledge and skill to understand and interpret television and other distance communication messages beyond their face value to discover "hidden persuasions" and other forms of viewer manipulation. It is also used to loosely refer to the body of knowledge associated with the operation and use of high-tech communications.

INDEX

A

Adams, Russell L., 83
Advanced Large Scale Integration Development Laboratory, 96
Advanced societies, 35, 37, 83
Adinkra People, 13
Adobe Photoshop, 60, 61
Aerospace Corporation, 91
Affirmative Action, iv, 22, 215, 216
Africa, 89, 140, 141, 203; telecommunication network and, 203
African American market, 11
African Civilization, 61, 76, 95
African Diaspora, viii
African Methodist Episcopal Church (AME), 247
Africa One (African Optical Network) 203
Afrocentric, 109, 140, 222, 244
Age of Light, 5, 45, 151
AIDS, 151
AirTouch Communications, 200, 207
Amdahl Corp., 169, 170

Alameda, 164
Algebra, 36
America, 6, 7, 8, 15, 47, 67, 68, 102, 133, 139, 141, 166, 175-179, 182, 183, 184, 187, 188, 191, 196, 198, 201, 248; workers and, 68; rural and metropolitan, 68; civilization of, 65; history of, 86
American Bell Telephone, 84-86, 189
American Bar Association, 221
American Telephone and Telegraph Company (AT&T), 39, 92, 180, 184, 189, 190-195, 202, 203, 214
American Engineering, 84, 85
American Federation of Labor and the Congress of Industrial Organization (AFL & CIO), 143
Ameritech, 193
analog phonograph, 46
analog systems, 207
Anchorage, Alaska, 69
androids, 71

ABOUT THE AUTHORS

Photo by J. Miccolo Johnson

Timothy L. Jenkins is currently chairman and chief executive officer of Unlimited Vision, Inc. Multi-media and the former publisher of the Smithsonian's *America's Visions* magazine. He was the founder of the international management firms, The MATCH Institution and the Near East Division of the Development Assistance Corporation, devoted to Third World economic and management solutions. He was appointed by the President and confirmed by the Senate to be a Governor of the U.S. Postal Service in the 1980s, where he helped to define the national concepts of electronic mail. Jenkins served as a Trustee, Professor of Admistrative Law and Outstanding Professor of Law at Howard University. He was instrumental in creating the first all-black on-line forum on the Internet and sits on the board of directors of National Instructional Television (NITV), with an interstate network of FCC licenses. For five years he was the Chief Lobbyist for the Student Nonviolent Coordinating Committee (SNCC). Jenkins earned his Juris Doctor Degree from Yale University Law School and his Bachelor of Arts degree from Howard University.

Khafra K Om-Ra-Seti is the author of *World Economic Collapse: The Last Decade and The Global Depression,* a contemporary work which examines the forces of politics and trade. He is currently a professional stockbroker and institutional trader for a large international brokerage firm headquartered in northern California, and is the CEO of KMT Publications, a publishing company. He is a recognized proponent of fundamental analysis and long wave macroeconomic theory. Mr. Om-Ra-Seti's keen interest in computer technology and related issues, evolves from his work with mainframe computers in the latter 1970s and early 1980s. He was educated at San Francisco State University with BA and MBA degrees in finance and marketing. His Master Thesis, *Analysis of the Optical Disk Industry & Business Plan for a Start-up Company - KMT, Inc.,* written in 1987, was a first in predicting the revolutionary power and potentials of laser technology in PC applications and storage improvements.

To Order Additional Copies of
BLACK FUTURISTS In The INFORMATION AGE
by Timothy Jenkins and Khafra K Om-Ra-Seti

(For volume discounts please contact the publishers)

KMT Publications
P.O. Box 881913
San Francisco, CA 94188-1913

UNLIMITED VISIONS, INC.
815 Florida Avenue N.W.
Suite 300
Washington, D.C. 20001

Please send _____ copies of BLACK FUTURISTS @ $19.95 each
(add $6.00 postage and handling for the first copy, $1.00 for each additional copy: DC residents add 5.75% Sales Tax; California residents add 7.25% sales tax) to:

NAME _____

ADDRESS_____

CITY/STATE/ZIP _____

Please allow 2-4 weeks for delivery